Narratives of Agency

Narratives of Agency

Self-Making in China, India, and Japan

Wimal Dissanayake, editor

University of Minnesota Press

Minneapolis

London

Chapter 1 was originally published in *Positions* 1 (Spring 1993). Copyright 1993 by Duke University Press. Reprinted by permission of the publisher. Chapter 2 is a revised version of an article published in *East-West Film Journal* 5, no. 2 (July 1991).

Published by the University of Minnesota Press
111 Third Avenue South, Suite 290, Minneapolis, MN 55401-2520
Printed in the United States of America on acid-free paper

Library of Congress Cataloging-in-Publication Data

Narratives of agency : self-making in China, India, and Japan / Wimal
    Dissanayake, editor.
        p.   cm.
    Includes bibliographical references and index.
    ISBN 0-8166-2656-1. — ISBN 0-8166-2657-X (pbk.)
    1. China—Civilization.   2. India—Civilization.   3. Japan—
Civilization.   4. Self.   5. Individuality.   6. Subjectivity.
I. Dissanayake, Wimal.
DS721.N37   1996
950—dc20   95-25562

The University of Minnesota is an equal-opportunity educator and employer.

Contents

Acknowledgments

This book grew out of the work of the Localism and Globalism project jointly coordinated by Kwok-kan Tam (Chinese University of Hong Kong), Terry Siu-han Yip (Hong Kong Baptist University), and myself. We are very grateful to Ho Sin Hang Memorial Fund for supporting the project. I must express my deep sense of gratitude to Kwok-kan Tam and Terry Siu-han Yip for their many valuable suggestions and support throughout.

Since the beginning of the project Janaki Bakhle showed great interest in it and encouraged me in numerous ways. I am very grateful to the two anonymous reviewers of the University of Minnesota Press who made excellent suggestions. They are, of course, in no way responsible for the shortcomings in this volume. Mary Byers, Biodun Iginla, Becky Manfredini, Jeff Moen, Robert Mosimann, and Kathy Wolter were unfailingly helpful and admirably efficient.

I wish to thank Andrew Arno, Harumi Befu, Rob Borofsky, Joan Chatfield, Virginia Dominguez, Marilyn Ivy, Vicente Rafael, Frank Tillman, and Rob Wilson for their support and interest. I am especially indebted to my wife Doreen and daughter Niru and son Sudeera for their innumerable acts of love and kindness.

Introduction / Agency and Cultural Understanding: Some Preliminary Remarks

Wimal Dissanayake

The broad objective of the essays gathered in this volume is to focus on the concept of human agency and its importance in cultural understanding and cultural redescription. The word "agency," like the words "selfhood," "individuality," "subjectivity," and "personhood," with which it is imbricated, does not admit of simple and clear definitions. All these words inhabit overlapping positions in a semantic field and conceptual cartography that are increasingly attracting the scholarly attention of both humanists and social scientists alike. In this introduction, and indeed in this book as a whole, no attempt will be made to affix immutable meanings to these terms, as if the problem of semantic definitions could be settled once and for all. Such an effort, even if it were possible, would not yield much by way of hermeneutic payoff. What I propose to do, therefore, is to focus on the notion of agency as a way of opening up a discussion on its importance in cultural and cross-cultural reunderstanding, and recuperating the term from neglect at the hands of some dominant cultural theorists. It is important not to treat the notion of human agency, as some are wont to do, as a transdiscursive and nonproblematic category. Our emphasis should be on the historical and cultural conditions that facilitate the discursive production of agency, and on useful ways of framing the question of agency so that we would be in a better position to understand the contours of the cultures that we study. The essays included in this book, I hope, will contribute to this effort from their different disciplinary and conceptual vantage points.

Rather than seek to define terms like "agency" and "subjectivity" in a precise manner, I indicate the broad outlines of my usage of them, with the sole intention of promoting a discussion of these terms. In this regard, the elucidations of Paul Smith, although not unproblematic, have much to offer toward the exploration of the terms and their problematic nature. Following his lead, I wish to use the term "self" to denote the imaginary register consisting of identifications, narratives, formulations, and images that serve the notion of the individual. This imaginary singularity is largely a product of self-reflection. The term "individual," as its etymology suggests, refers to the undivided source of consciousness, meaning, and action; it is an illusory whole that gives the appearance of a free and self-determining being. The subject, on the other hand, is a disciplinary construct; it is constituted by social and cultural formations, language, and political and institutional discourses, and does not suggest the sense of autonomy, sovereignty, and initiating power that the term "individual" carries with it. Closely related to the subject is the idea of subject-position. A subject is always subject to some discourse, and there are an enormous number of them; they are, in their shape and nature, different, changing, and at times even antipathetic to each other. Hence, there can be a plurality of subject-positions, depending on the various discourses that the subject is subject to. The "agent," as I use the term, denotes the locus from which an action can be initiated, whether it be one of reconfirmation or resistance, mainly from the interstices between various subject-positions. And I use the term "person" to denote one who has agency, and therefore the terms "agent" and "person" are used synonymously.

As Paul Smith rightly observes, a person is not merely an actor who follows a pregiven ideological script, as the concept of subject suggests, but is also an actor who reads it with the aim of inserting himself or herself into it.[1] The term "agency," which was originally popular among social scientists, is now increasingly making its presence felt in humanities scholarship and cultural redescriptions as a way of counteracting some of the dangers of idealistic and structuralist formulations of personhood. Following Smith, I conceive of the human agent as the locus from which reconfirmations or resistances to the ideological are produced or played out, and therefore not as equivalent either to the individual or to subjects, as I have described these terms. Paul Smith remarks, "The term 'agent' will be used to mark the idea of a form of subjectivity where by virtue of the contradictions and disturbances in and among subject-positions, the possibility (indeed actuality) of resistance to the ideological pressure is allowed for (even though that resistance too must be produced in an ideological context)." This is broadly the sense in which I employ the term "agency."[2]

I have indicated the broad outlines of my usage of the terms "self," "individual," "subject," "subject-position," and "agency." Naturally, these descriptions are unlikely to command general assent. Indeed, some of the authors of the essays collected in this volume employ the terms in ways that are different from mine. The important point, though, is to open up a discussion with particular focus on the concept of agency and its importance in cultural understanding. This book should be seen as a modest step in that direction and nothing more.

The nine essays contained in this volume serve to open a discursive space for the interdisciplinary exploration of a topic that I believe is both theoretically important and practically relevant. The topic is the importance of the recuperation of the concept of human agency in our effort to gain a deeper understanding of the cultures of China, India, and Japan. Two major conceptual trajectories have served to undermine and diminish the importance of agency in cultural descriptions of these societies. On the one hand, traditional Western approaches to the study of these cultures have emphasized, unduly and counterproductively, the pervasive influence of family and clan (China), caste and fatalism (India), and groupism (Japan), to the exclusion of the salience of agency. On the other hand, modern critical approaches such as postmodernism, poststructuralism, new historicism, and so on, which are being increasingly used in the study of these cultures, have sought to displace the autonomous, self-present, sovereign individual that is mistakenly believed to be the originator of meaning and action, and posit a decentered and deconstructed self without any epistemic or moral privilege. The upshot of these two main conceptual trajectories has been to severely undermine the notion of human agency, with adverse consequences. In this book, through discussions of a wide range of cultural practices, signifying economies, and institutional discourses in China, Japan and India, the aforementioned theoretical mappings are interrogated, sometimes directly, sometimes obliquely. The essays contained within the covers of this book underline the importance of understanding the operations of human agency and how it is trans-coded in various cultural grammars.

By and large, many of the Western writings on Asian cultures have erred in the direction of emphasizing too much the analytical cate-gories of caste, clan, community, family, group, and so on, to the vir-tual exclusion of human agency and personal intentionality. These have assumed the status of master tropes in the analysis of Chinese, Indian, and Japanese cultures. Terms such as "Chinese culture," "Indian cul-ture," and "Japanese culture" are used in such a way as to impose an unwarranted and unjustified cultural homogenization on this collec-tivist trope. The trouble with such collectivizing gestures and strate-gies is that they tend to give short shrift to the very real individual differences within groups and to ignore questions of personal desire, intentionality, or agency in a given collectivity. For example, the an-thropologist Lila Abu-Lughod, pointing out the need to pay close at-tention to particular individuals and their changing relationships within a given community (in this case the Bedouin community), says that such a move enables the subversion of the most problematic con-struction of culture: homogeneity, coherence, and timelessness.[3] Such a theoretical move becomes even more compellingly significant in the case of larger societies like those of China, India, and Japan. Com-menting on her own chosen terrain of research, Lila Abu-Lughod re-marks, "In the face of the complexity of individual lives even in a single family, a term like 'Bedouin culture' comes to seem meaningless, whether in the service of rules that people follow or of a community that shares such rules."[4] It is important to bear in mind that mem-bers of a community have to make personal choices, struggle and in-teract with others, argue about positions, confront new challenges, face up to new circumstances, engage new desires, and negotiate mean-ings, all of which involve intentionality and human agency. Many of the essays in this book seek to enforce this point.

The question of human agency has been framed in humanistic writ-ings largely by two distinct theoretical discourses, namely those of lib-eral humanism, which stresses the autonomous agent, and structural-ism, which disperses the agent in the play of textuality. According to the liberal humanist understanding, the agency is transhistorical, trans-discursive, sovereign, self-transparent, and self-identical, and is the orig-inator of action and the locus of truth. In their desire to focus on a transcendent essence of the human, the liberal humanists ignore the cultural differences and the role of social formations and ideological discourse in the constitution of agency. The structuralists (and poststructuralists, as well, despite their other differences) posit a decentered agency that is determined by the power of discourse and the interpellative force of ideology.

The theorists associated with both these conceptual pathways have, in a sense, overstated their case, much to the detriment of human agency and its undeniable role in culture. In one case, the fault is one of exaggeration; in the other, of total neglect. Let us, for example, consider the notion of interpellation or hailing enunciated by Althusser, which forms a vital strand in poststructuralist thought. He believes that persons are interpellated as subjects through ideological discourse that generates the reproduction of social relations. This notion of a monolithic ideological discourse tends to oversimplify what is a very complex and multifaceted process into a simple subjection and positioning, where the subject has very little room for resistance. As Anthony Giddens remarks, "Althusser's agents are structuralist dopes." Althusser is positing a unified subject determined by a unified ideological discourse that leaves little room for multiple ideological discourses and multiple subject-positions. The net effect of this is to rob human agency of any ontological status and strategic value.

It is against this line of thinking that Paul Smith's theorization of human agency as resistance, growing out of the interplay of multiple subject-positions, is important. He seeks to enunciate a concept of human agency that both amalgamates and moves beyond the frameworks of humanists and structuralists and poststructuralists. He situates human agency in the play of social and cultural forces, on the one hand, and personal desire, interest, and intentionality, on the other. Going beyond the liberal humanist theorizations, as well as those of Althusser, Barthes, Derrida, and Foucault, he foregrounds resistance as the condition of human agency. Despite the fact that he does not make clear the ontological status of agency and its indispensable link to strategies of resistance, his mode of thinking has much to offer by way of illuminating the problematic of agency. He sees agency as exceeding subjectivity.

There are others who would argue that agency often subverts subjectivity. For example, Judith Butler says that to be constituted by discourse is not to be determined by discourse. She says that as a process, signification harbors within itself what the epistemological discourse refers to as agency. As she remarks, "The subject is not determined by the rules through which it is generated, because signification is not a founding act, but rather a regulated process of repetition that both conceals itself and enforces its rules precisely through the production of substantializing effects. In a sense, all signification takes place within the orbit of the compulsion to repeat; 'agency,' then, is to be located within the orbit of the compulsion to variation on that repetition."[5] The notion of human agency is a complex and multivalent one, displaying a great measure of cultural variability. For example, in my own continuing work on the idea of human agency in Sinhalese Buddhist village culture in Sri Lanka, I find that the ideas of networks of communication, webs of affiliation, and intimately shared cultural spaces are central to the operation of agency. Rather than conceiving of human agency as solely individual-based and person-centered, the villagers in Sri Lanka whom I studied made me realize that agency can and does manifest itself in and through networks of interaction. The interplay of different axes of intimacy and confidentiality serve to legitimate human agency in these contexts. Human agency, so far from being the product of atomistic and isolated persons, can be the outcome of a group-centered ethos and orientation.

The need to understand human agency in an institutional context in which that agency gains in power and definition through diverse institutional mechanisms is underlined by Lydia Liu in her essay in this book. There she demonstrates how journals and related forms of communication in the public sphere, rather than unmediated individual subjects, act as vital agents in the political and intellectual domains of early republican China.

Another useful way of understanding the concept of human agency and foregrounding it is to see it in relation to what Kathy Ferguson terms "mobile subjectivities."[6] This concept has to be understood in the context of recent feminist theorizations on gendered subjectivity. In contradistinction to what she terms Praxis Feminism, Cosmic Feminism, and Linguistic Feminism, she enunciates the concept of mobile subjectivities that are products of interpretation; they are "standpoints of a sort, places to stand and from which to act." But as she points out, they are fluid and multiple, and defy essentialization because their concreteness does not lend itself to abstract formulation. Ferguson says, "Mobile subjectivities are too concrete and dirty to claim innocence, too much in-process to claim closure, too interdependent to claim fixed boundaries."[7] They are temporal and move across axes of power without fully residing in them. Her enunciation of the concept of mobile subjectivities comes close to the idea of agency that I have been advancing in this essay.

The need to focus more and more on the concept of agency is important not only in terms of theory but also in terms of praxis, and needless to say, the two are imbricated. There is a significant political dimension to the concept of agency. Just when feminists, minorities, gays, and lesbians are seeking to assert their identity, some of the theorizations associated with postmodernism seem to cut the ground from under their feet by denying agency and positing a passive and totalizing subjectivity that is at the mercy of discursive power. This has the effect of denying these groups the ability and the opportunity to offer a radical critique of the mainstream positions from their own distinctive vantage points. For example, Nancy Hartsock asks: "Why is it that just at the moment when so many of us who have been silenced begin to demand the right to name ourselves, to act as subjects rather than objects of history, that just then the concept of subjecthood becomes problematic? Just when we are forming our own theories of the world, uncertainty emerges about whether the world can be theorized. Just when we are talking about the changes we want, ideas of progress and the possibility of systematically and rationally organizing human society become dubious and suspect."[8] In addition, there is also the nagging feeling that the attempt to debunk human agency springs from a purely Eurocentric agenda that has very little connection or relevance to the experiences of the non-Western worlds. It is indeed true that poststructuralism and postmodernism (there are, of course, differences between the two in terms of theoretical and historical projects) have had the effect of displacing the autonomous, sovereign individual as the originator of meaning and action and as the locus of truth. Not all would agree with the contention that poststructuralism and postmodernism have ignored the importance of agency. What these theorists linked to postmodernism and poststructuralism have done is to problematize the notion of agency by focusing on the discursive construction of subjectivity. Certain feminists like Trinh T. Minh-ha, Rey Chow, and perhaps to a lesser extent Teresa de Lauretis are using poststructuralist frameworks to reclaim and redefine agency even while focusing on historical and political processes of subject formation. Other feminist scholars like Jane Flax, Nancy Hartsock, Linda Nicholson, Susan Bordo, and Christine de Stefano have, from their distinctive theoretical angles, sought to foreground the implications of poststructuralism and postmodernism for the understanding and dissection of agency, resistance, and political action.

The tangled question of human agency, subject formation, and poststructuralist thought finds compelling articulation in the work of feminist theorists. Nancy Miller underlines the need to differentiate between the universal subject and the female subject. She makes the point that the postmodernist decision that the author is dead, and the subject along with him, does not apply for women.[9] This move has the unfortunate consequence of prematurely foreclosing the question of agency for them. In a similar vein, Gayatri Chakravorty Spivak enunciates the notion of "strategic essentialism" as a way of getting around this difficulty.[10] The recuperation of human agency, then, has both theoretical interests and practical political consequences of great import. What is urgently needed is a theory of agency that recognizes that agents are shaped irreducibly by social and cultural discourses and that they have the potentiality to clear cultural spaces from which they could act in accordance with their desires and intentionalities.

As we ponder the complexities of human agency in the light of newer theories of language, culture, and society, we might, I believe, usefully examine the relationship between "strategy" and "agency." The term "strategy" has become a highly valorized term in contemporary cultural discourse and analysis. Strategies associated with various cultural practices, texts, discourses, economies of signification, and rhetorics of presentation are foregrounded with much enthusiasm. What is the relation between agency and strategy? Is agency doing its work elsewhere under false pretenses? The writings of prestigious French thinkers such as Michel Foucault, Jacques Derrida, Pierre Bourdieu, and Michel de Certeau have contributed significantly to the framing of the concept of strategy. The important question is, Can there be purposeful strategies without a sense of agency, as theorists like Habermas have pointed out? Clearly, the way the term "strategy" is deployed in contemporary discourse carries with it connotations of intentionality. If so, how do these two terms intermesh? Does the concept of strategy allow thinkers of a poststructuralist persuasion to introduce through the back door the sense of intentionality that they have so vigorously challenged and negatively valorized? These are questions that merit closer scrutiny.

The nine essays gathered in this volume are grouped in the three categories of Chinese, Indian, and Japanese cultures. This is only a means of imposing a rather loose geographical structure, and should in no way be taken as an effort to reify these cultures. There is no attempt here to delineate three separate cultural areas, each with its own unity. As a matter of fact, there are many variations within a single cultural area, as indeed there are many commonalities among the three cultural areas. One of the objectives of this volume is to promote a fruitful conversation among the three cultures in terms of human agency, and any hint of reification will go against that aim. Many of the essays contained in the book underline the need to examine the cross-cultural implications of making use of the ideas of self, individual, subjectivity, subject-position, and agency for cultural investigation. This involves epistemological, theoretical, and methodological questions of great consequence. How do we acquire a knowledge and understanding of the operation of agency in different cultures? Are Eurocentric models of subjectivity and agency currently in circulation among academics working on Asian cultures adequate for the task at hand? Do the abdications of Western-inspired discourses signify a retreat into a cultural essentialism? What commonalities of intent and approach do we find among Chinese, Indian, and Japanese cultures? These are important questions that merit close analysis. What this book does, I hope, is to focus on these vital issues — although often in an indirect manner.

There are three essays dealing with self, subjectivity, and agency in Chinese cultures. The opening chapter, by Lydia H. Liu, raises a number of significant issues related to the problematic of the self and its representation in literary texts. She makes important and valid distinctions between the concepts of self, individual, subject, and agency and the implications of these for identity politics. She makes a strong case for devalorizing the transhistorical and transdiscursive notion of self and recognizing the need to locate the self as a historical category, contingent as much upon specific social, cultural, and political conjunctures as on the discursive terrains of discipline. Liu explores the inscription of selfhood, individuality, and subjecthood in various Chinese texts so as to illuminate the complex relationships between human agency and questions of cultural modernity and nationhood. Through the analysis of her chosen literary texts she has sought to trace the discursive shifts and discontinuities in discourses of self in modern China.

The second chapter in this volume is devoted to an analysis of the Chinese film *Samsara,* with particular reference to the constitution of the self and the complexities of visual narrative. The centrality of narrative in understanding self, a point repeatedly made by philosophers like Paul Ricoeur and Alasdair MacIntyre and by sociologists like Anthony Giddens, is explored by Eugene Yuejin Wang with great subtlety and theoretical sophistication. His discussions of cinematic self-referentiality and of the self/the eye/the "I" in classical Chinese texts are most illuminating. His critiques of Lacanian conceptualities of the mirror stage and self-recognition are particularly valuable in light of one of the aims of this book, namely, to focus on the applicability and relevance of modern Euro-American theories of self and culture to non-Western societies.

The final chapter in the section dealing with Chinese culture is by Ming-Bao Yue. It thematizes the question of visual agency and ideological fantasy in three films by the well-known and internationally acclaimed Chinese filmmaker Zhang Yimou. The three films are *Judou, Raise the Red Lantern,* and *The Story of Qiuju.* Ming-Bao Yue maintains that cinema provides us with a powerful and rich area for exploring the construction of subjectivity. In this essay, through a sophisticated psychoanalytical discussion of the scopic field and its relation to libidinal economy, the author argues convincingly that the construction of subjectivity hinges upon two notions of great heuristic significance: fantasy and the gaze. The way this essay has sought to draw on the reconceptualizations of Lacan by Slavoj Žižek is interesting and opens the door to a whole range of significant investigations into human agency and cinematic representation.

Next we come to the essays dealing with Indian culture. There are three chapters in this section, two of them drawing on cultural anthropology and the other on modern cultural studies. The chapter by Owen M. Lynch examines the contested and contesting self-identities among Mathura's Chaubes. His focus is on the complex ways in which self is constituted through narratives of multiple identities in different social situations. This approach persuasively undercuts the widely held belief among humanists that the self is experienced and manifested in one totalized whole. How these narratives of self-identity are imbricated with interests is clearly brought out. The notion of a public space of disclosure through languages raises important issues related to agency and culture. The interplay between identity, place, and mythological beginnings, which is central to Lynch's argument, is delineated with great sensitivity and a nuanced cultural understanding.

Chapter 5, by the anthropologist Richard G. Fox, explores the ways in which self can become hegemonic, the struggles that surround these hegemonies, and how conceptions of self are realized in everyday practices and politics. The author makes a concerted effort to avoid the false and counterproductive notions of monolithic Indian and Western concepts of self; instead he focuses on everyday lives and politics. His desire to locate the emergence of self-identities and subjectivities in terms of ongoing political struggles introduces a new and fascinating avenue of inquiry into concepts of Indian selves. The way the author foregrounds the tensions between Hindu nationalism and other hegemonic "Indian" conceptions of subjectivity serves to strengthen the importance of inquiring into the political situatedness of self.

Chapter 6, by Vijay Mishra, addresses the issue of defining selfhood in terms of Indian literary and filmic texts. His focus is on the ways in which selves are artificially constructed agencies in works of the imagination. Mishra's aim is not to offer a definition of a "true" Indian self, which can be a dubious undertaking, but to suggest ways in which classical understandings of the Hindu self impinge on our readings and assessments of works of the imagination. At the conclusion of his essay, the author says that the culture's representation of the self "is marked by levels of ambiguity and contradiction that make problematic the truism of cultural relativity itself." This is indeed an insight that connects to the ground base of this volume of essays.

The last three essays in the book address issues of selfhood, agency, and cultural representation as they relate to Japan. The opening chapter in this section, by Emiko Ohnuki-Tierney, focuses attention on the symbolism of rice as a dominant metaphor of the Japanese. She points out how the Japanese notion of self has taken a distinct trajectory as a different historical other has emerged, and how the Japanese have sought to use rice as an instrument of thought in these processes. An examination of rice as a trope of the Japanese self, as Ohnuki-Tierney indicates, is imbricated with questions of the ways in which people fashion powerful representations of themselves and the ways multiple representations within a given culture are reconciled. The issue of agency figures interestingly in this effort. What is fascinating about this essay is the manner in which the different aspects of the symbolics of rice and selfhood have undergone transformations in responding to encounters with other cultures, and the way in which political contingencies have been explored.

In Chapter 8, Wimal Dissanayake discusses the complex relationship between self, agency, and cultural knowledge by examining three well-known Japanese films. For this purpose he has chosen the Japanese concept of *seishin* (spirituality) as a way of foregrounding his problematic. The three films discussed are Kon Ichikawa's *Harp of Burma,* Akira Kurosawa's *Ikiru,* and Hiroshi Teshigahara's *Woman in the Dunes.* Interestingly, all three films, when seen from a Western perspective or in terms of Western categorizations, display a high modernist and existentialist desire. The essay underlines the need to adopt a more complex and nuanced approach to the study of self and collectivism in Japanese culture and the importance of recognizing the discursive space that it provides for the fashioning of agency.

Marie Thorsten Morimoto, in Chapter 9, examines the protests of Hayashi Takeshi against the restrictions of the Japanese education system. Focusing attention on such issues as the legacy of military-like authoritarianism in Japanese education, the clash between egalitarianism and competitiveness, and the received wisdom about the hierarchy of schools and jobs, the author has demonstrated the way in which Hayashi cleared a discursive space for the purpose of challenging some of these deficiencies and giving expression to marginalized and dissenting voices. Based on long interviews with Hayashi, this chapter exemplifies the importance of agency and its relevance to Japanese culture, and underlines the need to abandon stereotypes in understanding Japanese culture, as indeed any other culture.

The nine chapters in this volume, then, from their distinctive disciplinary and cultural vantage points, have sought to illuminate the tangled questions of selfhood, subjectivity, agency, and cultural redescription. Many of the essays in this book enable us to avoid the totalizing and reductionist concepts of self, individual, and subject propounded by both humanists and poststructuralists. The importance of understanding the nature and significance of agency and its location in specific historical, cultural, political conjunctures is emphasized throughout the book. As we examine the ways in which agency has been encoded in different cultural idioms, it is important to bear in mind that the notion of culture conceived in terms of symbolic systems located in readily identifiable spaces or territories is being problematized by several contemporary scholars. The writings of Appadurai, Dirlik, and Gupta and Ferguson exemplify this line of thinking.[11] The heterogeneities within cultures and the play of localism and globalism serve to complicate cultures, whether they are Chinese, Indian, or Japanese.

Notes

1. Paul Smith, *Discerning the Subject* (Minneapolis: University of Minnesota Press, 1988) p. xxxv.

2. Ibid.

3. Lila Abu-Lughod, *Writing Women's Worlds* (Berkeley: University of California Press, 1993), p. 14.

4. Ibid., p. 19.

5. Judith Butler, *Gender Trouble* (New York: Routledge, 1990), p. 145.

6. Kathy E. Ferguson, *The Man Question* (Berkeley: University of California Press, 1993), p. x.

7. Ibid., p. 154.

8. Nancy Hartsock, "Foucault on Power: A Theory of Women?" in *Feminism/Postmodernism,* ed. Linda Nicholson (New York: Routledge, 1990), p. 163.

9. Nancy K. Miller, "Changing the Subject," in *Coming to Terms: Feminism, Theory, Politics,* ed. Elizabeth Weed (New York: Routledge, 1989), p. 6.

10. Gayatri Chakravorty Spivak, *In Other Worlds: Essays in Cultural Politics* (New York: Methuen, 1987).

11. Arjun Appadurai, "Disjuncture and Difference in the Global Cultural Economy," *Public Culture* 1, no. 2: 1989; Arif Dirlik, *After the Revolution: Waking to Global Capitalism* (Hanover, N.H.: University Presses of New England, 1994); Akhil Gupta and James Ferguson, "Beyond 'Culture': Space, Identity, and the Politics of Difference," *Cultural Anthropology* 7, no. 1: 1992.

1 / Translingual Practice: The Discourse of Individualism between China and the West

Lydia H. Liu

The meaning of a word is its use in the language.
LUDWIG WITTGENSTEIN

The concept of the self, subject, or individual (as well as the slippage between them) has been a main target of criticism in the academic West since the emergence of poststructuralist scholarship. A good deal of that critique is bent on deconstructing the post-Enlightenment European notion of the subject. This move has been greeted with challenge by critics of deconstruction—feminists and others—who try to (re)introduce concepts such as political agency, strategic identity, and multiple subjectivities into the contemporary debate.[1] As someone who specializes in a non-European language, I find this debate fascinating within the context of Euro-American academia but somewhat unsatisfactory at certain theoretical levels. For instance, I am often struck by the fact that the terms and ideas contested by contemporary critics in those kinds of debates tend to circulate within the self-referential framework of the discursive/linguistic traditions of the West and often have the effect of reinforcing, rather than disrupting, the system of knowledge that is being brought under critical examination. What I mean is that theories that invest so heavily in self-contemplation on behalf of metropolitan European languages cannot but replicate Eurocentrism in the act of criticizing it. After all, attacks on European culture from some hallucinatory non-European perspective in the West have always been a dynamic part of the European intellectual tradition since the time of the Enlightenment, if not earlier. My point here is not to seek some authentic non-Euroamerican position, which would have to be constructed against its Euroamerican opposite, hence forfeiting any claim of authenticity; nor do I wish to concern myself with the need to raise the voice of the third world. Where is the third world? Who names it? And who represents it anyway? Instead, I would like to raise the possibility of rethinking the condition of contemporary theory in terms of contestation of languages, by which I mean national, ethnic, and regional languages and dialects in a literal sense rather than the Saussurian *langue* versus *parole* or Bakhtin's notion of heteroglossia.[2] Inasmuch as theory, like other discursive practices, is linguistically specific as well as context-bound, I see the relationship between languages as one of the central issues that it is incumbent upon comparative scholarship to address.

This essay will look at the discourse of individualism in the context of what I call translingual practice between East and West. I will focus on the ways in which this "Western" discourse was deployed by Chinese intellectuals in theories of the modern nation-state during the early decades of the twentieth century. My emphasis on the act of deployment is intended to shift the critique of the post-Enlightenment European concept of the subject to a site where meaning does not belong to European philosophical traditions alone (even though the concept itself might have "originated" there), but "travels" and gets reinvented in the constant flux of historical practices, not the least of which is the encounter between languages through translation and translingual practice. I hope that this line of inquiry will enable me to engage with the contemporary theoretical debate on the subject, difference, culture, and nation at a time when it is becoming increasingly difficult to conduct "cross-culture" studies or theorize about national differences without giving primary attention to the complexities of historical transaction between languages.

Translingual Practice

What happens when a word, category, or discourse "travels" from one language into another? In the nineteenth-century colonial and imperialist discourse, the travel of ideas and theories from Europe to the rest of the world usually evoked notions of expansion, enlightenment, progress, teleology, and so forth, whereas in what has become known as postcolonial theory, the word "travel" is anything but innocent and often has to be put in quotation marks. Depending on the perspective one takes with regard to the above question, there is a world of difference between one theoretical position and the other.

In *The World, the Text, and the Critic,* Edward Said proposes the notion of traveling theory precisely to address the migration of ideas across space and time. This notion enables him to depart from previous Marxist theorists, who take capitalist economy as a critical model for literary production, and to introduce a different concept of literary practice that will emphasize the element of influence, creative borrowing, appropriation, and the movement of ideas and theories from place to place in an international environment. Apropos of the manner in which theories and ideas travel, Said gives four main stages:

> First, there is the point of origin, or what seems like one, a set of initial circumstances in which the idea came to birth or entered discourse. Second, there is a distance transversed, a passage through the pressure of various contexts as the idea moves from an earlier point to another time and place where it will come into a new prominence. Third, there is a set of conditions—call them conditions of acceptance or, as an inevitable part of acceptance, resistances—which then confronts the transplanted theory or idea, making possible its introduction or toleration, however alien it might appear to be. Fourth, the now full (or partly) accommodated (or incorporated) idea is to some extent transformed by its new uses, its new position in a new time and place.[3]

Having introduced his general framework, Said proceeds to examine the intellectual development of three major Marxist literary critics, Georg Lukács, Lucien Goldmann, and Raymond Williams, with Foucault thrown in toward the end, in order to measure the individual career of each critic against his historical background. For some inexplicable reason, however, his discussion does not go beyond the usual argument that theory is always a response to changing social and historical circumstances.[4] The traveling aspect of his theory is somehow abandoned in the course of his discussion. As I tried to figure out a way to explain why Said's notion of traveling theory got sidetracked so easily and failed to deliver that which it had promised, it occurred to me that perhaps the notion itself lacked the kind of intellectual rigor needed for its own fulfillment. Indeed, who does the traveling?

Does theory travel? If so, how? Granted that theory does possess such subjectivity, a further question is entailed: What is the means of transportation? Is it aircraft, automobile, rickshaw, train, man-of-war, or space shuttle? Commenting on Said's oversight, James Clifford suggests that "Lukacsian Marxism in his essay seems to travel by immigrant boat; theory nowadays takes the plane, sometimes with round-trip tickets."[5] But I would like to take this point a step further, for not only does the concept of traveling theory tend to affirm the primacy of theory (or Western theory, in the context of Said's book) by endowing the latter with full-fledged, mobile subjectivity, but it neglects to account for the vehicle of translation. With the suppression of that vehicle, travel becomes such an abstract idea that it makes no difference whatsoever in which direction theory travels (from West to East or the other way around) and for what purpose (cultural exchange, imperialism, or colonization?), or in which language and for what audience one translates in the first place.[6]

It is not as if Said has not paid attention to the question of translation. In fact, his widely influential book *Orientalism* and later writings all tackle the representation and translation of cultural difference in the Orientalist textual tradition of the West, and Said himself has become a leading contemporary critic of the history of colonialism, imperialism, and ethnocentrism in the West.[7] It is ironic, therefore, that his notion of traveling theory is generally interpreted as if theory (read Western theory) were the incarnation of a hero from a European picaresque narrative who initiates the trip, encounters obstacles en route, and always ends up being accommodated one way or the other by the host country.[8] Inasmuch as language transaction is always a contested territory in national and international struggles, one must rethink one's priorities in theorizing the migration of ideas and theory and ask what role translation and related practices play in the construction of relations of power between the so-called first and third worlds. Indeed, what happens when languages meet during the East-West encounter? Are the relations of power between the two always reducible to patterns of domination and resistance? Is the cultural critic not risking too much for granting too little to the agency of non-Western languages in East-West transactions?

Tejaswini Niranjana's book, *Siting Translation: History, Post-Structuralism, and the Colonial Context,* is probably one of the few attempts to place the problem of translation at the heart of colonial history. Writing about the experience of colonial India, the author sees translation as "part of the colonial discourse of Orientalism" and as "British efforts to obtain information about the people ruled by the merchants of the East India Company."[9] To the extent that the author points to translation as an important site of colonial control, she offers a most powerful critique, indeed; but to the extent that her discussion privileges European languages as target languages in those linguistic transactions and in her own research (for instance, three of her chapters are devoted to discussing Paul de Man, Walter Benjamin, and Derrida), the book leaves the other side of the story untold: What happens when a European language gets translated into a non-European language? Can the power relationship between East and West be reinvented (if not reversed) in that case? If so, how?

In raising those questions, however, I must take care not to endorse new constructs of binary opposition in place of the old ones, no matter whether they take the form of Western theory versus Chinese reality or the more sophisticated one of oppositional discourse. In the case of the former, the theory-reality divide reintroduces the old binary of theory and practice and thus compounds the historical burden that it is supposed to unpack. Perhaps a more meaningful question to ask in this kind of investigation is what type of relationship exists historically between Western theory and Chinese theory, rather than asking, say, whether Western theory is relevant or irrelevant to Chinese reality.[10] On the other hand, the concept of oppositional discourse that prevails in contemporary scholarship on postcoloniality creates a different set of problems, although this idea is far more interesting than the theory-reality opposition mentioned above. My difficulty with the idea of oppositional discourse is that it tends to reduce the complexities surrounding the power relationship between East and West to that of Western domination versus native resistance.[11] There is a certain amount of danger in reifying the patterns of resistance and domination along the East-West divide, since the boundaries between the two are frequently permeable and subject to changing conditions. In my study of translingual practice, therefore, a non-European language does not automatically constitute a site of resistance to European languages. Rather, I see it as a much neglected area where complex processes of domination and resistance can be observed and interpreted from within the discursive context of that language, as well as in connection with other linguistic environments.

I am proposing the notion of translingual practice in order to ground my study of an earlier moment of historical transaction between China and the West in language practices. Since the modern intellectual tradition in China began with translation, adaptation, appropriation, and other interlingual practices in relation to the West, it is inevitable that this inquiry should take translation as its point of departure. Yan Fu's interpretative translation of Huxley's *Evolution and Ethics* (1898) made an enormous impact on China and helped fashion a whole generation of Chinese intelligentsia in his time. In literature, Lin Shu became immensely popular for having rendered over a hundred foreign works into literary Chinese, and his work predated the publication of Lu Xun's first modern short story (1918) by many years.[12] However, I must hasten to add that the focus of my study of translingual practice is not translation in a technical sense, but the *condition of translation* and discursive practices that ensue from initial interlingual contacts between languages. Broadly defined, I will be looking at the process through which new words, meanings, and discourses arise, circulate, and acquire legitimacy within the target language because of, or in spite of, the latter's contact—or collision—with the source language. Meanings, therefore, are not so much "transformed" when concepts pass from the source language into the target language as (re)invented within the local environment of the latter. In that sense, translation is no longer a neutral event untouched by the contending interests of political and ideological struggles. Instead, it becomes the very site of such struggles, where the source language is forced to encounter the target language, where the irreducible differences between them are fought out, authorities evoked or challenged, ambiguities dissolved or created, and so forth, until new words and meanings emerge in the target language itself. I hope the notion of translingual practice will eventually lead to a vocabulary that helps account for the process of adaptation, translation, introduction, and domestication of words, categories, and discourses from one language to another and, furthermore, explains the modes of transmission, manipulation, deployment, and domination within the power structure of the target language.[13]

Self and *Ji*

What is the Chinese equivalent of "self"? This question often rests on the assumption that equivalence of meaning could be readily established across different languages. Does not the existence of bilingual dictionaries testify to the fact? I hear people ask. Isn't it true that the category of the "self" has existed all along in the Chinese philosophical tradition? What about the Confucian notion of *ji*? In my view, those questions are themselves open to question because they ignore the fact that the trope of equivalence between the English word "self" and the Chinese *ji* or other such words has only recently been established in the process of translation and fixed by means of modern bilingual dictionaries.[14] Thus, any linkages that exist between the two derive from historical coincidences whose meanings are contingent on the politics of translingual practice. Once such linkages are established, a text becomes "translatable" in the ordinary sense of the word. However, problems arise immediately—and I cannot stress this point enough—when a comparative theory between languages allows itself to be built upon the basis of an essential category, such as that of "self," whose linguistic identity somehow transcends the history of translation. To give an example, I would like to mention Tu Wei-ming's work on Chinese philosophy in English, as he is the foremost theorist in the United States to expound on the differences between the Neo-Confucian *ji* and the Western notion of the self. Tu Wei-ming's humanist notion of *ji* is predicated on the idea that the former can be readily translated into the English word "self" without the mediation of the modern history of translation. In a number of his works, such as *Humanity and Self-Cultivation: Essays in Confucian Thought* and *Confucian Thought: Selfhood as Creative Transformation,* his argument appears tautological: the Neo-Confucian *ji* differs from (by which he means is superior to) the Western notion of the self, but it remains a notion of the "self."[15] In other words, difference comes to be conceived only at the level of ontological makeup but not at the level of the constitutive category where the question of linguistic transaction must be brought in. The assumed homogeneity between *ji* and "self" inevitably blots out the history of each word, as well as the history of translation of "self" and related words in modern Chinese. His knowledgeable study of Neo-Confucianism notwithstanding, Tu Wei-ming's comparative approach has the disadvantage of circumventing the question of analytical categories by assuming transparency in translation.

In order to open up the equivalence of meanings across different languages that bilingual dictionaries guard so jealously, it is necessary to interrogate the dynamic history of words and related concepts, categories, and discourse beyond the realm of common sense or dictionary definition. For example, it is one thing to know that the English word "self" can be translated as *ziwo, wo, ji,* and so on, but a different thing to realize that each of those translations commands a discursive field that carries its own history. In modern Chinese, *ziwo* is probably a neologism imported from Meiji Japan, where a huge number of Chinese characters had been used to translate concepts from European languages. The other translations of "self" are appropriated from classical Chinese philosophy, Neo-Confucianism in particular, although with a radical and important shift in meaning.[16] To complicate the situation further, there is also a family of words in modern Chinese — *geren, gewei, geti,* translations of the English word "individual" — that are sometimes used interchangeably with the family of *ziwo.*[17] Thus, the slippage of *ziwo, wo, geren, gewei, geti,* and *ji* not only inherits the slippage of meaning between "self" and "individual" in the English original but reflects the complex scenario of translingual practices and its politics in the Chinese context.

Indeed, the notions of *ziwo, wo, geren, gewei, geti, ji,* and the like have come down to us as part of the rich legacy of modern Chinese history.[18] How do we understand and explain this situation? What kind of knowledge does it bring to light besides a popularized image of Westernization, iconoclasm, and antitraditionalism? Is it possible to pose it as a theoretical problem in the context of Chinese modernity rather than foreclose it as an established fact or one of those timeless motifs?

The inaugural issue of the journal *Xin chao* (The renaissance or new tide), published by students of Beijing University at the peak of the New Culture Movement, carries a polemic piece by Chen Jia'ai entitled "Xin" (The new). This article spells out the rhetoric of modernity in a series of tropes. "The new is singular and the old is plural," says the author, "The former is singular for being absolutely unique whereas the latter is plural for being open to infinite multiplication."[19] Armed with the figure of inflective grammar, the author then proceeds to elaborate his point about old and new using the metaphor of genealogy: "It takes two, man and wife, to make a single son at a time (even twins come one after the other). Conversely, parents who give birth to the son were in turn brought into the world by the grandparents, who owed their lives to the great-grandparents, *ad infini-*

tum" (ibid.) Far from being a treatise preaching filial piety, the essay is trying to make the point that "old" ideas, like the older generation, are bound to be replaced by "new" ones, which the author defines in the rest of the essay as singular, unique, modern, and therefore superior.

In the context of the New Culture Movement, the loaded terms of old and new set up a binary opposition between tradition and modernity, which typically intersects with the cultural antinomy of East and West that assigns superiority to the latter. This unique intersection characterizes the historical experience of modernity in China as distinct from that of the West, which also had its share of the *querelle des anciens et des modernes*. While Europe sought the expansion of its territory in the name of progress, China had to endure the violence of imperialism in order to come to terms with "modernity," namely the West.[20] As can be seen, such violence is internalized by the author of the above essay, whose argument for the new and the unique is couched, not surprisingly, in the trope of Indo-European grammatical number: *danshu* (the singular) versus *zhongshu* (the plural), not available in the Chinese language. Inasmuch as the figure of speech in this passage draws on the resources of the inflective Indo-European language, the allegorical thrust of the text may, therefore, be read as privileging the categories of the modern, Western, and individual (symbolized by the son), as opposed to those of the traditional, Chinese, and familial (represented by the older generation). Such rhetoric turns into a driving force behind most of the radical discourses of selfhood, nationhood, and modernity in the May Fourth era.

Since the inflected grammar of the modern self is embedded from the first moment in a history of contested meanings within which the idea of nationhood looms large, it is difficult, if not impossible, to treat the self as an isolated site of unique personal identity. The sources of this difficulty, as I see it, lie not so much in the ontological, psychoanalytical (as in Lacanian theory), or linguistic considerations that usually enable our academic deconstruction of the unitary subject or in the so-called unbroken tradition of holism in Chinese culture, as in the particular kind of history that China and the Chinese have been forced to undergo since the mid–nineteenth century. In other words, the violence of China's encounter with the West forces nationhood upon selfhood, and vice versa, under those unique circumstances. Yet the modern self is never quite reducible to national identity. On the contrary, it is the incongruities, tensions, and struggles between self-hood and national identity, as well as their mutual implication and complicity, that give full meaning to the lived experience of Chinese modernity.

Individualism

Geren zhuyi (individualism) happened to be one of those concepts that held out great promise to help resolve the problematic of modern self-hood and nationhood, but, as I will demonstrate below, it turned out to complicate the whole situation instead. This neologism, like many others, was earlier invented by Meiji intellectuals in Japan to translate Western liberal and nationalist theories of "individualism" (*ko-jin shugi*). Introduced into China at the turn of the century, it soon grew to be a chief signpost on the discursive terrain of the self in modern China. In order to tease out the meaning of individualism in the Chinese context, let me begin by making a brief comparison between two antithetical views about individualism and its relevance to China. The first view is expressed in an article entitled "Gewei zhuyi" (Individualism) that was published in *Dongfang zazhi* (The Eastern miscellany) in 1916. Jia Yi, who signed this essay, says: "Individualism is utterly alien to the Chinese mind. Inasmuch as the clan, local district, state, and society hold absolute dominance, there is no chance for the individual to emerge."[21] A contrary view will be found in Bertrand Russell's *The Problem of China* (1922), in which the author states that "individualism has perished in the West, but in China it survives, for good as well as for evil."[22] Both authors seem to subscribe to a notion of individualism that predicates a core of fixed values, yet their views are mediated by a profound sense of crisis about the state of their nations, that is, Jia Yi's poverty-stricken China and Russell's post–World War I Europe, and by a desire for the other (although on both sides that desire seems embedded a priori in the economy of Western Enlightenment ideology). The contrast provided by their individual positions has major methodological implications for me, because it renders any potential quest for an essential and fixed meaning of the individual and individualism futile and misguided. What really matters here is the discursive practice surrounding the notion of individual, self, and individualism, as well as the politics of such practice.

The above point, however, is not as self-evident as it appears. On the contrary, much of the existing historiography on the theme of Chinese enlightenment in the New Culture Movement treats the concept of individualism as a given value. Li Zehou and Vera Schwarcz, for instance, hold May Fourth nationalism chiefly responsible for bringing the New Culture Movement to an untimely end and consequently jeopardizing the project of enlightenment of which individualism formed an integral part.[23] Both scholars seem to take the grand narrative of the European Enlightenment as a fixed, unproblematic site of meaning against which the Chinese enlightenment is to be measured for its degrees of success (or failure), instead of investigating the latter as part of a dynamic historical process capable of generating its own meanings and terms of interpretation. In so doing, they end up reading history according to a set of master codes, while eliding the subtleties, complexities, and contingencies of given meanings and situations that emerged from the twists and turns of events.[24]

Among mainland Chinese scholars currently engaged in revisionary historiography, there is a general tendency to dub the May Fourth conception of the individual "inauthentic" on the ground of its incommensurability with the original notion from the West. According to that view, Li Zehou was wrong to grant to the New Culturalists a role—short-lived as it was—in the dissemination of the idea of individual freedom. Supporters of this view argue that the tragedy of Chinese intellectuals in this century is that they tend to place the highest premium on society, nation, people, and the state but never on the individual, and that "it is absurd to believe that the 'May Fourth' conception of the 'liberation of individuality' came anywhere close to sending the true message of 'individual freedom.' "[25] While I agree that the May Fourth notion of the individual is always tied up with those of the nation, state, and society, I find it difficult to take the idea that the "original" Western notion of the individual is exempted from those external considerations, nor do I see the Chinese notion as simply a distorted image of the Western idea. Anthony J. Cascardi points out in his book *The Subject of Modernity* that the Enlightenment notion of subjectivity in the West is part of the legitimation question in the theory of modernity and that "the culture of modernity is given shape as a divided whole that can only be unified through the powers of an abstract subject, or its political analogue, the autonomous State. Indeed, it can be said that the State gains power and scope precisely insofar as it provides a means through which the divided subjects of modernity can be made whole."[26] In light of Cascardi's analysis of the political theory of Hobbes, Hegel, Heidegger, Weber, and others in that book, one can hardly maintain an essentialist and ahistorical understanding of the individual without upholding a myth of the West. That being the case, the critique of the Chinese concept of the individual as inauthentic is but a recuperation of the reductive rhetoric of Chinese collectivism versus Western individualism and, therefore, fails to provide a historical explanation as to why the Western notion of the individual or individualism, authentic or otherwise, had been introduced into China in the first place.

In one of his early essays, "Wenhua pianzhi lun" (On misorientation of culture, 1907), Lu Xun offers an explanation that at least situates the problem of the individual and individualism in the context of the Late Qing reform:

> In less than three or four years after the word *geren* [individual] was introduced into China, progressive intellectuals began to shun the idea like leprosy. Whoever had the misfortune of having the label of the individual tagged to his person, he would be regarded as a scoundrel, for it is commonly believed that individualism privileges self-centeredness at the expense of others. The reason that such a misunderstanding is able to thrive is that nobody has ever bothered to look into the true meaning of the word. However, as soon as we investigate the idea in its historical setting, the truth will come to light.[27]

To redeem the authentic meaning of the individual and individualism, Lu Xun draws on diverse European intellectual traditions of the eighteenth and nineteenth centuries. Rousseau, Kierkegaard, Hegel, Schopenhauer, and Henrik Ibsen are invoked as the voices of dignified individuals, whereas frictions or incongruities that exist among those thinkers pass otherwise unnoticed. Such treatment of post-Enlightenment European thought is no doubt extremely reductive, but its reductionism demands a historical explanation. In the context of this essay and elsewhere, such as "Moluo shili shuo" (The power of Mara poetry, 1907), Lu Xun's rhetoric of (in)authenticity with regard to individualism is deployed for the purpose of criticizing the constitutionists for their worship of wealth and military power. In so doing, he challenges their hold on intellectual authority on its own ground (that is, knowledge of the West). Individualism is seized upon as a potential antidote to what he sees as the vice of rampant materialism of his time. For example, he argues that Western civilization has been consistently misrepresented by those Chinese who pursue power, fame, and wealth in the name of progress. In his opinion, the true spirit of the West lies beneath the surface of its nineteenth-century materialism, its essence being the noble ideals of the French revolution, like egalitarianism, freedom, and political rights of the individual. To capture that spirit, one must say "no to materialism" and "yes to the individual" (ibid., p. 185). This view of the individual is interesting less because it anticipates the New Culture Movement by many years than because it provides a contextual basis for the study of the discourse of individualism and, particularly, its subsequent metamorphoses.

In a study of the intellectual legacy of Meiji Japan, to which theorists of Chinese modernity, including Lu Xun, were heavily indebted, Andrew E. Barshay points out that it is important to grasp the meaning of individual and individualism with utmost attentiveness to the rise of modern Japanese nationhood. "We cannot treat individual and state as mutually opposed," he argues; "we are not dealing with alienated personalities." Barshay's discussion of Uchimura and the latter's influence on Nanbara Shigeru demonstrates that even in the case of spiritual quest, "religion did not form an 'exit option' from earthly — read national and organizational — duties. The nation was to be the object of religious action transmuted into expertise."[28] Likewise, James Fujii's recent study of Sōseki and other modern Japanese writers (some of whom Lu Xun read and liked) shows that the strategies of narrativizing subjects in the works of these writers reveal "resistance and capitulation to, uneasiness and complicity with, the discourses of national consolidation and modernity, which discourses mediated the relationship of writer to state in early twentieth-century Japanese literature."[29] In other words, the performative texts of the *kindai shosetsu* are the very site on which the individuated subject, nationhood, textual production, and modernity enter into a meaningful relationship at the moment of their occurrence and interaction.

Indeed, the historical contingency of meanings requires that the notion of the individual be studied as a historical category rather than assumed as a superior, transcendental value. So, instead of taking up a position to valorize the ideology of individualism on behalf of a localized narrative of progress, my study will try to situate the claims of individualism, such as postulated by the theory of Chinese modernity, within their specific historical contexts and subject them to critical examination. My argument is that, contrary to that which is commonly believed, the discourse of individualism stood in a rather ambivalent relation to the master narrative of the nation-state in the early republican period. Like all other prevalent discourses of the time, it invested in the major process of power reconfiguration in ways that defy simplistic closure (that is, authentic versus inauthentic individualism). As my analysis will show, individualism does not always constitute itself as the counterdiscourse of nationalism, nor does the enlightenment see itself as the other of national salvation. Tensions between the two discourses seem to derive from the instability of their historical meanings just as much as from their mutual implication and complicity.

Journalistic Debates

In this section, I will focus on some of the most interesting debates on individualism in the early republican period; they appeared in the following journals: *Dongfang zazhi* (The Eastern miscellany), *Xin qingnian* (New youth), and *Xin chao* (The renaissance or new tide). My discussion will deal mainly with the period between the mid-1910s and the early 1920s, which was the relatively short but crucial time that encompassed the New Culture Movement and the May Fourth Movement, as well as the founding of the Chinese Communist Party (CCP). I choose to focus on the agency of journalistic debates partly because those journals are seminal historical documents of the time and partly because I wish to avoid treating the concept of individualism as a keyword.[30] On the other hand, I conceive of my study as an investigation of the *rhetorical practice* of journalistic writing rather than a straightforward account of what was written in these journals. This approach, I hope, will allow me to disengage my study of translingual practice from what is generally known as the history of ideas. To be sure, the above-mentioned journals are not alone in bringing to public awareness the problem of the individual and his or her relationship with the modern nation-state. Nevertheless, they represent some of the most influential voices of the time and, by unraveling the kinds of rhetoric in them, I wish to bring out the stakes of the discourse of individualism in the nation-building process of early modern China.

The *Eastern Miscellany,* founded in 1904, was one of the oldest and most influential journals published by the Commercial Press. It started out as an open forum for the discussion of politics, national economy, foreign policy, education, and other public issues. After Du Yaquan became its new editor-in-chief in 1911, he began to introduce drastic changes in terms of format and content, placing increased emphasis on the issues of self, gender, and psychology. Although the question of the individual long preceded the existence of the *Eastern Miscellany* as part of the theory of the nation-state in the writings of Huang Zunxian, Yan Fu, Liang Qichao, and others,[31] Du Yaquan's article "Geren zhi gaige" (Reforming the individual), published in the June 1914 number of the *Eastern Miscellany,* represented one of the first major journalistic efforts to bring this question to the attention of the new republic in the aftermath of the 1911 revolution.[32] In this essay, the author points out that the types of social reform implemented in the past few decades have focused exclusively on macrolevel politics, the educational system, and the business economy, whereas proper attention should have been devoted to the reform of *geren,* or the individual (a subtle displacement of Liang Qichao's *xinmin,* or new citizen). As a result, even though the new republic replaced the old imperial order, the reform has not fundamentally changed the old bureaucracy, which continues to do business as usual and, moreover, turns reformers themselves into bureaucrats who now go by the name of civil servants of the republic. Genuine reform, he emphasizes, must originate at the level of the individual, including those self-appointed reformers. Until the individual begins to face the reality of "his own frail and unhealthy body, his impotent and weak spirit, his shallow and incapable mind, and his disordered and purposeless life, social reform will be no more than a remote dream."[33] The mere fact that Du Yaquan stresses the centrality of the individual in the reform program does not imply that he endorses the Enlightenment notion of individualism. On the contrary, it is the limits of the individual that he sees and addresses here.

It is worth noting that the concept of individualism had not yet acquired the kind of ideological and emotional baggage that it would accumulate a few years later when the New Culture Movement got under way. For Du Yaquan, the meaning of individualism is ambivalent and needs redefinition: "We are not individualists," he says, "but socialism must be imagined on the basis of individualism. Confucius means precisely that when he says that a scholar should study for self-improvement, so does Mencius when he adjures us to cultivate our inner being" (ibid., p. 3). What strikes me most about Du's use of individualism is that he sees it as fully compatible with socialism and Confucianism. That brings out two points. First, the concept of individualism is undergoing a semantic conversion that aims to redeem it from the negative image in which it has been cast by Liang Qichao's theory of the nation-state. In his *New Citizen* and *On Liberty*, for example, Liang Qichao has allowed the nation-state to take absolute precedence over the individual and has tried to maintain a careful distinction between the liberty of a people and individual freedom while opposing the former to the latter.[34] What Du Yaquan attempts to do in this essay is to reconcile the two. Second, individualism has not yet become radicalized at this particular juncture of history, either as the polar opposite of Confucianism or as the other of socialism. The first of such polarizations, as I will explain later, occurred around the New Culture Movement (1917) and went on through the May Fourth Movement, when individualism came to invest heavily in the political indictment against traditional Chinese culture. The next wave of polarization set in during the Communist revolution in the middle and late twenties, when individualism acquired the negative status of bourgeois ideology and was opposed to socialism. In Du Yaquan's view, however, individualism is but a modern version of Confucianism that emphasizes the need for self-reform, and at the same time it articulates a version of socialism that predicates the interest of the average members of society. This peculiar (re)interpretation of Confucianism, socialism, and individualism helps throw light on the reform agenda of Du's own time. Since his text and context were thoroughly embedded in the historical circumstances under which he wrote, it is beside the point to argue whether his particular interpretation of any of these ideas is authentic or not. Insofar as the condition and the production of knowledge are concerned, interpretations and misinterpretations (if there is any such thing) both obtain and participate in the making of real historical events. As Edward Said points out, calling one work a misreading of another's or relating that misreading to a general theory of interpretation as misinterpretation is "to pay no critical attention to history and to situation."[35] The question that interests me, therefore, is why the author interprets the way he does and what new meanings are produced in this process.

Du Yaquan's article is probably one of the first journalistic attempts to bring *geren* (the individual) into public discussion after the founding of the new republic. But the essay does not go beyond constituting the individual as a privileged site of reform, and therein lies his affinity with Liang Qichao. In Min Zhi's article, "Wo" (I, or self), which appeared in the same journal in 1916, the individual begins to evolve into something of an absolute value. The author preaches self-reliance with an acute modern historical consciousness, although much of what he says is couched in the language of ancient Chinese philosophy.[36] Min Zhi situates his argument in the total bankruptcy of the ancient world, pointing out that, at a time when the country disintegrates and poverty, unrest, and catastrophe reign everywhere, the individual is left with no resources. Whereas in the old imperial age a man would take consolation in the thought that he could read the sorrows of the people and bring them to the attention of the emperor, nowadays one can do absolutely nothing. Under those circumstances, the best thing one can do is to fall back on one's own self. Self-reliance thus becomes a necessary means of survival in the modern world. In order to justify his claim that the self is the raison d'etre of existence, Min Zhi draws a distinction between *siwo* (private self) and *gongwo* (public self) and elaborates the dialectic of the two on the basis of a worn metaphor. Just as a candle illuminates every corner of the room when it gives out light, he argues, so the pursuit of self-interest will also benefit others. *Gongwo* and *siwo* are thus interconnected and mutually reinforced, except that the former is set apart from the latter by a sense of moral commitment in its relentless crusade for individual *quanli* (rights). But when he claims that *gongwo* (the public self) "must fight those who block its way until the desired objective is achieved" and that it will "thrive in *jingzheng* (competition)," this public self sounds more like a social Darwinist than a beneficial candlelight (ibid., p. 16).[37]

The next issue of the *Eastern Miscellany* (1916) carries the article "Gewei zhuyi" (Individualism), by Jia Yi, whom I mentioned earlier. Jia Yi openly champions the Western Enlightenment notion of the individual.[38] Individualism, he argues, is the single most effective medicine to cure China's illness, the root of which lies in her weakness for totalistic thinking. The modern world abhors *longtong* (totality), and everything under the sun must be subjected to the scientific law of specification, division, and subdivision. To him, the master trope of modernity is *fen* (to divide, separate, classify, differentiate): "What is modern civilization? By way of illustration, there are branches in science, division of labor in society, liberated individuals, independent personalities and whatnot" (ibid., p. 7). The case of individualism is borne out, moreover, by established modern disciplines such as psychology, sociology, and ethics, all of which are designed, in his view, to assist in "the development of the individual" and his "self-realization" (ibid., p. 8). The modern individual is now opposed to social collectives. State, society, community, and family are all supposed to provide for the individual and not hinder his growth. This kind of oppositional rhetoric would soon help unleash a tremendous amount of political energy during the New Culture Movement and the May Fourth period. But the paradox is that, throughout the essay, the author himself remains oblivious to his own totalistic impulse in prescribing individualism as *the* cure for China's illness.

In the next year, Du Yaquan brought out a new article entitled "Geren yu guojia zhi jieshuo" (The boundary between the individual and the state) in the *Eastern Miscellany*. He set out to specify the relationship between the individual and the state. Du insists that the line between the individual and the state be scrupulously drawn so that neither will encroach upon the rights or interests of the other. The oppositional rhetoric that we noted in Jia Yi's article is now expressed in an unequivocally conflictual framework. "It is commonly believed that the state represents totality whereas the individual belongs to this totality as a member, who may thus be submerged in the totality."[39] The author then proceeds to criticize such subordination of the individual to the state. In fact, throughout the article one senses a good deal of anxiety about the increasing hold of the state and nationalist discourse on the individual. "Who represents the state?" he asks. "Perhaps it is just a handful of administrators who decide to sacrifice the interest of the majority to their own will" (ibid., p. 4). In a less cynical moment, he points out that the architecture of the state is founded on the building blocks of the individual. Without due respect for the integrity of the latter, there cannot be reliable support for the former. On the surface, this sounds like an idea taken directly from the theory of German Romantic thinkers, such as Wilhelm von Humboldt, who opposed state action on behalf of the welfare of the citizens because such action, in his view, misunderstood the dignity of man.[40] But, on deeper levels, there is something more interesting going on here than the mere assertion of the *Humanitätsideal*, for Du Yaquan's argument clearly assumes that modernity is quite capable of placing the average individual in unmediated relation to the nation-state, as opposed to the earlier forms of social organization. The author may well criticize the oppression of the individual by the state, but his critique cannot disrupt the state-individual continuum that he describes so lucidly. The very act of elaborating a dialectic between the two is to reproduce that continuum. In order for the nation-state to claim the individual in some "unmediated" fashion, the individual must be "liberated" in the first place from the family, clan, or other traditional ties that claim his or her loyalty. The discourse of individualism performed precisely that liberatory role in the early history of modern China. As Tse-tsung Chow points out in a slightly different context, "While the disintegration of the old ethics probably emancipated the individual somewhat from the bond with his family and clan, it also cleared the way for placing the individual in bondage to state, party, or other social and economic organizations."[41] I would also argue that the discourse of individualism has probably accomplished something more than liberating the individual from family to state. It has contributed to the process of inventing *geren* for the goals of liberation and national revolution. In that sense, despite its apparent clash with the nation-state, the discourse of individualism finds itself in complicity with nationalism. Being a discursive formation of modernity, the unmediated continuum of the individual and the nation-state seeks to contain the conflicts it generates, which explains why the critique of the state's subordination of the individual can be so readily recuperated by the object of that critique.

Gao Yihan's 1915 essay "Guojia fei rensheng zhi guisu lun" (The state is not the ultimate goal of human life) in *Youth Magazine* (later *New Youth*) criticizes the modern state in a similar vein, but he also introduces the notion of *renmin* (the people), an aggregate of individuals, and treats it as a potential opposite of the state. Like most journalistic writings of the time, this essay contains numerous references to European philosophy and political science, sometimes via the work of Japanese scholars. Since the enlightenment theory of the nation-state dictates the terms of his critique, the author remains blind to the fact that *renmin* (the people) is just as much a product of the modern nation-state as the individual. What I find most peculiar about his argument, however, is not so much the concept of *renmin* as his translation of the individual as *xiaoji*—a word appropriated from ancient Chinese philosophy—instead of the usual word *geren*. *Xiaoji* evokes *daji* (the Greater Self), which serves as a trope for *guojia* (nation-state) and occasionally for *shehui* (society).[42] The author elucidates the relationship of *xiaoji* and the state in the words of a Japanese scholar as follows: "'The development of *xiaoji* [individual] is the concern of the state. Without the proper development of the individual there can be no proper development of the state'" (ibid., p. 7). This is reminiscent of the earlier dialectic examined above, but here I also see a subtle slippage of meanings and categories. The word *xiao* (small) opens the thinking of the individual to the metaphoric realm of substitution, displacement, and analogy in which the word *da* (big or greater) reigns. In other words, *xiao* is related to *da* not only as its antithetical other but as its hierarchical other, or the lesser of the two. The implication of this linguistic mechanism for our understanding of the problematic of the individual versus the state is manifold, particularly in light of the fact that publications in *New Youth* during this period were chiefly responsible for disseminating the modern idea of *xiaoji* and *daji*.[43] Inasmuch as the individual is named *xiao* and the state *da,* the critique of the state on behalf of the individual cannot transcend the hierarchical order of a language that names and determines such a relationship. Furthermore, as the concept of the greater *self* seems to project full-fledged subjectivity onto the state, it displaces the individual as agency and site of power on the discursive level. Indeed, never has the individual been so inextricably tied up with the nation-state and so ineluctably claimed by it as when *xiaoji* and *daji* began their dialectic career.

With the advent of *New Youth* on the eve of the New Culture Movement, the discourse of individualism began to turn in a new direction. In "Rensheng weiyi zhi mudi" (The sole purpose of life), for example, Li Yishi accuses traditional Chinese philosophy of sacrificing individual happiness and self-interest for the sake of ritual and social morality. By way of contrast, he extols the virtues of individualism exhibited by the Anglo-Saxon race and admires their power and wealth, which he attributes to individual-centered Western philosophy. No doubt this is a far cry from Du Yaquan's understanding of Confucianism that I analyzed earlier. The radical polarization of individualism (as a privileged signifier of the West) and Confucianism (as the equivalent of Chinese tradition) that would prevail subsequently in the discourse of the New Culture Movement is already anticipated in this 1915 essay of *New Youth*. To the author, Confucianism encourages slave mentality because it ritualizes the dependency of the subject on the ruler, of son on father, and of wife on husband: "Like slaves and beasts of burden, these tragic creatures could not aspire to self-autonomy, to say nothing of self-development. The true law of the universe is *weiwo* [egoism] and it must be maintained at all cost."[44] He then cites science, sociology, psychology, and nineteenth-century European ethics in support of his theory of self-aggrandizement. But if the author's argument is to be taken seriously at all, it is not difficult for us to see that his rhetoric derives its power from contradictory sources. Individualism is perceived not only as thoroughly homogeneous with nationalism by virtue of its being associated with the superior Anglo-Saxon nations, but as anticipating and nurturing it. This observation is not intended as a critique of the author's lack of sophistication, although that is certainly true if we compare him with Gao Yihan, but serves as a reminder that the discourse of individualism, which never had a stable center of meanings, was undergoing a dramatic process of transformation around the New Culture Movement, out of which new configurations of power would emerge.

Chen Duxiu, editor of this iconoclastic journal, seized on the idea of individualism as a powerful weapon to launch his wholesale attack on Chinese tradition. Among the numerous essays he wrote at this stage, the one published in the December 1915 number of *New Youth*, entitled "Dongxi minzu genben sixiang zhi chayi" (The fundamental difference between the intellectual traditions of Eastern and Western peoples), probably best represents his early views. Chen assesses the relative strengths or weaknesses of the East and the West by the importance they attach to individualism. He argues:

Western nations give priority to individualism whereas Eastern nations value family and clan. From the ancient times down to the present, Westerners have always been nations of thoroughgoing individualism, including the British and Americans, as well as the French and Germans. The same can be said of Nietzsche and Kant. Their state and society place ethics, morality, politics, and law before everything else and uphold the free rights of the individual and his happiness. The freedom of speech precisely guarantees the development of individuality. Before the law, all individuals are equal. As the free rights of the individual, called human rights, are protected by the Constitution, the state cannot take them away.[45]

Although Chen Duxiu's rhetoric would undergo an interesting reversal after the May Fourth Movement several years later, the above-quoted view illustrates very well the changing rhetoric of this ongoing debate on individualism, in which tradition is being targeted as the chief enemy.

Indeed, it is in this context that the New Culture Movement, literary revolution, and their shared antagonism toward tradition should be grasped. In 1916, Li Dazhao published an article in *Chenzhong bao* (Morning bell) entitled "Qingchun zhonghua zhi chuangzao" (Creating a youthful China), in which he maintains that the creation of a new culture falls upon the shoulders of iconoclastic thinkers who have the courage to challenge tradition with original thinking, to assert the authority of their *ziwo* (self), and to advocate self-awakening.[46] When Hu Shi envisions literary reform in his two seminal essays "Suggestions for Literary Reform" (1917) and "Toward a Constructive Theory of Literary Revolution" (1918), he calls on the genuine voice of the individual to replace the ancient classical canon.[47] Likewise, in Zhou Zuoren's writing, individualism and humanism are proposed as the guiding spirit for modern Chinese literature, the underpinning argument of which is that classical Chinese literature has failed to live up to humanistic goals and must, therefore, be discarded.[48] Indeed, if one were to summarize the remarkable role played by the New Culture Movement in modern history, one might say that this movement successfully constituted Chinese tradition and its classics as the polar opposite of individualism and humanism, whereas the nation-state, which used to occupy that antithetical position, was now largely taken for granted.

The discussion of individualism during the New Culture Movement was by no means confined to theoretical debates, since such considerations lay at the very heart of literary reform. A significant event took place in the stylistics of fiction when May Fourth writers began to translate and introduce modes of psychonarration, free indirect style, lengthy interior monologue, and other narrative strategies from European fiction into their own works. The impact of this stylistic change has yet to be fully grasped in detailed analysis of individual texts, as my reading of *Camel Xiangzi* attempts to show in the next section, in light of comparative stylistics. By way of suggestion, let me just point out that the new stylistics of fiction allows Chinese writers to locate the protagonist in a new symbolic context, one in which the protagonist no longer serves as a mere element within the nexus of patriarchal kinships and/or in a transcendental, divine scheme, as in most premodern Chinese fiction, but dominates the text, instead, as the locus of meaning and reality in possession of psychological and moral "truth." Not surprisingly, the May Fourth period was also a time when huge quantities of first-person fiction and autobiography written in a "Western" form appeared.[49] The modern autobiographical subject—one that takes itself seriously, asserts its autonomy against traditional society, and possesses an interiority representable in narrative—made its entry into Chinese literature exactly at the time when the individual and tradition were constructed as polar opposites.[50] To modern writers, this individual self can be immensely empowering, because it enables him or her to devise a dialogic language with which to attack the status quo, as Lu Xun does in "The Diary of a Madman." But it can also be problematic, because the individual often turns out to be a misfit in the hostile environment of a rapidly disintegrating society. The Russian "superfluous man," who figures so prominently in Yu Dafu's works, thus becomes a perfect embodiment of the typical dilemma of modernity.

Yet, to conclude that subjectivism and individualism characterize May Fourth literature is to miss the point here. What I am trying to suggest is that the discourse of individualism enabled May Fourth intellectuals to open up a new battlefront in their struggle to claim modernity. It is not as if the individual were valorized at the expense of society or nation. Even as Chinese tradition fell under attack, nationalism and social collectivism were never abandoned. On the contrary, the latter now inhabited the same homogeneous space of modernity as individualism. One need only recall Yu Dafu's protagonist in "Chen lun" (Sinking), where the crisis of modernity is experienced as one of selfhood, manhood, and nationhood simultaneously. Hu Shi's 1919 essay "Bu xiu" (Immortality) in *New Youth* bears further witness to the May Fourth conception of the individual, nation, and society. In it Hu Shi names the individual "I" as *xiaowo,* whose extension or multiplication in society is called *dawo* (greater self).[51] *Xiaowo* is mortal and incomplete, as opposed to *dawo,* which is immortal and capable of renewing itself. Hu Shi's dialectic of the two selves echoes that of Gao Yihan's *xiaoji* and *daji,* except that in the anti-imperialist context of the May Fourth Movement the nation-state is no longer perceived as antithetical to the individual, so *dawo* here stands for modern organic society with which the individual must come to terms under the aegis of the nation-state. It should be pointed out, however, that Hu Shi's subordination of *xiaowo* (individual) to *dawo* (society) does not indicate regression from individualism or enlightenment on the part of the New Culturalists. I see his position as a logical expression of the theory of modernity, which does not seek to liberate individuals so much as to constitute them as citizens of the nation-state and as members of a modern society.

It is no surprise that the first essay in the initial issue of the *Renaissance* (1919) is devoted to the question of the place of the individual in modern society. Fu Sinian, author of this article, begins by establishing the superiority of Western scientific and humanist knowledge against several indigenous intellectual traditions—Taoism, Buddhism, and Confucianism—none of which, according to him, embodies the truth of human life. In his opinion, one must look for the truth in biology, psychology, sociology, and so forth, because modern scientific knowledge is subject-centered and humanistic. Finally, Fu brings out his favorite slogan in both Chinese and English: "The free development of the individual for the Common Welfare." [52] In an attached footnote, he confesses that the Chinese language is inimical to his modern way of thinking, so he is compelled to use English. This sounds almost like a burlesque of language reform to a post–May Fourth ear. If the author were to follow this logic all the way through, would he perhaps end up finding the free development of the individual inimical to the common welfare of the nation as well? This is precisely the point at which leftist and Marxist intellectuals would enter and stake their claims in the aftermath of the May Fourth Movement.

Fu Sinian's liberal-humanist ideal was soon displaced by a leftist ideology that cast grave doubts on individualism and capitalized on the conflictual relationship between individual and society. In 1921, the *Renaissance* published an article entitled "Wu he wo" (Matter and self) by Wang Xinggong, who tried to bring the autonomy of the individual into question. The author begins by rejecting the notions of "physical self" and "spiritual self," maintaining that this autonomous

"I" we call self does not really exist: "If the self at the age of twenty were to encounter the self at the age of forty on the street, they would probably not recognize each other. Nor would any one else imagine that they were one and the same person. If the identity of the 'I' changes constantly as time goes on and is utterly heterogeneous with itself, can we still maintain that it is a fixed, permanent, and unchanging essence?"[53] The upshot of his argument is that self is a form of experience, forever changing and forever adapting, whose meaning is solely determined by the material world. Therefore, to emphasize the importance of the individual is to misplace one's priority. It is interesting that the author uses Confucianism as a scapegoat for misplaced priorities. In his view, the idea of self-cultivation in Confucianism means placing exclusive emphasis on the improvement of the individual, with the implication that a perfect personality would bring about a perfect society. He dismisses that idea as sheer illusion. In his opinion, no fundamental change in society will occur until the sociopolitical system is tackled. Therefore, the question of society must take absolute precedence over that of the individual. Now, it is not for me to decide in this book which social theory, Confucianism or socialism, is more desirable for China, because I am interested only in the ways in which the terms of the debate are set or the uses to which either of those theories is put. In other words, to interpret individualism in terms of Confucianism in the antitraditionalist context of the May Fourth period is to incriminate it and turn it into a negative idea. We have come full circle from Du Yaquan's reconciliation of the two terms, in which the opposite effect was intended.

Chen Duxiu's reversed position on individualism in 1920 is even more illuminating in that respect. In "Xuwu de geren zhuyi ji ren ziran zhuyi" (Nihilistic individualism and laissez-faire theory) he attacks individualism as a socially irresponsible, nihilist idea. Instead of aligning it with Confucianism, as Wang Xinggong does, he sees it as originating from the Taoist philosophy: "The evils that have hindered the development of culture and scholarship in China can be traced back to the nihilist individualism and laissez-faire philosophy of Lao Zi and Zhuang Zi."[54] To be sure, this accusation is anachronistic in the extreme. However, my purpose is not to defend Taoism against ludicrous charges but to call attention to the changing scenario of the discourse of individualism between 1920 and 1921. When one connects individualism with traditional Chinese culture in the May Fourth context, be it Confucianism (Wang Xinggong) or Taoism (Chen Duxiu), one is in fact naming it as the roadblock of social progress and the opposite of socialism or Communism. Of course, what we witness here is not the suppression of the discourse of individualism but the reinvention of it so that the discourse could serve the desired political end in a changing historical context.

One of the earliest sophisticated critiques of individualism as bourgeois ideology, in my view, was offered by Deng Feihuang in his essay entitled "Geren zhuyi de youlai jiqi yingxiang" (The origin and impact of individualism), which appeared in the *Eastern Miscellany* in 1922.[55] In this lengthy article, the author traces the development of individualism through the rise of the free market and capitalism in the West and through the Industrial Revolution and the European Enlightenment. He concludes by saying that, as a bourgeois ideology, individualism is passé and should be replaced by socialism. This is, of course, a familiar Marxist critique that at least shows some respect for the etymology and historicity of individualism, but, as knowledge and power are inextricably linked together, it is not enough to grasp what a discourse says, and one must be attentive to what the discourse does, as well. In the context of the national politics of the early twenties, the Marxist evolutionist view of history is used to open up a political future whereby new power configurations involving the Communist Party, the Nationalist Party, warlords, and imperialist powers begin to surface and engage in intense local struggles.[56] By the same token, the critique of bourgeois individualism introduces a rhetoric of social collectivism that can be used to advance the politics of the left, in much the same way as did the earlier liberatory discourse of individualism that had first established the individual-state continuum.

In the mid-1920s through the early 1930s, the discussion of "*puluo wenxue*" (proletarian literature) among writers and critics on the left led to a major rethinking of the earlier iconoclastic literature.[57] Once again, the notion of individualism came under gunfire as the new rhetoric began to stress the importance of class-consciousness in literary production.[58] Leftist critics and writers tried to promote what they called *geming wenxue* (revolutionary literature), *dazhong wenyi* (art for the masses), and proletarian literature. Cheng Fangwu, the leading theoretician of the Creation Society, called for the "revolutionary intelligentsia" to negate themselves and acquire class consciousness.[59]

In order to depict the life of the working class and to produce a non-elite literature, he argued, writers must abandon bourgeois individualism and familiarize themselves with the language of workers and peasants. Likewise, Lu Xun had renounced his earlier position on individualism by this time and had begun to question the idea of *pingmin wenxue* (plebeian literature), a humanist notion promoted earlier by his brother Zhou Zuoren. Lu Xun held that *pingmin wenxue* was a self-contradictory term, for literary production had always been the sole prerogative of the upper class. "Until workers and peasants themselves are liberated from the dominant ideology of the elite class, there can be no literature for ordinary people in the real sense of the word."[60] Lu Xun was sympathetic with revolutionary literature, although he himself never intended to write proletarian fiction. Yet it is a profound irony that his earlier fiction came under attack by the radical left, especially by Taiyang she (The sun society), for more or less the same reasons he outlined in the above quote. Qian Xingcun, a leading critic of the Sun Society, wrote in 1928, proclaiming the death of individualism and of the liberal ideas of petit bourgeois intellectuals.[61] He contended that Lu Xun's cynical, elitist, negative portrayal of the Chinese peasant class in "The True Story of Ah Q" and other stories must be replaced by a revolutionary literature that anticipates and encourages the coming of class consciousness. It is no surprise that Jiang Guangci's short novel *Shaonian piaobo zhe* (The youthful tramp, 1926) was singled out by the Sun Society as the earliest example of such proletarian fiction.[62]

The changing rhetoric surrounding the individual, class, state, and social collectivity tells us a great deal about the historical situatedness of Chinese modernity during the period examined here. To conclude, I would like to jump ahead of this essay by making a few general remarks about the subsequent metamorphosis of the discourse of individualism after the founding of the People's Republic in 1949, for one can observe interesting linkages between the period I have discussed and the later decades, as well as profound changes that have taken place since. The founding of the People's Republic marked a major turning point mainly because discursive authority was now placed squarely in the hands of the state. Although much of the CCP rhetoric was inherited from the earlier leftist criticism of bourgeois ideology, the state successfully transformed the idea of individualism into a synecdoche for a negative West, as the discursive struggle surrounding this meaning began to play an important role in China's reinvention of the power relationship between East and West, as well as that between the state and its intelligentsia. In other words, the state had a political stake in presenting the idea of individualism to its people as *un-Chinese*. Paradoxically, the anti-Western rhetoric of the state is most effective when it sends its opponents to rally around individualism in the predictable gesture of pro-Western defiance. What tends to be neglected, forgotten, or suppressed in these endless contentions for or against the West is the potent history surrounding the discourse of individualism within China, a century-long history of translingual practice fraught with political exigencies. As late as the mid-1980s, there was a major controversy over critic Liu Zaifu's theory of literary subjectivity in mainland China.[63] In many ways, that controversy carried over some of the familiar overtones from the earlier debates on individualism, but it also took on a character of violence reminiscent of the Cultural Revolution.[64] Yet, there is another kind of violence not so acutely felt but all the more damaging, which is amnesia, a forgetting of the discursive history of the past.

Notes

1. In the opinion of Paul Smith and other critics of deconstruction, Derridean critique of the subject forecloses the possibility of human agency and deprives marginalized social groups of the ground for political action. However, the facile equation between the individual/subject and agency made by these critics suggests that the subject-centered philosophy of the West may well persist at one discursive level even as it is being rejected at another (see Paul Smith, *Discerning the Subject* [Minneapolis: University of Minnesota Press, 1988], and Nancy K. Miller, "Changing the Subject," in *Coming to Terms: Feminism, Theory, Politics,* ed. Elizabeth Weed [New York: Routledge, 1989]). Stephen Heath's suggestion of "taking the risk of essence" and Gayatri Chakravorty Spivak's notion of "strategic essentialism," on the other hand, articulate an identity politics that aims to empower feminist, ethnic, gay, and other minority communities in North America without sacrificing the contingencies of adopted identities (see Stephen Heath, "Differences," *Screen* 19, no. 3 [1978]: 50–112; and Gayatri Chakravorty Spivak, *In Other Worlds: Essays in Cultural Politics* [New York: Methuen, 1987]). However, as critics have pointed out, one cannot afford to surrender the subject unconditionally to the general hegemony of Identity in spite of the political gains promised therein, because new identities could also be problematic and oppressive. There is a great deal of scholarship on this debate in feminist, gay, and postcolonial theory, as well as in ethnic studies, but it is not my purpose to engage or reiterate them here. The following works merit special attention: Donna Haraway, "A Manifesto for Cyborgs: Science, Technology, and Socialist Feminism in the 1980s," in *Coming to Terms: Feminism, Theory, Politics,* ed. Weed, pp. 173–204; Henry Louis Gates Jr., ed., *Race, Writing, and Difference* (Chicago: University of Chicago Press, 1985); R. Radhakrishnan, "Eth-

nic Identity and Post-Structuralist Difference," *Cultural Critique* 6 (Winter 1987): 199–220; and a group of essays on feminism under the title "The Essential Difference: Another Look at Essentialism," *differences* 1, no. 2 (Summer 1989). For me, whose interest lies in the critique of categories, a different kind of problem arises from the above scenario. I am concerned that the strategic impulse of identity politics might sidestep the question of the self as a historical and analytical category, not to mention not problematizing it in any sustained manner. Hence the impoverishment of our understanding of the whole problem on a theoretical level.

2. In an essay entitled "The Concept of Cultural Translation in British Social Anthropology," Talal Asad poses the question of unequal relationship between the languages of the East and West in the field of social anthropology: "To put it crudely, because the languages of Third World societies—including, of course, the societies that social anthropologists have traditionally studied—are 'weaker' in relation to Western languages (and today, especially to English), they are more likely to submit to forcible transformation in the translation process than the other way around. The reason for this is, first, that in their political-economic relations with Third World countries, Western nations have the greater ability to manipulate the latter. And, secondly, Western languages produce and deploy *desired* knowledge more readily than Third World languages do. (The knowledge that Third World languages deploy more easily is not sought by Western societies in quite the same way, or for the same reason)" (see *Writing Culture: The Poetics and Politics of Ethnography,* ed. James Clifford and George E. Marcus [Berkeley: University of California Press, 1986], pp. 157–58). It seems to me that Asad's critique of ethnographic practice applies equally well to the overall linguistic situation of contemporary theory.

3. Edward W. Said, *The World, the Text, and the Critic* (Cambridge, Mass.: Harvard University Press, 1983), pp. 226–27.

4. Besides, Said focuses only on the European side, as in his earlier book *Orientalism,* where the bibliography comprises works written exclusively in the metropolitan European languages English and French.

5. James Clifford, "Notes on Travel and Theory," *Inscriptions* 5 (1989): 185.

6. Said's concept of traveling theory has drawn some serious attention from historians, anthropologists, and literary critics in this country. The journal *Inscriptions,* for instance, published a special issue, "Traveling Theories and Traveling Theorists," in 1989, which I believe is a major collective effort to apply and revise Said's theory. Nearly all eight fine essays and three commentaries contained in that volume center on the question of location. Lata Mani's essay "Multiple Mediations: Feminist Scholarship in the Age of Multinational Reception" illustrates the politics of location by comparing the differing receptions of her own historiography on *sati* in the United States, Great Britain, and India. Following Chandra Mohanty's definition of the politics of location as "the historical, geographic, cultural, psychic and imaginative boundaries which provide the ground for political definition and self definition," Mani emphasizes that "location" is not a fixed point but a "temporality of struggle" and that its politics is characterized by processes of movement "between cultures, languages, and complex configurations of meaning and power" (Lata Mani, "Multiple Mediations: Feminist Scholarship in the Age of Multinational Reception," *Inscriptions* 5 [1989]: 5. The quotes come from Chandra Mohanty, "Feminist Encounters, Locating the Politics of Experience," *Copyright* 1 [Fall 1987]: 31, 40, 42).

By focusing on the complexity of the self-positioning of the theorist in the postcolonial context, this move helps revise Said's original conception of traveling theory. At the same time, however, traveling theory is here replaced by the postcolonial traveling theorist as the privileged subject in the multiple mediations of different locations. To the extent that the fuzzy notion of location helps cut a discursive space for post-colonial theory and the third-world "diaspora" in the first world, it might work very well, but it is not very clear to me exactly how the postcolonial theorist relates to the "third world" except that he or she travels in and out of it and points out its differ-ence from that of the "first world."

David Scott's analysis of the postcolonial situation in "Locating the Anthropologi-cal Subject: Postcolonial Anthropologists in Other Places" in the same issue of *In-scriptions* suggests that the direction in which the postcolonial travels matters just as much as the difference of locations when he or she leaves one place for another: "The postcolonial is now, in Derek Walcott's felicitously ironic phrase, a 'fortunate traveller.' However, even as we recognize this irreversible redistribution of the postcolonial map (one which Louise Bennett has so inimitably satirized in such poems as 'Colonization in Reverse'), we should not lose sight of the fact that these movements are rather *one* way than the other. Colonial and postcolonial peoples were/are going *west*" (David Scott, "Locating the Anthropological Subject: Postcolonial Anthropologists in Other Places," *Inscriptions* 5 [1989]: 75). Ironically, as immigrants arrive by large numbers in the *West*, theory is simultaneously penetrating the *East*. In her essay "Postcolonial Feminists in the Western Intellectual Field: Anthropologists *and* Native Informants?" Mary E. John points out that "the choice of the term itself is telling—not emigrant, but immigrant" (ibid., p. 57).

The linkages between the two phenomena can hardly escape one's notice. In this aspect it is doubtful that the postcolonial condition differs much from that of the old colonial era. But I will defer the subject of immigrant culture to the scholars of dias-pora, whose excellent work has attracted increased attention in this country, and con-centrate instead on the subject of traveling theory between East and West. My ques-tion is this: what happens when theory that has been produced in one language gets translated into another?

7. See Said's recent book, *Culture and Imperialism* (New York: Knopf, 1993).

8. See the *Inscriptions* special issue, "Traveling Theories and Traveling Theorists" (vol. 5 [1989]).

9. Tejaswini Niranjana, *Siting Translation: History, Post-Structuralism, and the Colonial Context* (Berkeley: University of California Press, 1992), p. 11.

10. This is the view expressed in Zhang Longxi's essay entitled "Western Theory and Chinese Reality" (*Critical Inquiry* 19 [Autumn 1992]: 105–30). In it Zhang cites Lu Xun's much-quoted phrase of *nalai zhuyi* ("grabbism") to justify the Chinese ap-propriation of Western ideas. Although I agree that the meaning of a theory is always determined by the uses to which it is put, I think it is a naive gesture to celebrate Lu Xun's "grabbism" as some kind of a happy solution to the traumatic relationship be-tween East and West in modern history. Precisely because of that history, a reverse for-mulation of Chinese theory versus Western reality cannot even be conceived. In my view, it is more important to explain the historical condition that gave rise to Lu Xun's "grabbism" than simply to endorse it or reinforce the hegemonic relationship between Western theory and reality elsewhere in the world.

11. Among scholars of postcolonial history, Partha Chatterjee is aware of this prob-lem and tries to negotiate it in his book *Nationalist Thought and the Colonial World: A Derivative Discourse* (Tokyo: Zed Books, 1986).

12. See Leo Ou-fan Lee, *The Romantic Generation of Modern Chinese Writers* (Cam-bridge, Mass.: Harvard University Press, 1973), p. 44. I would like to add that the ma-jority of early modern writers started out as translators and many remained in that

capacity throughout their individual careers. Lu Xun himself translated numerous Russian and Japanese works into Chinese. His very first book, as we know, was *Yuwai xiaoshuo ji* (Anthology of foreign fiction, 1909), translated in collaboration with his brother Zhou Zuoren during their student days in Japan. Speaking of the influence of foreign literature Lu Xun says, "I had no preparation for the story [The diary of a madman] other than the hundred or more foreign stories I had read and a smattering of medical knowledge." It goes without saying that the rise of modern journalism in metropolitan centers such as Shanghai and Beijing played a crucial role in all this. Take *Xiaoshuo yuebao* (The short story magazine), for example. The importance of this journal is often grasped in terms of its contribution to modern fiction. However, I find its role as a broker between Chinese and foreign literatures far more interesting and significant than anything else. Between its reorganization by the Literary Association in 1921 (vol. 12, no. 1) and its demise in January 1932, this monthly set up sections and numerous programs, the majority of which related to the introduction of foreign literature, theory, and criticism. By comparison, the original works of fiction and poetry we now call modern literature took up only a fraction of the total space. Among the regular sections featured by the journal, there is "*Yi cong,*" or translation series; "literature abroad"; and "criticism," which devotes well over half of the essays to the discussion of foreign literature. In addition, there are serialized studies on foreign literature, including Russian literature (supplementary issue, 1921); French literature (supplementary issue, 1924); a special number entitled *Literature of the Damaged Nations* (1921), which contains translations of the literature of marginal European nations such as Poland, Czechoslovakia, Finland, and Greece.

13. A word about my own positioning in this essay. Working simultaneously with two languages, Chinese and English, I find myself occupying a shifting position: moving back and forth between these languages and learning to negotiate the irreducible differences. The concept of translingual practice, therefore, applies to my personal situation as an analyst just as much as to the earlier historical encounter between China and the West that I will explore in this essay.

14. I find Douglas Robinson's term "trope of equivalence" useful for describing what happens when languages meet in the process of translation and meaning-making. Robinson employs that concept to criticize the idea of substantial equivalence that prevails in the traditional theory of translation and language. See Douglas Robinson, *The Translator's Turn* (Baltimore, Md.: Johns Hopkins University Press, 1991).

15. Tu Wei-ming, *Humanity and Self-Cultivation: Essays in Confucian Thought* (Berkeley, Calif.: Asian Humanities Press, 1979) and *Confucian Thought: Selfhood as Creative Transformation* (Albany: State University of New York Press, 1985).

16. In Meiji Japan, neologisms such as *jiga* and *kojin* were used to translate "self" and "individual," respectively.

17. A common practice among modern Chinese writers is to have the original and the Chinese translation appear together; for instance, the English word "individual" or "self" would follow the Chinese words *geren* or *ziwo*.

18. Of course, the traditional meaning of the word *ji* continues to exist in connection with Neo-Confucianism and related scholarship. What interests me here is not its old meaning but the newly established equivalence between *ji* and the English word "self," or some other foreign words for that matter, in the process of translingual practice. The complexity of this situation has huge implications for those of us engaged in comparative scholarship. To give an example, in an early essay entitled "Zizhi yu ziyou" (Autonomy and freedom) published by *New Youth* (1, no. 5 [1916]), Gao Yihan uses *xiaoji* and *daji,* respectively, to translate Bernard Bosanquet's notion of

"individual" and "greater self" in *Philosophical Theory of the State* (chapter 6). What Gao does in that essay is to place the Chinese translation side by side with the foreign original (p. 1).

19. Chen Jia'ai, "Xin" (The new), *Xin chao* 1, no. 1 (1919): 36. All English translations are mine.

20. I wish to stress this historical difference, because to measure the Chinese experience of modernity with the yardstick of the Western Enlightenment is to downplay the history of imperialism.

21. Jia Yi, "Gewei zhuyi," *Eastern Miscellany* (hereafter cited as *EM*) 13, no. 2 (1916): 9.

22. Bertrand Russell, *The Problem of China* (New York: Century, 1922), p. 215.

23. See Li Zehou, *Zhongguo xiandai sixiang shi lun* (A study of the intellectual history in modern China) (Beijing: Dongfang chuban she, 1987), especially pp. 7–49; and Vera Schwarcz, *The Chinese Enlightenment: Intellectuals and the Legacy of the May Fourth Movement of 1919* (Berkeley: University of California Press, 1986).

24. The intellectual tradition of the European Enlightenment is itself fraught with heterogeneous elements and counterdiscourses. For instance, the critique of modernity has always been part of the Enlightenment legacy from the Romantics, Nietzsche, Marx, and Heidegger to Horkheimer, Adorno, Foucault, Derrida, and Habermas.

25. Gan Yang, "Ziyou de linian: 'Wusi' chuantong zhi queshi mian" (The ideal of freedom: Negative aspects of the "May Fourth" tradition), in *Lishi de fanxiang* (Resonances of history), ed. Liu Qingfeng (Hong Kong: Joint Publishing), p. 70.

26. Anthony J. Cascardi, *The Subject of Modernity* (Cambridge: Cambridge University Press, 1992), p. 179. See his chapter "The Subject and the State."

27. Lu Xun, "Wenhua pianzhi lun" (On misorientation of culture), in *Lu Xun quanji* (The complete works of Lu Xun) (Beijing: Renmin wenxue chuban she, 1957), vol. 1, pp. 186–87.

28. See Andrew E. Barshay, *State and Intellectual in Imperial Japan: The Public Man in Crisis* (Berkeley: University of California Press, 1988), pp. 55–56.

29. James Fujii, *Complicit Fictions: The Subject in the Modern Japanese Prose Narrative* (Berkeley: University of California Press, 1992), p. 10.

30. I am referring to Raymond Williams's keyword approach to history. See his *Keywords* (New York: Harper and Row, 1976).

31. For a study of earlier discussions of individualism, see Benjamin Schwartz, *In Search of Wealth and Power: Yan Fu and the West* (Cambridge, Mass.: Harvard University Press, 1964); Hao Chang, *Liang Ch'i-ch'ao and Intellectual Transition in China, 1890–1907* (Cambridge, Mass.: Harvard University Press, 1971); and Zheng Hailin, *Huang Zunxian yu jindai zhongguo* (Beijing: Sanlian shudian, 1988).

32. For a survey of the political events (warlordism, government corruption, imperialist invasion, and so on) between 1911 and 1919 that underlie Du's attitude toward the Republican Revolution of 1911, see Tse-tsung Chow, *The May Fourth Movement: Intellectual Revolution in China* (Cambridge, Mass.: Harvard University Press, 1960). Also see Benjamin I. Schwartz, ed., *Reflections on the May Fourth Movement: A Symposium* (Cambridge, Mass.: Harvard University Press, 1972).

33. Cang Fu (Du Yaquan), "Geren zhi gaige" (Reforming the individual), *EM* 10, no. 12 (1914): 2.

34. See Liang Qichao, "Xinmin shuo in *Yinbing shi heji, zhuanji* (Collected works and essays from the ice-drinker's studio: topics), 3:4 (Shanghai: Zhonghua shuju, 1936), pp. 1–162; and "Ziyou shu," in ibid., 2:2, pp. 1–123. Also see Hao Chang, *Liang Ch'i-ch'ao and Intellectual Transition in China, 1890–1907*.

35. Edward Said, *The World, the Text, and the Critic,* p. 237.

36. "Wo" (I), *EM* 11, no. 1 (1916): 13–16.

37. The influence of Yan Fu's translation of Huxley's *Evolution and Ethics* is clearly discernible in Min Zhi's argument.

38. Jia Yi, "Gewei zhuyi" (Individualism), *EM* 13, no. 2 (1916): 6–10. Individualism is translated in this article as *gewei zhuyi* rather than the usual *geren zhuyi,* probably because it evokes a corresponding sociological (scientific?) term, *geren benwei zhuyi* (the doctrine of the individual unit, p. 7).

39. Gao Lao (Du Yaquan), "Geren yu guojia zhi jieshuo" (The boundary between the individual and the state), *EM,* p. 2. Gao Lao and Cang Fu are pen names Du Yaquan frequently uses in these essays.

40. Wilhelm von Humboldt's formulations about the limits of the state are contained in his classic work *Ideen zu einem Versuch die Grenzen der Wirksamkeit des Staats zu bestimmen* (Ideas on an attempt to define the limits of the state's sphere of action), published in English as *The Limits of State Action,* ed. J. H. Burrow (London: Cambridge University Press, 1969).

41. Tse-tsung Chow, "The Anti-Confucian Movement in Early Republican China," in *The Confucian Persuasion,* ed. Arthur F. Wright (Stanford, Calif.: Stanford University Press, 1960), p. 312.

42. Gao Yihan, "Guojia fei rensheng zhi guisu lun" (The state is not the ultimate goal of human life), *Youth Magazine.* In this particular article, the author uses the word *xiaoji* alone, but with the implication that *daji* is its antithetical counterpart.

43. Hu Shi later takes up this dialectic in an essay entitled "Bu xiu" (Immortality), but, for him, the greater self stands for *shehui* (society) rather than the state.

44. Li Yishi, "Rensheng weiyi zhi mudi" (The sole purpose of life), *EM* 1, no. 2 (1915): 5.

45. Chen Duxiu, "Dongxi minzu genben sixiang zhi chayi" (The fundamental difference between the thoughts of Eastern and Western peoples), *New Youth* 1, no. 4 (1915): 284.

46. Shou Chang (Li Dazhao), "Qingchun Zhonghua zhi chuangzao" (Creating a youthful China), *Chenzhong bao,* August 15, 1916.

47. See Hu Shi, "Wenxue gailiang chuyi" (Suggestions for literary reform) and "Jianshe de wenxue geming lun" (Toward a constructive theory of literary revolution), in *Zhongguo xin wenxue daxi* (Compendium of modern Chinese literature), ed. Zhao Jiabi, vol. 1 (Shanghai: Liangyou tushu gongsi, 1935–36), pp. 34–43; pp. 127–40.

48. Zhou Zuoren, "Ren de wenxue" (Humane literature), in *Zhongguo xin wenxue daxi,* ed. Zhao Jiabi, pp. 193–99.

49. See Lydia H. Liu, "The Politics of First-Person Narrative in Modern Chinese Fiction" (Ph.D diss., Harvard University, 1990).

50. The "autobiographical subject" is a narratological term here. It refers to the autodiegetic narrator *within* the text rather than the author. For a distinction between homodiegetic and autodiegetic narratives in the first person, see Gerard Genette, *Narrative Discourse,* trans. Jane E. Lewin (Ithaca, N.Y.: Cornell University Press, 1980), chapter 5.

51. Hu Shi, "Bu xiu," *New Youth* 6, no. 2 (1919): 118.

52. Fu Sinian, "Rensheng wenti faduan" (Introduction to the problem of human life), *Renaissance* 1, no. 1 (1919): 15.

53. Wang Xinggong, "Wu he wo" (Matter and self), *Renaissance* 3, no. 1 (1921): 2–3.

54. Chen Duxiu, "Xuwu de geren zhuyi ji ren ziran zhuyi," *New Youth* 8, no. 4 (1920): 638.

55. Deng Feihuang, "Geren zhuyi de youlai jiqi yingxiang," *EM* 19, no. 7 (1922): 35–46.

56. See Arif Dirlik, *The Origins of Chinese Communism* (New York: Oxford University Press, 1989).

57. The word *puluo* is the Chinese transliteration of the English "proletariat." As in the case of the majority of such Chinese transliterations, such as the word "democracy" (*demokelaxi; minzhu*) and "bourgeoisie" (*bu'erqiaoyasi; shisan kaikyu-*), this transliteration coexisted with the Japanese loanword translation *musan kaikyu-* and was soon replaced by it.

58. There was an interesting exchange between Huang Yaomian and Shi Heng on this issue in 1928. See Huang, "Fei geren zhuyi de wenxue" (A nonindividualistic literature), and Shi, "Geren zhuyi de wenxue ji qita" (Individualistic literature and other concerns), in Li Helin, ed., *Zhongguo wenyi lunzhan* (Debates on Chinese literature and art), ed. Li Helin (Shanghai: Zhongguo wenyi she, 1932), pp. 298–302.

59. Cheng Fangwu, "Cong wenxue geming dao geming wenxue" (From literary revolution to revolutionary literature), in *Chuangzao she ziliao* (Research materials on the Creation Society), ed. Rao Hongjing et al. (Fuzhou: Fujian renmin chuban she, 1985), p. 169. This essay was written in 1923 and first published in the February 1928 issue of *Chuangzao yue kan* (Creation monthly).

60. Lu Xun, "Geming shidai de wenxue" (Literature in a revolutionary age, 1927), in *Lu Xun quanji*, vol. 3, p. 422.

61. See Qian Xingcun, "Si qu le de Ah Q shidai" (The age of Ah Q is dead), in *Xiandai zhongguo wenxue zuojia* (Modern Chinese writers of literature) (Shanghai: Taidong shuju, 1929), pp. 1–53.

62. For a discussion of Jiang Guangci and his involvement with the Sun Society, see C. T. Hsia, *A History of Modern Chinese Fiction, 1917–1957* (New Haven, Conn.: Yale University Press, 1961), p. 259. Also see Liu, "The Politics of First-Person Narrative," pp. 189–98. *Shaonian piaobo zhe* was first published by Yadong Tushu Guan in 1926 and is now included in *Jiang Guangci wenji*. A prolific writer and an active member of the Sun Society, Jiang contracted pneumonia and died in 1931 at the age of thirty.

63. For a discussion of this debate, see Liu Kang, "Subjectivity, Marxism, and Cultural Theory in China," in *Politics, Ideology, and Literary Discourse in Modern China: Theoretical Interventions and Cultural Critique,* ed. Liu Kang and Tang Xiaobing (Durham, N.C.: Duke University Press, 1993), pp. 23–55.

64. See Liu Zaifu, "Lun wenxue de zhuti xing" (On subjectivity in literature), in *Liu Zaifu ji* (Works of Liu Zaifu) (Harbin: Heilongjiang jiaoyu chuban she, 1988), pp. 72–125. Initially published in *Wenxue pinglun* (Literary criticism) (no. 6 of 1985 and no. 1 of 1986), this essay was attacked by an official critic named Chen Yong.

2 / *Samsara:* Self and the Crisis of Visual Narrative

Eugene Yuejin Wang

The Closing Sequence That Is Not an End

In the darkness of the young couple's bedroom, the woman starts to sob. The concerned husband—his name is Shiba—swears his love for her. The wife flares up and accuses the man of loving no one in the world except himself. "Stop cheating me and yourself," the wife snaps. At this, Shiba slaps her on the face and shuffles into the living room—he is a cripple. Confronting a large mirror, he is suddenly seized by a fit of self-odium at seeing his own image reflected in the mirror. With one violent stroke, he smashes the mirror. The sulking young man then finds himself near a lamp. He tips the lamp so that it slants. Posing in a manner emulating some classical sculptured figures or some bodybuilders' show or a slave breaking out of his chains,[1] he lets the overturned lamp project the shadow of his poised figure onto the wall. He goes up to the black wall, draws the imaginary configuration of his body's blown-up contour with his cane, steps back, and sinks into his sofa to gaze at the drawing of his body on the wall. Shiba then steps out onto a high-rise balcony overlooking the Beijing streets. He stares at the moon. Cut to the moon, which takes up the full frame. What follows is a series of shot–reverse field shots alternating between Shiba, with a blank expression, and the full presence of the blank moon. Framed frontally, Shiba climbs over the rail and slips down, out of the frame. Cut to a high-angle shot overlooking the night scene. Fade into darkness. A march breaks out on the sound track while the ending subtitle states that six months later, Shiba's wife gives birth to a boy, who is named Shi Xiaoba. There follows the credit and the ending of the film: *Samsara* (*Lunhui,* Xi'an Film Studio, 1988).

The film is directed by Huang Jianxin with screenplay by Wang Shuo, from whose novella the film was adapted.[2] A succinct synoptic account of the film runs like this:

> The chief protagonist in *Samsara* ... lives without a family: his parents, high-ranking cadres, have died. Shi Ba makes a living in the private sector greatly expanded by Deng Xiaoping's economic reforms of the 1980s. Like other entrepreneurs with social and political connections, Shi Ba dabbles also in some illegal business. Success brings threats of blackmail. Resistance to the demands brings a severe beating. From then on Shi Ba drifts. Refusing to join a friend in blackmailing foreigners, he marries Yu Jing. This relationship proves a disaster. One evening, in a macho act, Shi Ba throws himself off a balcony.[3]

The closing sequence of the film is disturbing and provocative in many ways. The suicide is unexpected, and it is staged with a certain mannerism teetering on a dividing line between nonchalant cynicism and poignant pathos. For our purposes here, however, the ending sequence of *Samsara* thematizes well the problems involved in the representation of self.

Self has often been evoked as (1) a linguistic phenomenon,[4] (2) a narrative construct,[5] and (3) a spatial topology involving imaginary doubling and specular activities.[6] All these aspects are dramatized in the ending of the film. Insofar as the ending evokes the reflection in the mirror, the linguistic problem of "I" and its referential other emerges; insofar as it is an ending, a denouement, a *narrative* problem comes to the fore; insofar as the sequence is about the specular activities — mirror and self-reflection, projecting and watching one's shadow on the wall — questions of *the visual* constitution of self come up.

These aspects are closely linked. "I" as a linguistic entity necessarily differs from the referential "I" — an other, so to speak. The so-called self is often played out in the space involving the desiring "I" and a utopian or masked other — an antithesis against the articulating "I" — whom the "I" claims or wants to become. The inner tension underlying the drama of self is often the act of desiring or pretending to be what one is not. It is one of the problems essential to *Samsara,* one that is closely tied up with the problem of narrative.

The film is predicated upon the riddle and the unriddling of the true self of Shiba. Such a game of concealment and revelation is something of a narrative imperative, as self is largely a narrative construct. "Self-identity," as Giddens puts it, "as a coherent phenomenon, presumes a narrative."[7] "We grasp our lives in a *narrative* ... our life exists in a space of questions, which only a coherent narrative can answer."[8] If we find a character baffling in the beginning, we know that by the end of the narrative, the true self will come out.

Samsara mocks our expectations. We initially recognize three facets of Shiba. First we see the sardonic, iconoclastic cynic lurching through the vanity-fair world, scornful of sentimentality, defying conventions, engaged in illegal dealings without a sense of guilt. In fact, he carries an air of "being more sinned against than sinning." Second, there is another Shiba, related to the cynic, who justifies his unconventionality as based on a dignified ethical vision of being true to himself, having no use for deception either to others or to himself. Third, the flamboyant display of sardonicism and the ethical self-righteousness, precise because of its degree of self-consciousness and its calculated excess, betrays a hidden self vulnerable to what he openly rejects, susceptible to conventional sentimentalities, longing for what has been denied him, and capable of warmth and passion in spite of his outward display of nonchalance. The hidden self seems to be unveiled in rare moments when he pulls down the cynical mask and proves himself capable of genuine love for the ballerina, marked by his flat refusal to get involved in the mean scheme of trapping unsuspecting victims. The film thus titillatingly offers the tip of a submerged iceberg of the self. It promises to be an interplay between inner integrity and outer dissembling. The cynic seems all but a mask at war with the "hidden self," even though this charade undermines the very claim to sincerity and authenticity — Shiba's true-to-myself ethical avowal.

Parallel to this antinomy is the interplay between the unprepossessing outer physiognomy and the inner moral strength. Shiba starts out as an unglamorous figure, short and lean. To make things worse, halfway through the film, he falls prey to a horrible blackmail and is mutilated and crippled. Self-pity and sentimentality attending such pathetic occasions are consciously avoided. When his girlfriend asks to see the wound, he calmly refuses: "I do not want to display my muscles in public." He abruptly and unceremoniously ends his relation with the girl. Without displaying the wound, he is nevertheless displaying his put-on grim austerity. The self-inflicted harshness and the pretense of laughing at his own suffering and misfortune again seem to posit an outer mask and an inner self: an exhibitionist mask that rises above the situation by making light of the suffering, philosophically absorbing the evil of the world with a grim smile of scorn, and a hidden self distraught with pain and unwilling to swallow the injustice of the world. The mask is unflinchingly austere, sardonically grim, and capable of laughter even at the darkest moment too poignant for tears; the hidden self is mired in the normal human reactions to external forces. The film is, therefore, poised to suggest that the "I" of Shiba, for all its excessive indifference, is not what it claims to be.

However, this inner-outer interplay crumbles in the final moment when his wife suddenly cries out: "You care for nobody else except yourself!" We are startled. The assumption of the inner-outer discrepancy has all this while assured the spectator of the final unmasking and revelation. When it comes, it turns out to be precisely opposite to our expectation. Instead of seeing the "integral" honest soul unveiling itself, we are told that the mask is his true self.

Shiba's slapping of his accuser on her face is ambiguous: it could be a deeply hurt gesture of denial—fretting at the thought that even his wife fails to see his inner self; the slap could also be taken to show his indignation at the uncompromising disclosure of a painful truth with which he himself has been reluctant to come to grips. At this point, we no longer know whether the instability of self is largely caused by a narrative indeterminacy, or vice versa.

The theatrical solipsism of the final sequence breaks away from the preceding part of the film in several ways. It dismisses the preceding inner-outer antinomy as an illusory charade that ultimately reveals nothing about the self. It dismisses all the other characters in the film as legitimate spectators wrongly burdened with the role of seeing Shiba's true self—hence the narcissistic enclosure or a space of specular solipsism. In this darkness, however, what has been dismissed returns. Having excluded all other spectators-in-the-film, he himself replaces them to watch his own mirror image and shadow. The distance and discontinuity between the "I" and the other within himself are reenacted again. With the initial setup of the artifice of inner-outer discrepancy dismantled, Shiba now frets at the failure of his own mirrored physiognomy to represent what he really is, or wants to be. The smashing of the mirror is only the final desperate act or protest at the undestroyable inner-outer discrepancy.

If the whole film holds out an initial promise of finally unveiling the self of Shiba, the fulfillment of that cinematic-narrative promise is no more than reiterating the initial promise. If Shiba has been immersed in role-playing in front of the spectators-in-the-film ("Stop the role-playing," his actress-girlfriend pleads), he nevertheless is unable to step out of the role of role-playing even when locked in facing himself. Role-playing may be a charade to others, with the implicit assumption that the role could easily be transcended. The film ends, however, with the frustrating moral: that once out of the role, he still has to play a role to be convinced that the role may not be part of himself or some other self. The self-as-spectator is nonetheless perplexed at the self-as-projection. The bewilderment is still the uncertainty of whether the mask he puts on is condemned to be an eternal part of him, whether there is a hidden true self behind the mask, or whether he could be other than this body.

Is There a Self to Be True To? Moral Dilemma as Narrative Problem

Narrative of self unfolds in a moral space. The crisis in the narrative of self as manifested in *Samsara* is a moral one. The film appeared in the historical moment when the moral cosmos in China was in chaos. In the Maoist era, the notion of self was a much more definite, if not regimented, one. One gained one's self-identity in orientation toward an external order or social hierarchy. The moral sources that one was urged to identify and aspire toward were altruism, larger-than-life heroism, and commitment to public causes. Social responsibilities and stratified class status relegated people into different group identities: one was a "successor to the Communist causes" or a member of a "black gang."

The post-Mao era was lived through as a reenactment of Enlightenment and reexperiencing of modernity. The blind faith in Communist causes was seriously questioned and rejected. Ideals of higher order were replaced with an affirmation of certain ordinary life values. Class identities with their attached pride and humbleness disintegrated. The loss of frameworks in which to situate oneself led to a loss of orientation. The sensitive Chinese in the early 1980s began to have a modern sense of meaninglessness, lack of purpose, and emptiness. The famous letter, written by Pan Xiao, a twenty-three-year-old, to the editor of *Zhongguo qingnian* in 1980, spoke for a whole generation and captured the ethos of the early 1980s. The noble visions and higher ideals she had been indoctrinated with had all but crumbled and faded. She sought refuge in writing, not for some noble public causes, but for "the self." "All human beings," so she declared, "whether surviving or creating, live for the self subjectively, and for others objectively."[9]

Pan Xiao's declaration of the primacy of self was carried further. Nan San, the heroine in *When the Sunset Glow Fades* (1983), a meditative philosophical treatise in the guise of fictional discourse, voiced a total disenchantment with the grandeur of epic history and the myths of revolution and searched for a cultivated private space.[10] The disenchantment reached its climax in Xu Xing, "Variations without a Theme."[11] The protagonist-narrator begins his story by wondering: "I am not clear what I want besides all I have now. What is this 'I'? What is even more damning is that I am not waiting for anything."[12] Xu Xing's story may not have had a wide appeal in 1985, although it caused serious concern from some critics who deplored this cynical self-preoccupation and cried out for a restoration of heroic values and responsibilities.[13] However, Xu's novella laid out a basic pattern with which Wang Shuo gained prominence after the mid-1980s. Like Xu's "Variations without a Theme," Wang's novels are mostly told by a first-person narrator who is also the protagonist. Cynical and playful, they stand the hitherto commonly held moral values on their heads.

In 1988, China was swept by a "Wang Shuo Wave." Four of Wang Shuo's novellas were adapted to the screen within a matter of a year, between late 1988 and 1989: *Samsara* (*Lunhui,* 1988), *Rogues* (*Wanzhu,* 1988), *Heavy Gasp* (*Da chuanqi,* 1988), and *Half Seawater, Half Flame* (*Yiban shi haishui, yiban shi huoyan,* 1989). Wang Shuo became the center of media attention. Symposiums were held by *Chinese Film Weekly, Film Art,* and the Chinese Film Critics' Society to assess the Wang Shuo films. The critical and public reception was divided. The Wang Shuo films were applauded by some for their provocative edge and their wide spectrum of parodies, ironies, and satires, which reveal the complex dimension of social realities.[14] Praised for capturing the fragmentation and dislocation of space and time in modern urban life, they were also hailed as representing the post–Fifth Generation films.[15] The Wang Shuo films were also overwhelmingly deplored by others as socially irresponsible, decadent, diseased, trivial, and ultimately nihilistic.[16]

The polarization in public reception of Wang Shuo reflects the inner tension in his works, of which the best formulation comes, uncannily enough, from Hegel. In reading Diderot's Rameau, Hegel spells out a trajectory for Spirit's historical itinerary. The "honest soul," inhabited by Diderot's Moi, assumes a constant relationship with external forces; therefore it is integral. This "noble" consciousness is destined to move toward a "base" self, exemplified by Diderot's Lui, a distraught, disintegrated, and alienated consciousness in rebellion against external forces.[17] In the post-Mao era, the change from blind allegiance to external power to autonomous self-expression, from pious subscription of the collective "noble" spirit to the "debased" form of integration, from submission to a traditional morality to moral defiance, has all but acted out the Hegelian move from the noble self to the base self. With the rejection of the archaic noble vision, the base self attains a self-determining freedom that Hegel celebrates.

The move has its price. The self has to undergo "renunciation and sacrifice." "Assuming a negative relation with external powers, meting out depreciatory judgement which rends and tears everything," the base self has to go through the pain of a disintegrated, alienated, and distraught consciousness. The nobility of the base self consists in forbearing this pain: "But of its baseness there is no doubt. The truth of the self, at a certain stage of its historical development, consists in its being not true to itself, in there being no self to be true to: the truth for self, for Spirit, consists precisely in deceit and shamelessness."[18] The moment of finding the self is the moment of its loss. This is the dilemma confronting Shiba and the cynical generation this screen character represents. The identity of self is parasitic on what it seeks to break away from. As Charles Taylor puts it: "First, it is parasitic on its adversaries for the expression of its own moral sources, its own words of power, and hence for its continuing moral force. But second, since it undermines all previous formulations of the constitutive good which could ground the life goods it recognizes, without putting any in its place, it also lives to some degree on these earlier formulations."[19] Flouting the smug moral sentimentalism, lampooning the falsities, Shiba needs to put on a mask that is relentless, uncompromising, and outrageous in order to obtain the scathing power of destruction, while implying that behind the mask there is also another self that is honestly humane. Yet the promised or implied hidden self behind the mask turns out to be a moral void. Shiba has indeed moved from the despised "noble spirit" toward the celebrated "base self." The cynical mask may well be a mask that conceals something behind—which means the mask is deceptive, not true of or to the hidden self. But the mask grows into something that can no longer be lifted. The concealed behind becomes a moral lacuna. The mask becomes intransitive—it is a mask of nothing, of emptiness. Shiba may well want to be true to himself, but then there is no self for him to be true to.

Problems of the Medium and of the Self

The moral dilemma underlies the narrative crisis and undermines specular credibility. For all Shiba's excessive self-exhibitionism, there is a wearied distrust of visual representation of self. Upon his girlfriend's request for his photo, so that she could at least evoke the bittersweet memory of their relations by looking at his picture, Shiba's response is almost negative. No picture, he insists, could truly capture his true self. Thus said, he nevertheless fishes out a—or rather, the—picture for her: a photo showing the baby version of Shiba, whom he no longer is, with its completely naked body. With the self becoming increasingly "epistemologically unreliable,"[20] it could only hope to moor its anchoring onto its tangible tropological structure whenever the very topology of self is evoked. The specular structure itself replaces finally what it is structure of, having moved from the transitive to the intransitive. The representation of the self is substituted by the self-representation, while that which is to be represented is eternally deferred. Self becomes the quest itself, no more than a specular structure. The mise-en-scène of Shiba's engagements with mirrors, shadows, and the moon becomes the ultimate answer to the quest of self.

Likewise, the successive confrontations with mirror, shadow, and the moon in the last sequence move toward an increasingly more blank and less individually differentiated visual representation. This mounting repudiation of specular objects parallels the questioning of the validity of selfhood as being visually conceived. The interrogation is directed toward the very act of seeing, the mode of specularity, and spectatorship, which constitute the most expedient methods of an epistemological quest. This is suggested by the cinematic choreograph in the final sequence of *Samsara*.

After slapping his wife on the face, Shiba walks from the depth of field toward the camera. As he draws near the camera, the film cuts to a similar frontal shot framing Shiba gazing into the camera at a slightly oblique angle. The continuity of the shot with the preceding shot is such that we assume the cut to be no more than bridging a temporal gap of the otherwise prolonged walk toward the camera, and Shiba's final positioning is the resting point of the preceding movement. The spatial relationship between Shiba and the camera remains the same. Shiba's stern gaze into the camera grows more intense. He raises his cane and strikes at the camera. In the wake of the sudden clattering and shattering, we see the configuration of the broken glass, and realize that Shiba has actually confronted a mirror instead of the camera. The film seems to have deliberately omitted some expository shots of Shiba's positioning before the mirror, thereby creating the visual illusion that Shiba was actually confronting the camera.

This equation of the mirror and the camera is disquieting. Shiba does violence to his own mirror image—that goes without saying; by doing so, he also symbolically does violence to the camera, since it substitutes here as the mirror in experiencing Shiba's "murderous gaze."[21] Why does that menace implicate the camera, which is a synecdoche of the film medium? To say that the smashing of the mirror also symbolically smashes the film medium may have overstated the matter. Yet a look at how the semantics of the film is bound up with cinematics may make the correlation less than idle speculation.

To explore the self is to explore the labyrinth of the consciousness. What is cinema if not a persistent exploration of the ways in which the mode of consciousness can be visualized? It is therefore not surprising to reflect that a majority of the greatest films in history—*Persona, Citizen Kane, Last Year at Marienbad,* to name only a few—in purporting to explore the condition of the human mind necessarily explore the medium and instrumentality of cinema itself. With each step deeper into the labyrinth of the human subjective world, cinema discovers its own new possibilities, stylistically or formally. With this uncanny correlation in mind, one finds that, with a film like *Samsara,* which is obsessed with the problem of the self, the exploration of the self is necessarily equivalent to the exploration of the cinematic condition.

By projecting his own shadow onto the wall in the final sequence and posing in front of the lamp, Shiba becomes his own director, actor (that is, impersonator), spectator, and even screenwriter (he draws on the wall by tracing the projected but now vanished contours of his posture). The structure of cinematic properties stands in lieu of what is filmed—the configuration of the self. Thus, while the shadow play and shadow watch act out the tropological structure of the self, they at the same time become an explicit gesticulation of cinematic self-referentiality. While figuring the self/other with the implication of a willed self-delusion and self-recognition, the projection of the shadow at the same time logically refers to the condition of cinema.

What marks the final sequence off from the preceding body of film in *Samsara* is a completely different mood: somber, pathetic, and above all, reflexive. The film sinks into a brooding pantomime: its excessive muteness becomes a sign of reverie. Is it the mode of silent film—the origin of film history—that has been unconsciously evoked here? The main body of *Samsara* strikes one as a relentless, self-conscious play with iconoclastic witticisms (so self-conscious and strained that they fail to be witty). In fact, the original novella (by Wang Shuo, who is also the coscreenwriter) from which the film is adapted is fiercely indulgent in explosive linguistic cracks. The film inherits the same tone—until, however, the final sequence, which asserts the autonomous status of the "cinematic self" unmatched by the novelistic discourse. In fact, the whole final sequence is absent from the original novella. The only way cinema here claims its power is by reverting to the silent mode of shadow play, the origin of the cinematic medium. Thus the film retrospectively questions itself by disavowing and negating the preceding modalities of representation. As if in keeping with the screen character's painful soul-searching and self-questioning, the film itself needs its parallel interrogation of its own mode of existence/expression. When Shiba shuts his scathing mouth, the film shifts off its noisy gears and sinks into muteness. If Shiba disowns his reflected image or his mask, the film formally disavows its preceding modalities and generic tendencies. As Shiba has been bent on searching for his true self, so is the film equally bent on finding out its generic incarnation and stylistic anchoring.

The film has up to the final moment flirted with various generic possibilities, presuming them, proceeding with them, and finally casting them behind. Romance fails to mature. Shiba meets one of his old acquaintances, a now rich but downcast woman returning from abroad, disillusioned and hence starving for emotional fulfillment. Yet the planned ménage à trois after the encounter never amounts to anything. Shiba's love and then marriage with his ballerina-lover promises to hover over the working out of the deus ex machina—here an allegory of the fallen man blessed with the reviving kiss of the descending angel. Yet the film does not even allow a single spectacle of the ballerina on stage, in stark contrast with the original novella, in which Shiba frequently sat in the first row to gaze on his angelic lover-wife on stage.[22] The whole affair proves to be love's labor lost. The film noir at moments threatens to take over, yet it only leaves the imprint of a horrifying spectacle of torture (the electrical, mechanical drilling into Shiba's leg); then it careens into the grotesque, the black humor of the crippled man trying to balance himself on the high-rise railing. The comedy of repartee sporadically has its glories, yet the final silent sequence of the film, with its heavy muteness and grimness, retrospectively dismisses all the preceding linguistic exuberance as mere indulgence in gibberish. It is as if the film narrative motor had its own discontent, its own anxiety. The discontent is with all the available modes of expression, the cinematic rituals that fail to stage contemporary problems and sentiments. In this light, Shiba's violent act against the mirror staged as a smashing of the camera logically amounts to a symbolic act of violence toward the camera—the film medium. The film, frustrated along the way toward fleshing out a cinematic narrative, finally brings its grievance/vengeance against itself. Hence the final lapse into silence. It is here that film finally settles on the most congenial generic and stylistic mooring: a quiet, inward-looking, and reflexive mise-en-scène of mirror/shadow/moon.

The soul summoning (a search for the lost self) goes hand in hand with the cinematic self-reflexivity, that is, the return to its origin. Thus to summon the soul of the existential self is at the same time to call back the soul of the cinema—the semantics and the cinematics are indistinguishably related. In representing the self, the cinema necessarily represents *itself*. "It must represent," writes Foucault, "but that representation, in turn, must also be represented within it." Thus

> the binary arrangement of the sign ... presupposes that the sign is a duplicated representation doubled over upon itself. An idea can be the sign of another, not only because a bond of representation can be established between them, but also because this rep-

resentation can always be represented within the idea that is representing. Or again, because representation in its peculiar essence is always perpendicular to itself: it is at the same time indication and appearance; a relation to an object and a manifestation of itself.[23]

So the representational problem is at once that of the fictional character's and that of its auteur, director Huang Jianxin.

Huang distinguished himself in the eighties as a cutting-edge filmmaker celebrated mostly for his sumptuous stylistic novelties: the use of strong color schemes, peculiar camera angles, glitzy and geometrical decors, allegorical characterizations, and so on. Unlike the majority of outstanding Fifth Generation filmmakers, who made their debut by setting their films in "exotic" landscapes (Tibet, Mongolia, or the barren yellow land of northwest China) and who captured worlds more or less removed from contemporary city life, Huang has insistently focused on contemporary urban scenes—and sometimes even futuristic scenarios.[24] If the 1980s China reexperienced modernity in the wake of the Cultural Revolution, Huang is among the Chinese "avant-garde" obsessed with modernity. His notion of cinema as part of modern experience is materialized in a world of glitzy decors and dazzling colors that are subjective mental projections. His heroes are consequently often wearied and disenchanted antiheroes.

Huang is best known, however, for his tireless search for an expressive film language and adequate generic trapping, signaled by his celebrated *Black Cannon Incident* (1985). The film fits a political satire into the genre of a detective thriller—a pseudothriller at that. It ends with the hero, or rather, the awkward antihero, wandering around. The ending sequence is pregnant with meaning. A couple of kids, having stood numerous bricks in a meandering line, start to push the bricks to bring about a domino effect. The camera follows the successively falling bricks until it comes to the end of the line, where the protagonist stands. He gives a wry smile and then walks away. Much of the cinematic narrative as a chain of absurd events is thematized here with a logical imperative. No words are spoken. The visual mise-en-scène speaks everything—and nothing at all. It is narratively self-referential.

Samsara is one more instance of Huang's cinematic explorations—only the exploration is now exhausted and confused. The ending sequence of pantomime is both an extension of Huang's signature style of mannerism and its own critique. Three tropes — mirror reflection, shadow projection, and moon viewing — are respectively staged and then ruled out. The film ends with a note of discontent — not only Shiba's with himself and his world, but also the film's with itself. Huang succeeds where he fails.

Visual Tropes and the Tension between Tradition and Modernity

The final sequence in *Samsara* strikes one as peculiarly and definitely archaic (not in its negative sense). The successive and excessive engagement with mirror, shadow, and the moon seems a visual transcription of some classical Chinese tropes or topoi. This is ironic when we think of the film as poised in a search for a modern self by being self-consciously mutinous and iconoclastic toward the received cultural formulae.

The specular engagement in classical literary experience posits a special modality of viewing. It generates a peculiar classical vision of the self. Crassly put, the self arising out of specular moments moves toward a nonself. The self-formation is more of a state of merging between the self and the external world: "Man is (lit. I am) crowded together with the myriad other things in the Great Changingness, and his (lit. my) nature is one with that of all other natural things. Knowing that I am of the same nature as all other natural things, I know that there is really no (separate) self, no (separate) personality, no (absolute) death and no absolute (life)."[25] If self is seen as tropologically shaped, then in the classical Chinese culture, the most emphatic moment of self-assertion is cast into the rhetoric of dissolution. The boundary between the interior and the exterior is to be traversed and abolished. The attainment of the self is the moment of uncertainty as to what is the external world and what is the self. This is not unlike what Freud described as the "oceanic feeling": "a feeling of an indissoluble bond, of being one with the external world as a whole," the feeling of "limitlessness and of a bond with the universe."[26] There is, however, a difference. Freud spelled out a trajectory from the oceanic bond to the separation of the self and the universe. The Chinese chart is precisely its reverse.[27]

Closely related to this tropological self is the idea of the disembodied eye or gaze. The theory of the mode of viewing, best articulated by

Shao Yong (1011–77) of the Song dynasty, encourages viewing the *wu* (external objects) with the eye of *wu*. It posits an imagined spectatorial position where the "I" is renounced; the external world is seen with the disavowed subjective vision, as if the world were seen through the *wu*'s eye. The idea thus generates the notion of a "universal eye": "Because I know I am an other, and the other is also 'me.' Both I and the other are equally *wu*. Therefore it is possible to adopt the universal eye as my eye, which is capable of viewing everything [or, literally, from which nothing can fail to be viewed]."[28] The idea of the universal eye or gaze finds its extreme expression in Wang Shouren's (1472–1528) formulation: "The eye has no body; it takes the myriad colors as its body."[29] The ontological status of the eye/gaze is disowned and disembodied. If we follow the (Western?) aesthetics that prioritizes the eye (especially in the cinema culture) and assigns the subjective gaze the primary condition of stepping into subjectivity, then this subjectivity seems all but disavowed in the Chinese context following the disembodiment of the eye. Consequently what might have been deemed by the modern imagination as the threshold experience of self-recognition is often — in classical Chinese contexts — the moment of self-annihilation or the merging of the self with the nonself.

The mirror has been excessively deployed in the Lacanian algebra to symbolize the intermediate phase leading to the final stage of self-recognition, the preparation for entering into the symbolic order in which the child could articulate "I." The cultural use of the mirror in classical Chinese tradition bespeaks otherwise. One looks into the mirror not so much to see oneself as to evoke and remember the other, with whose identification one has a vague sense of the "self" equivalent to nonself. One might say this other is represented in the Lacanian vocabulary as the mother or the maternal body. Yet the psychoanalytic scenario drives toward the difference or separation between the maternal body and myself, while the Chinese scenario leans toward the fusion. One does not have a distinct sense of self until one can find oneself merged with the other — call it the mother in the Lacanian phraseology. If we continue with the mother-son trope as figuring the self-other antinomy, we may take hermeneutical liberty with a historical tale in which the Chinese experience of mirror viewing is best thematized. In A.D. 74, Emperor Ming of Han was so grieved over the late Empress Yin (Yin Taihou), his departed mother, that he went to visit Yuanlin, her tomb. Bending over to scrutinize the departed dowager's toilet and mirror, the emperor looked into the mirror into which his mother used to cast her gaze. Completely overwhelmed with a sharp poignancy, the emperor cried. His retinue all lay prostrate on the ground, not daring to look up. This historical event, originally narrated in *Hou Han Shu,* was seized upon by Sima Guang, a later historian of the Song dynasty, author of *Zizhi tongian* (The mirror of universal history—the title itself includes a metaphor of mirror). With slender textual clues, Sima Guang imagined that Emperor Ming must have been deeply touched by looking into the mirror into which his mother had looked. Emperor Ming looked into the mirror to see not himself, but an Other. Now the actual psychological experience is impossible to verify. But what is revealing is that Sima Guang's historical exegesis of an otherwise inaccessible experience of mirror viewing in itself already posits a mode of viewing.

Articulating the "I" in classical cultural discourse is often a matter of finding a figure of identification whose articulation stands in lieu of that of mine. Since personal grievance and the pathos of self have been fully articulated by Qu Yuan, to express the self, for the later born, is to express the Qu Yuanian expression. In the late Han dynasty, when bronze mirrors began to figure self-consciousness, the two most common figures of identification were Wu Zhixu, frequently iconographically represented on the back of bronze mirrors, and Qu Yuan, often textually echoed in mirror inscriptions. The inscriptions often complain of how one is misunderstood by the world. By evoking Qu Yuan, one feels a better sense of the self. To look into the mirror, then, is to remember Qu Yuan. The act of self-recognition is equivalent to the act of remembering the other.[30]

Likewise, the moon is often evoked as a figure of identification with the bygone ancients:

> The living do not see the ancient moon,
> Yet the present moon did once shine on the ancient man;
> The ancient and the living man are like the flowing river,
> Sharing the moon as it is.[31]

The primary conferring of the self comes from the remembrance or the evocation of the absent interpersonal other. The recalled other almost takes precedence over, substitutes for, and replaces the "I" that does the recalling. I see, therefore I remember; I remember, therefore I am. Since I am by way of remembering the other, therefore what I am is what I am not, or vice versa. The fullest sense of self arises precisely in this total identification with either the external world or the historical collective other.

The typical self-expression employing the trope of the moon is that the suffering individual feels himself misunderstood by the world. It is only with the moon's receptive gaze that one is capable of some communion. Although the moon is frequently evoked with the implication of a mirror,[32] the identification is essentially with a communal entity that has been gazed on, hence shared by, all the sages and like-minded suffering individuals in the past, present, and future. Thus one seeks a spiritual communion with the vast transcendent otherness embodied in the moon in order to disavow this blind temporal world. "The world is a dream," declared Su Shi, the greatest poet of the Song dynasty, "[I'd] better hold up my wine cup to the moon over the river."[33] The moon prompts the desire toward self-annihilation in seeking union with it. The gaze at the moon often borders on rejection of this world. The sequentiality of the move from the mirror to the moon in *Samsara* implies the willed choices and rejections in settling for a supreme figure of identification. The sequentiality is perfectly in keeping with the classical poetic logic. The move is from the phase of mirror image (in which the configuration of the bodily self is more graphically registered) to the shadow-of-the-body phase (which oscillates between the appearance and disappearance of the body, hence between a self and nonself), and finally to the moon-as-mirror phase, which absorbs the gaze without returning any configuration of the self's body. What the blankness of the moon reflects is the "image" of the dispersed self, the realm of nondifferentiation. The disfiguration of his "true self" by the blind world prompts Shiba to restore the true image of the self. Neither the reflected mirror image (the unliftable mask) nor the self-created shadow on the wall could accurately embody his self. It is by looking into the moon that he sees the perfect reflection: the annihilated bodily form. One attains the self via the negative. The explicit rejection and embracing of these different mirrors as figures of identification betray the film's complicity with the classical scenario.

Shiba attains a selfhood by acting out a classical scenario that has already been acted by a galaxy of historical personae, ranging from Qu

Yuan to Wang Guowei, or even to Master Hong Yi. Upon his self-willed death, Master Hong Yi left a swan-song-like note concluding with the following tranquil lines:

If [one] presses the images for meaning,
the difference is a thousand miles wide of the mark;
Ask me what is proper, I forget the words,
The spring is fully present on the verdant branches, the moon,
the heaven's mind, is round.[34]

This mode of viewing and the traditional associations clustered around the mirror/shadow/moon naturally collapse into the mise-en-scène of these tropes in *Samsara*. What we have, then, is a symbolically ambiguous space that allows vacillations between two modalities of specularity, the classical Chinese and the modern (Western?). Mirror experience is one of the most semiosymbolic engagements in the Western critical consciousness. Two factors prevent the film from being locked in a completely archaic Chinese space—the fact that we are in an age of openness and exposure to Western ideology and aesthetics and the fact that film apparatus is a Western "language" with its embedded "unconscious." The question—a little absurd maybe—is, What kind of mirror is Shiba facing? If we insist on contextualizing it in its immediate textual-narrative proximity, then this is the mirror that certainly generates the classical Chinese musings, but if we contextualize it in the recent trend of Chinese films—the new surging cinematic interest, excessive, self-consciously stylized—and align it with its peers, such as *Obsession* (1989),[35] for instance, we feel that somehow the archaic reading of the sequence is a little biased. The film is actually caught between these two claims. Therein lies the problem of the self—that it not only has to find an expression, but it may also fall short of the control over the range of implications generated by the expressive expediencies. The mirror/shadow/moon images as tropological device in this film inevitably drift in two directions—the nonself, on the one hand, and self-recognition, on the other. It is not the choice of expressive adequacy that is at stake here; rather, it is the inevitability of the fate of the modern Chinese self to be caught between traditional textuality (the net whose nodal point is the self) and the new impulse toward restructuring the traditional textuality. So the war is not merely between the mask and the inner soul, but more of and between books, cinemas, symbolic languages, modes of perceptions, and traditions. The anxiety rankling within the breast of Shiba is a lesser hermeneutical issue compared with the agitation of formal expressions and their hermeneutical slipperiness.

One may also conjecture a possibility of transition: precisely because the "coefficiency" of the two different values congealed in the same visual tropes—the nonself merging and self-recognition—it could well be imagined that the field of visual tropes becomes the foremost space in which the transition in the modes of visual/cultural discourse is effected. The old values may well be edged out or phased out, substituted or usurped by the new mode of self-consciousness. In this respect, the filmic images charged with cultural values and historical memories will also carry the historical burden of changing the mode of discourse, or rather shortchanging the inner meanings of the inherited discursive forms.

There might be, however, disquieting consequences. The final sequence of *Samsara* is compelling precisely because it thrives on the symbolic richness accumulated from a rich tradition and on the historical weight and memories unleashed from these classical topoi. Once the sedimented residues are disengaged from these tropological devices, will they hold equal aesthetic appeal for us? That may, of course, depend on the identity of this "us." If it is a forgetful generation, then the historical whisperings never make any difference.

The poignant irony is that *Samsara,* with a pointed edge of iconoclasm and defiance toward tradition, is helplessly caught in the historical cycle—the *ricorso* to the past with which it seeks to break. The aesthetic choice of the most traditional tropes repudiates its political radicalism. The discrepancy reverts to some radical iconoclasts of the May Fourth Movement: seeking to break away from all traditional forms of discourse, they nevertheless found that it was in the archaic prosodic forms that they could best express their personal or innermost grievances. This explains that, as a film avowedly driven by the desire to search for a modern Chinese self, *Samsara* fails in many ways to stage the ineffable pathos of the self; the moment of its true powerful mastery of formal articulation occurs when it reverts to the formal mechanism that has the potential of annihilating the self. Again, to reiterate the paradox set forth earlier, the moment of finding the self is the moment of its loss.

Notes

In preparing for the publication of this essay, I have benefited from exchanges with Weigang Chen (Harvard University) and Professor Qingming Ke (Taiwan University).

1. The connotation of chain-breaking is suggested by Li Xinye, "Bingtai shehui bingtai jingshen de zhenshi xiezhao" (The authentic portrait of a diseased society and a diseased spirit), *Wenyi lilun yu piping* 4 (1989): 36.

2. The original novella is titled "Fuchu haimian" (Emerging out of the sea). See Wang Shuo, *Wang Shuo xiequ xiaoshuo xuan* (Selected light-hearted novels by Wang Shuo) (Beijing: Zuojia chubanshe, 1990), pp. 241–353.

3. Paul Clark, "Chinese Cinema in 1989," in *The Ninth Hawai'i International Film Festival* (Honolulu, East-West Center, 1989), pp. 40–42.

4. Paul de Man, *Allegories of Reading: Figural Language in Rousseau, Nietzsche, Rilke, and Proust* (New Haven, Conn.: Yale University Press, 1979), pp. 160–87.

5. Alasdair C. MacIntyre, *After Virtue: A Study in Moral Theory* (Notre Dame, Ind.: University of Notre Dame Press, 1981); Jerome S. Bruner, *Actual Minds, Possible Worlds* (Cambridge, Mass.: Harvard University Press, 1986); Paul Ricoeur, *Time and Narrative*, trans. K. McLaughlin and D. Pellauer (Chicago: University of Chicago Press, 1984–88).

6. Martin Jay, *Downcast Eyes: The Denigration of Vision in Twentieth-Century French Thought* (Berkeley and Los Angeles: University of California Press, 1993), pp. 295–97, 346–75.

7. Anthony Giddens, *Modernity and Self-Identity: Self and Society in the Late Modern Age* (Stanford, Calif.: Stanford University Press, 1991), p. 76.

8. Charles Taylor, *Sources of the Self: The Making of the Modern Identity* (Cambridge, Mass.: Harvard University Press, 1989), p. 47.

9. Pan Xiao, "Rensheng de lu a, weisheng mo yuezhou yuezai" (Why is it that the more we walk down the road of life, the narrower it becomes?), *Zhongguo qingnian,* 1980, no. 5:5.

10. For a survey of the critical reception of Nan San's novella, see *Jiefangjun bao,* December 8, 1983.

11. Xu Xing, "Wu zhuti bianzhou qu" (Variations without a theme), *Remin wenxue* 310, no. 7 (1985): 29–41.

12. Ibid., p. 29.

13. See He Xin, "Dangdai wenxue zhong de huangmiugan yu duoyuzhe" (On the sense of absurdity and the outsider in contemporary literature), *Dushu,* no. 11 (1985): 3–13.

14. Bai Hua, "Wang Shuo dianying zuopin de yiyi" (The significance of Wang Shuo's works), *Zhongguo dianying bao,* March 15, 1989.

15. Chen Xiaoming, "Yawenhua: Wang Shuo de shenming congli" (Subculture: Wang Shuo's living impact), *Zhongguo dianying bao,* March 15, 1989; Ni Zhen, "Hou di-wudai dianying lailin" (The arrival of the post–Fifth Generation films), *Wenyi bao,* December 31, 1988.

16. Shao Mujun, "Wang Shuo dianyinre yuanhe erqi?" (What has made the Wang Shuo films so hot?), *Zhongguo dianying bao,* March 25, 1989; Shao Mujun, "Ren buneng zheyang huozhe" (Human beings should not live like this), *Jiefang ribao,* April 12, 1989; Liu Dan, "Rendao de jianwang he meixue de pinfa" (The disregard of humanity and impoverished aesthetics), *Wenhui bao,* April 11, 1989.

17. G. W. F. Hegel, *The Phenomenology of Mind,* trans. J. B. Baillie (New York: Harper and Row, 1967), pp. 509–48.

18. Lionel Trilling, *Sincerity and Authenticity* (Cambridge, Mass.: Harvard University Press, 1972), p. 44.

19. Taylor, *Sources of the Self*, p. 339.

20. Paul de Man, *Allegories of Reading*, 1979, p. 187.

21. I am here taking liberty with William Rothman's phrase without being able to retain the richness of its original import. For some detailed exposition of the notion, see Rothman, *Hitchcock: The Murderous Gaze* (Cambridge, Mass.: Harvard University Press, 1982), pp. 53, 104, 107, 346.

22. See Wang Shuo, *Selected Novels*, p. 336.

23. Michel Foucault, *The Order of Things: An Archaeology of the Human Sciences* (New York: Vintage Books, 1973), pp. 64–65.

24. Huang Jianxin has often been cast in the Western press as a member of the Fifth Generation. If one were to stick to the narrower definition of the term, which refers to the class of 1982 of Beijing Film Academy, then he would not be included. He was in the Beijing Film Academy for a one-year training course in the early 1980s.

25. *Guan Yinzi* (The book of Master Guan Yin), cited in Joseph Needham, *Science and Civilization in China*, vol. 2, *History of Scientific Thought* (London: Cambridge University Press, 1985), p. 444.

26. Sigmund Freud, *Civilization and Its Discontents*, trans. and ed. James Strachey (New York: Norton, 1961), pp. 12–15.

27. Although the Song scholars stress the initial merge—"The heaven and man initially were not different. There is no need to say 'merging'"—this insistent dismissal of the need to abridge the linguistic discontinuity between "I" and the "world" is only a negative index. It presupposes the cleavage between the two, and betrays an anxiety underneath the excessive desire for the merging that posits a difference between the imperfective tense and perfective tense, between what is or has been and what is not.

28. Shao Yong, *Huangji jinshi shu*, in *Qinding siku quanshu*, ed. Ji Jun et al. (Taipei: Taiwan Shangwu Yingshu guan, 1986), vol. 803, p. 1050 (my translation).

29. Wang Shouren, *Yulu—Chuanxi lu*, in *Wang Wen cheng gong quanshu, 2. Zhongguo meixueshi ziliao xuanbian*, 2, ed. Yu Ming et al. (Beijing: Zhonghua shuju, 1980), p. 105 (my translation). This statement by Wang Shouren is, however, quite uncharacteristic of him. Wang is one of the few exceptional Chinese philosophers—the other prominent representative being Yang Zihu of Southern Song dynasty—who do not quite share the mainstream notion of "putting the eye into the wu [external objects]." He believes in the primacy of the mind's filtering of the external world. The quoted statement suffices here to illustrate a concept whose subscribers, paradoxically, exclude Wang Shouren himself. For a succinct account of Wang Shouren's isolated position in relation to mainstream Chinese thought about selfhood, see Zhang Dainian, *Zhongguo zhexue dagang—Zhongguo zhexue wenti shi* (Beijing: Zhongguo shehui kexue, 1980), p. 8.

30. See Eugene Yuejin Wang, "Mirror, Death, and Rhetoric—Reading Later Han Chinese Bronze Artifacts," *Art Bulletin* 76, no. 3 (1994).

31. Li Bai, "Bajiu wenyue" (Questioning the moon with a wine cup in hand), in *Li Bai ji jiao zhu* (Complete works of Li Bai, with annotations), ed. Qu Tuiyuan and Zhu Jingceng (Shanghai: Guji chubanshe, 1980), pp. 1178–79.

32. See, for example, the odes to the moon in Li Fang et al., eds., *Wenyuan yinhua: Shi* (circa A.D. 1009), vol. 2. (Beijing: Zhonghua shuju, 1966), pp. 703–13 (my translation).

33. Shu Shi, "Nostalgia at Chibi," in *Songci xuan,* ed. Hu Yunyi (Hong Kong: Zhonghua shuju, 1970), pp. 75–76 (my translation).

34. Chen Huijian (Chen Huey Jiann), *The Life of Vinaya Master Huny I* (Taipei: Kangli shuwu, 1965), p. 482.

35. *Obsession* (*Fengkuang de daijia,* directed by Zhou Xiaowen, Xi'an Film Studio, 1989) explores the impact of a rape upon a young victim and the complex psychological nurturing of revenge accompanying the rites-of-passage of two sisters. The film self-consciously — if not heavy-handedly — uses some mirror devices to symbolize the burgeoning notion of self-recognition.

3 / Visual Agency and Ideological Fantasy in Three Films by Zhang Yimou

Ming-Bao Yue

Among China's diverse group of internationally acclaimed Fifth Generation directors, only Zhang Yimou has managed to make films that capture and maintain the West's undivided and unprecedented attention.[1] Although it is also true that Zhang's fellow director Chen Kaige has launched a potential Academy-award-winning epic with his latest film, *Farewell to My Concubine,* his work in general has not been greeted with quite the same degree of enthusiasm.[2] For viewers familiar with Zhang's hallmark artistic obsession with eroticism, this obvious discrepancy in audience reception is indicative of the powerful lure of Orientalism long thought dispelled, but now causing Hollywood critics and cynics of multiculturalism alike to triumph in their belief that the West's need for exoticism is still very much alive. Indeed, the fact that many of Zhang Yimou's films are actually considered to be unpalatably Westernized by the Chinese themselves strikes another sensitive note in the ongoing U.S. cultural debate on multiculturalism. Outside liberal academic concerns, the currency of ethnicity has rapidly created lucrative economic avenues for "cultural otherness" and "global consciousness."[3] Contrary to the popular belief, then, that multiculturalism merely constitutes an educational project within U.S. academic institutions, its ideological repercussions clearly encompass the economic sphere, as well.[4] Moreover, as Chinese films are fast becoming economic successes in the era of late, or what is also known as global, capitalism, the logic of culture is no longer comprehensible in strictly national or local terms.

To be sure, the whole notion of cultural autonomy effectively undermines the reality of social practice and its complex ramifications within the economic realm. This is certainly true for capitalist society structures where rigid compartmentalization of the human realm primarily and proportionally regulates the steady market flow of perceived lack and "healthy" consumption. Ideologically speaking, this means that the market economy relies on the discursive existence of a narrative structure that interpellates human subjects into individuals: in other words, the successful recruiting of the Self through the production of desire. Cinema provides a particularly rich field for analyzing this process and, through a psychoanalytical discussion of the scopic field and its relation to libidinal economy, this essay argues that the filmic construction of the Self crucially hinges upon two central notions: fantasy and the gaze — albeit neither as understood in its conventional meaning. My examples will be limited to three of Zhang Yimou's more popular films in the West: *Judou, Raise the Red Lantern* (*Da hong denglong gaogao gua*), and *The Story of Qiuju* (*Qiuju da guansi*). Although the last-named film at first appears to be a radical departure from the first two, I propose that all three films follow the same trajectory of visual agency and ideological fantasy in which issues of masculinity are at stake.

How Fantasy Screens the Field of Vision

Zhang Yimou's work is usually characterized by its strong visual appeal and its "progressive" attention to so-called women's issues. This is reflected in the fascination the films hold for the viewer; they typically construct a sensory experience of China that is at once beautiful and cruel: beautiful because of Zhang Yimou's superbly choreographed cinematography, and cruel because of the profound sense of emotional entrapment the filmic characters, generally the female lead, experience.[5] However, the way in which these two sensory perceptions are arranged establishes a hierarchy that gives clear superiority to the visual-aesthetic aspect, and, despite empathy with the tragedy displayed on the screen, the viewer is ultimately unable to evade the seductive powers of Zhang's artistic study of the image. In this way, the use of color and sound is allowed to overpower the much more oppressive aspects of his film: the portrayal of human cruelty in the form of physical and mental torture. In *Judou*, for example, we witness the desperate reality of a woman first condemned to a life of misery with her brutal husband, then denied the right to live with her lover, Tianqing, and finally tragically consumed in the final conflagration of the film. But all this somehow pales into lesser significance against the lush setting of the old dye-mill which, incidentally, was built according to Zhang's own design and, in the film, is further stunningly embellished by the shots of the dyed cloth hanging from the ceiling. Throughout the film, these sheets of color function as an emotional screen, both projecting the story's libidinal movement and capturing the viewer's pleasure in looking.

A similar effect can be observed in *Raise the Red Lantern,* in which the camera's almost obsessive focus on the lavish interiors (including the women's clothing) and on the raising and lowering of the red lanterns serves to create an erotic atmosphere that almost neutralizes the violence against women produced within that aesthetically appealing environment. When Songlian is first led into her quarters, the sight of red lanterns displayed all over the room momentarily produces a mixed sense of ambivalence and fascination. Against such a background, Songlian's hysteria and final madness and the cruel deaths of her maid, Yan'er, and the third concubine, Meishan, are not recognized as direct and inevitable results, but seem to be somewhat accidental and unfortunate side effects.

In the final film, *The Story of Qiuju,* the female lead neither commits suicide nor turns mad; on the contrary, she triumphs over the villain of the piece. But the victory she is granted is not the one she desires, and the film's final close-up of her face shows an expression of utter disbelief, as if to say: "Who is sane here and who is not?" This level of open-endedness is, however, not allowed to detract from the visual effects of a film bristling with shots of fire-red chili peppers and wide-angle, static camera views of bustling modern city life in an opening China.

How then, we might ask, is it possible to literally *over*look what is so clearly situated in the visual field? To answer this question, we need to turn to Lacan's claim that the scopic field is constituted by a split, a division between the eye and the gaze, which manifests the drive, or rather the lack, that constitutes castration anxiety.[6] Lacan's insistence on the split qua lack serves a twofold goal: to problematize subjectivity in the domain of vision and to articulate the relationship between the Real and the scopic drive. His first important conceptual revision with regard to the scopic field is, therefore, to insist on the antinomy of the eye and the gaze. For Lacan, the gaze is not to be confused with the "look" usually located on the side of the seeing subject. On the contrary, as Slavoj Žižek explains in his informed discussion of Lacan's theory of vision, the gaze is to be understood as "a point in the object (in the picture) from which the subject viewing it is already *gazed at,* i.e. it is the *object* that is gazing at me."[7] Focusing, then, on the ideological status of the gaze, Žižek astutely points out that, for Lacan, the gaze "functions like a stain, a spot in the picture disturbing its transparent visibility and introducing an irreducible split in my relation to the picture: I can never see the picture at the point from which it is gazing at me, i.e. the eye and the gaze are constitutively asymmetrical."[8]

In spite of the brevity with which the Lacanian notion of the gaze is presented here, it is apparent that Lacan is more concerned with mapping the spatial logic of vision than its temporal order. To emphasize that it is the subject's *locus of identification,* and not sight, that determines the gaze, Lacan offers a phrase that is possibly uttered when we are in love and are soliciting a look from the other that we then experience as "something is missing": "You never look at me from the place from which I see you!"[9] What is at stake in this utterance is the subject's desire qua ideological positioning within a visual trajectory of symbolic identification with the Other. As Lacan points out, "The gaze I encounter, is not a seen gaze, but a gaze imagined by me in the field of the Other."[10] It then follows that reality for Lacan is itself *already* structured by a visual illusion, that is, by a fetishistic inversion of the gaze that blinds us to the fact that we can never see ourselves from the place of the Other. In the Lacanian psychoanalytic scheme of things, however, this is a structural necessity of reality because the gaze as blind spot prevents our encounter with the Real, which must be forever postponed because of its traumatic impact. In the final instance, it is this inevitable visual and emotional restaging of the encounter as a *mis*-cognition that determines for Lacan our sense of reality. The important point to grasp in Lacan's theory of vision is that the gaze occupies the status of "ideological fantasy" because it literally and necessarily screens the subject's desire.[11]

The concept of screen should not be reduced to its conventional definition of censorship or filter but understood instead, in accordance with Lacan's paradigm of scopic drive, as a largely unmediated moment in the subject's ideological positioning. As a visual structure of representation, it is the screen that embodies the subject's *jouissance*— a term coined by Lacan to denote a form of excess produced by meaning. Departing from more conventional definitions of the term as postive energy or life force, this Lacanian notion of enjoyment-as-excess refers much more to an empty space, an impossible void, so to speak, that needs to be filled with something. Ideological fantasy basically fulfills this role of some-Thing, masking the no-Thing in its impossibility. This, then, is the theoretical motivation behind Lacan's statement that "the relation between the gaze and what one wishes to see involves a lure."[12]

Returning now to our previous discussion of Zhang Yimou's films, it is not difficult to see how Lacan's theory of vision offers a useful perspective on the ideological functioning of Zhang's staggering cinematography. Precisely because Zhang's images are intended as "lures" to seduce the spectator into a visual orgy with China, the camera is already caught up in a libidinal economy of disavowal and fetishization. Within this visual trajectory of desire, a beautiful, sensuous image of China screens the more sober and painful recognition of an ancient culture with a set of cruel, ritualistic social practices that ultimately cripples its people emotionally and even destroys them physically. I would argue that this artistically orchestrated sensory perception in Zhang's films amounts to a visual "mis-encounter" that is intimately linked to the director's preoccupation with issues of masculinity.

Male Impotence and the Gaze

Although the three films under discussion are ostensibly stories about women, they are foremost narratives of masculinity in which patriarchal power of control is mirrored by impotence and a loss of the gaze. In *Judou*, the beautiful and sensual body of Gong Li occupies the status of a fantasy screen for her husband, Yang Jinshan, and his adopted nephew, Tianqing, with whom she later begins an illicit love affair. For Yang Jinshan, the mill owner with sufficient purchasing power over women, Judou's body holds the promise of bestowing full masculinity by producing his long-awaited heir. Although he is clearly impotent, his disavowal is safely guarded by the mythical healing powers of ancient Chinese medicine and the socially sanctioned, violent control over Judou's body that he exercises. Sexual perversion, however, is not an end but only a seemingly necessary means to achieve the narcissistic goal of becoming a paternal producer, and after Judou gives birth to Tianbai, the sexual violence comes to an end. Paternal pride is now able to transform a previously abusive patriarch into a considerate partner quite blind not only to his own impotence but also to the fact that only Tianqing could have fathered Tianbai. To that effect, Yang Jinshan is outside the gaze: he does not possess the power to see in the same manner that he does not possess the power to inseminate.

Significantly, it is Tianqing who controls the gaze on the film's structural as well as diegetic level: as the voyeur. In a scene that shows Tianqing at work beneath a huge wheel, he is looking upward to Judou on the second floor walking through the cloth hanging from the ceiling. As the camera follows Judou, she becomes aware of the gaze and unexpectedly looks straight into the camera, thus recognizing Tianqing's desire for her. The use of the shot–reverse shot technique leaves no doubt that the camera's point of view here coincides with that of Tianqing. This is also true for another voyeuristic scene in the barn. When Judou discovers that Tianqing is secretly watching her, her initial reaction of shame turns to a recognition of her power over the gaze: by deliberately exposing her naked body to him, she arrests his pleasure in looking and, by extension, his illicit sexual longing for her. Ironically, though, this very gesture of exposing her knowledge of his desire for her at once alleviates and compounds her misery. Although Judou's situation markedly improves after the birth of her son, Tianbai, the social codes do not permit a legal union with her lover and her son's father.

As for Tianqing, his sexual potency does not automatically translate into patriarchal power of control and, on the contrary, he is punished by the law-of-the-father in more than one way. For example, when Tianqing, in his desire for acknowledgment, teaches Tianbai the word "father," the lesson in paternal nomenclature has unexpected consequences when Tianbai is only able to produce this form of address to name Jinshan. Tianqing's fate, to have to forfeit forever his "rightful" position, is thus sealed by this very act of enunciation, and his symbolic impotence becomes increasingly apparent as Judou's every attempt to escape patriarchal control is denounced by Tianqing as "unfilial." Even after Jinshan's accidental death, social codes of propriety demand that Tianqing no longer live in the mill, and he is shown powerless to resist and resolve an unbearable situation. In spite of the fact that he is actually not related by blood to Jinshan, the symbolic order must be maintained at all costs, and it is significant that, after Judou finally tells her son that Tianqing is his biological father, the consequences are fatal. In an attempt to clear his stained family name, Tianbai throws Tianqing into a pool of dye and beats him to death while Judou tries in vain to stop him. But her crying only aggravates Tianbai's temper further, and in the final scene, we are shown Judou setting fire to the mill. Tianqing's failure to seize control of the patriarchal gaze is also visible on another level: after Judou gives birth to Tianbai, the camera's point of view no longer coincides with that of Tianqing's, and open voyeurism altogether disappears from the film's diegetic level. Instead, it is the camera's and the spectator's point of view that now coincide to rejoice in a potent vision of China triumphing aesthetically even as its social order crumbles ethically.

In Zhang Yimou's *Raise the Red Lantern,* the theme of masculinity is closely linked to a paternal superego that compensates for emotional impotence. Embedded in a series of ritualistic practices coupled with their blatant fetishistic display, the raised red lanterns are fantasy objects that drive the interpretative movement of a phallic gaze. To that effect, the lanterns constantly remind the women of their status as objects of male desire. As they are raised, extinguished, removed, and occasionally covered up, the lanterns function as a libidinal barometer indicating women's precarious status within the patriarchal household. The rich merchant, Chen, is a paternal figure whose power of control over women's bodies is enshrined in the tightly enclosed space of the mansion, where the intricate architecture and interior design function as fantasy screens through which Chen's vision is fractured.

Each of the four women is confined to her own little courtyard that is the breeding ground for both private pleasure and public humiliation. Every evening, the women are forced to offer themselves in competition for their master's favors by presenting themselves in front of their main entrances to observe a fixed ceremonial procedure. The final choice is indicated by placing a red lantern in front of the selected woman. Demeaning as this gesture may be, the women's participation is rewarded with seemingly irresistible libidinal pleasures: before the master retires to the respective quarters, a soothing and thoroughly addictive foot massage is performed on the woman because, as the master explains, "it is important to take care of a woman's feet, a relaxing massage will make her feel good, and only then will she serve her master well." In addition to this special treat, the selected partner for the night is allowed to order her favorite dish for dinner the next day.

After his tireless efforts to find a suitable location for the film, Zhang finally chose a mansion-turned-museum in deeply rural Shanxi.[13] Indeed, both the setting and the women characters appear more as artifacts on display in a museum, as visual aesthetic "lures," which reinvent a distant time and space for spectators generally unfamiliar with Chinese history and culture.[14] But even if this is the case, it is nevertheless primarily the gaze itself that produces the lure. As in *Judou,* colors and setting contribute to the film's visual appeal and the camera's preoccupation with masculinity. But above all, *Raise the Red Lantern* is a story about the tenuous status of the phallic gaze and, by extension, the impossibility of sexual relations. Significantly, that impossibility is produced when the gaze meets the gaze of the other, that is, when the gaze is turned upon itself. Whenever this happens, the gaze is castrated; it loses its phallic status. For example, when Songlian realizes that her social standing and emotional well-being in the household can only be secured by "having" the red lanterns, she fakes a pregnancy. According to custom, from the moment the good news is announced, red lanterns and foot massages, not to mention a special diet, are to be lavished on the pregnant woman until delivery. In Songlian's case, however, after a relatively short indulgence in such attention, her scheme is unfortunately discovered and, in his wrath, master Chen orders that all red lanterns in Songlian's private quarters be immediately covered with black cloth, thus denying her the "phallus" and indicating her status as fallen object. In contrast, her maid Yan'er, who has won the sexual favors of master Chen but not the expected promotion to the status of his concubine, secretly decorates her sleeping quarters with old red lanterns, in spite of explicit house rules to the contrary, in stubborn defense of her "share" of the phallus. When Yan'er is betrayed by Songlian as an act of revenge, she is forced to kneel in the snow in front of a burning pile of her red lanterns until she is willing to repent. But Yan'er is determined not to disavow her possession of the phallus and resists until both she and her lanterns are extinguished.

The inability of a phallic gaze to produce satisfactory sexual relations is made even clearer in an episode involving the phallic object par excellence. When Songlian discovers that her flute, a precious gift from her late father, is missing and that master Chen, thinking it to be a gift from a lover, has burnt it, she becomes even more indifferent to his needs and her marital duties. Some time later, when she finds Feipu, the handsome and effeminate son of the first wife, playing a flute, she appears to become sexually aroused. In spite of the brevity of the encounter, she develops an affection for Feipu, but the impossibility of this relationship is evident from the very beginning as he is, first of all, her stepson and second, not at home enough to give her the emotional support she needs in order to survive the patriarchal control of master Chen.[15] Songlian finally resigns herself to her fate and is soon completely involved in increasingly bitter battles against the other women of the household. Deprived of any real power and genuine emotional support, though, Songlian's actions only serve to aggravate the situation she initially sought to turn to her advantage, and her final loss of sanity seals her fate as a typical feminine and domestic "detail" gone mad.[16]

Unlike *Judou* and *Raise the Red Lantern,* Zhang's more recent film, *The Story of Qiuju,* is set in contemporary China and centers on the life of the Chinese peasantry. Differences notwithstanding, *The Story of Qiuju* may be considered yet another variant of Zhang's thematic preoccupation with a paternal superego and male impotence controlling the interpretative movement of the gaze. The first thing to say is that, unlike *Judou* and *Raise the Red Lantern, The Story of Qiuju* revolves around a soberly unerotic plot and thus does not lend itself so readily to Zhang's preferred use of color and sound images to solicit the spectator's gaze. On the other hand, Zhang's resourceful exploitation of the medium of the camera, keeping it hidden from the actors while they move about the bustling city crowds, vividly captures China's current and aggressive self-image of a country moving rapidly along the road of modernity toward capitalist industrialization.[17] The stark contrasts throughout the film between the slick, modern city life and the naively innocent country mentality highlight this impression. This can be observed, for example, in the scene of Qiuju and her sister-in-law arriving in the provincial capital and feeling hopelessly lost. As a wide-angle take focuses on the two standing at a busy street junction, their expression is clearly one of feeling out of place.

This anxiety of *not* being in the picture, that is, outside the patriarchal gaze, is precisely what motivates Qiuju to file a lawsuit against the village chief, who has attacked her husband, Qinglai, by kicking him below the belt. The same anxiety is also what motivates the village chief to commit his act of aggression. On the surface, *The Story of Qiuju* celebrates the heroic attempt of one female peasant to challenge the formidable labyrinth of Chinese bureaucracy for an explanation of why the village chief has been allowed to injure her husband right there where "life resides." It remains highly questionable, however, whether Qiuju would have shown the same degree of tenacious persistence had her husband been kicked in a less sensitive area. So why is Qiuju so obsessed with her husband's reproductive organ? At the heart of the matter is a negative transference of guilt that involves a phallic gaze: that is, the village chief's inability to produce a male heir. Although Qiuju is pregnant and expected to deliver at any time, the baby could be a girl and thus pose a real threat to Qinglai's patriarchal lineage. In the context of modern China's prohibitions of polygamy and the one-child policy, this form of symbolic impotence provides a new discursive structure for exploring issues of masculinity. During an argument between Qiuju's husband, Qinglai, and the village chief, the latter's masculinity is called into question because he has no sons and only four daughters. This insensitive comment on the chief's symbolic castration naturally provokes retaliation, so the village chief kicks Qinglai below the belt precisely to render him as impotent as he is himself. Although the injury turns out to be slight, and Qinglai is willing to accept a monetary settlement, Qiuju becomes obsessed with the issue and demands a full explanation.

This is, of course, to demand the impossible, and not surprisingly, Qiuju does not receive her explanation from the village chief, nor does the state court settle her case to her satisfaction, and the many trips to the city and her tireless efforts to appeal the court's decision appear to have been in vain. In any case, the issue is suddenly superseded by the dramatic events surrounding Qiuju's emergency delivery. After her husband finally succeeds in soliciting the village chief's help, the villagers rush Qiuju to the city hospital in the chief's cart, and she gives birth to a boy. The joy over the newly born male dispels all hostility between the two parties and earns Qiuju respect as a "real woman" in the eyes of her "villain," and it is as if the injury to Qinglai's reproductive organ has never happened. Ironically, however, at the infant's one-hundred-day celebration feast, to which the whole village is invited, Qiuju unexpectedly receives the news from the city counsellor that the state court has revoked its earlier decision and ordered the arrest of the village chief. Qiuju immediately tries to stop the arrest, but the chief has already been taken away. The final scene shows her face in a close-up, and the expression is one of profound confusion. As she watches the car with the village chief in it disappearing into the distance, she seems to say: "I don't believe what I see!"

History and Nostalgia

In the West, the general reaction to *The Story of Qiuju* ironically mimics the film's final scene, and many Zhang Yimou fans seem to have lived through the same experience as the protagonist Qiuju: a sense of incredibility toward what they have seen. Within China, in contrast, the film was, in fact, Zhang's biggest success to date. Perhaps encouraged by hitherto unknown domestic recognition, Zhang's latest film follows the model of *The Story of Qiuju* rather than the more familiar, for Western audiences, *Red Sorghum* or *Judou*. At a time when Chinese filmmaking is still subject to stringent political censorship and attracting foreign investment is proving increasingly competitive with the emergence of new young Chinese directors, Zhang's move toward more domestic concerns can be seen as symptomatic of current Chinese cultural politics.[18]

The failure of many Fifth Generation directors to satisfy audiences within the home market is often ascribed to the fact that these films are so clearly directed toward overseas consumers.[19] Virtually all of Zhang Yimou's and Chen Kaige's films were funded by companies in Taiwan, Hongkong, and Japan, and it is also not unusual to hear Chinese critics at home and abroad complaining about Zhang Yimou's "pornographic" vision of Chinese history and society, that is, a vision that nourishes Western audiences' scopophilic drive.[20] However, making such an argument simply reduces the ideological ramifications of the gaze vis-à-vis the various scopic aspects and levels of the entire cinematic apparatus. What we cannot ignore is the fact that the films were made by Chinese directors whose presence is inscribed in the very materiality of their work. One way of accounting for this aspect, while not losing sight of the fact that the films were also intended for export, is to argue that Zhang's films are not so much pornographic as *nostalgic* in nature.

It has often been noted that Fifth Generation films are shot either in dramatically barren landscapes—of which *King of Children* by Chen Kaige is a classic example—or in beautiful but enclosed spaces, such as Zhang Yimou's *Judou* and *Raise the Red Lantern*. In addition, these films are also nominally set in a recent past, but as with space, they nevertheless create their own time. A case in point is *Life on a String*, in which the precise historical context is unspecified, not to mention *Li Lianying*, in which the historical continuity is constantly broken, or *Raise the Red Lantern*, in which the depiction of feudal order is far from accurate. But if, in other words, the envisioned China in the new wave films is merely an imaginary space, what can be said about the Fifth Generation's ideological fantasy supporting their reality? Bérénice Reynaud has made the following observation: "The films don't portray modern China, rather they deal with the trauma experienced by their makers during the Cultural Revolution when as teenagers, they were sent to work in factories or to the countryside. They have an obsessional quality: they explore secret wounds, re-enact the loss of innocence, and the collapse of utopia."[21]

In spite of many obvious differences that defy the use of any single, unifying category for the Fifth Generation directors, their personal histories are nevertheless remarkably similar and provide a basis for a collective identity. Like many young educated people, during the Cultural Revolution the directors were sent to remote areas in the countryside in order to "learn from the people," spending the formative years of their lives among peasants before admission to the newly reopened Beijing Film Academy in 1978 made it possible for them to return to urban life. Readjustment, to be sure, was not without its problems. They felt a sense of alienation from both Chinese urban life and traditional culture, a sense of having been at once seduced and victimized by the Cultural Revolution, and they now experienced an openly Western, foreign-oriented training at the film academy.[22] Whether we choose to define their work as postmodern or as hybrid forms, it is hardly difficult to perceive that all of the new wave films bespeak a lack, a permanent feeling of displacement that accounts for the fascination with a distant time and place typically associated with the nostalgic gaze.

According to Slavoj Žižek, nostalgia always invokes an object that either is lost or is one with which we no longer identify. For that matter, nostalgia is foremost a form of fascination with a *gaze itself*, which often, but not always, belongs to an innocent, naive child.[23] This is primarily because the power of fascination works to eliminate the antinomy between the eye and the gaze, that is, it conceals the traumatic impact of the *gaze qua object*.[24] Unlike the case with pornography, for example, where the gaze is "perverted" (because it is actually the subject-spectator who is the real intended object), in nostalgia, the gaze is concealed because the subject believes it "sees itself as seeing." That is to say, fascination effectively blinds us to the fact that the other is already gazing at us, that we are always already being looked at. Indeed, as Žižek maintains, "far from being the point of self-sufficient self-mirroring, the gaze qua object functions like a blot that blurs the transparency of the viewed image."[25]

Applying this understanding to film, Žižek points out that the blot can be identified as that element which appears as a meaningless stain, which "does not fit into the picture" or "sticks out."[26] The phallic metaphor invoked here by Žižek's choice of words is, of course, not accidental and highlights the blot's ideological functioning within the Lacanian paradigm of visual agency. Since Lacan's primary project is to elaborate the notion of the subject, the emphasis on the blot's irreducible materiality establishes its theoretical status as a symptom and begs the larger question of human consciousness or the subject's role in a signifying chain. In terms of the language of vision, what Lacan is interested in is to expose the onlooker/seer as part of a larger picture but one that escapes her own view. Here "escape" has to be understood in the Lacanian sense of ideological fantasy that offers us social reality itself as a way of mis-cognizing our traumatic encounter with the Real. In that respect, the blot is phallic because it ultimately embodies the Real—a traumatic kernel that resists symbolization.

Žižek's theoretical gloss on Lacan's notion of the blot offers us a way of discussing the Fifth Generation directors' films as constitutive of their own ideological fantasy, rather than mere entertainment products for Western audiences' consumption. If we now return to Zhang Yimou's films, we would have to say that, in *Judou*, the figure of Tianbai, her son, functions as a blot, a detail that does not belong, that is out of place and refuses to fit into the symbolic order. First of all, it should be noted that Zhang's deliberate attempt to portray Tianbai as a mentally abnormal child cannot be rationalized on the film's diegetic level. Tianbai is not socially recognized as Tianqing's son, nor as the product of an illicit union. Tianqing is, in fact, only an adopted nephew of Yang Jinshan, Judou's husband, and, therefore, not in any way blood-related to the Yang family clan. Secondly, although Tianbai has no knowledge of who his real biological father is, the emotional life of his early years appears to be little affected by the situation, since Yang Jinshan, Judou, and Tianqing all demonstrate their love for him in their own ways.

While the figure of Tianbai resists meaning in the context of a tragic love story, an allegorical reading of the film would suggest that Tianbai embodies the inexplicability of the Cultural Revolution. From his disturbing laughter upon seeing his symbolic father drown to the brutally calculated murder of his biological father, Tianbai is that irrational and uncanny element in his-story that both ensures and perturbs the rule of the Name-of-the-Father. Ideologically speaking, therefore, Tianbai embodies the traumatic Real that resists symbolization. And just as he stubbornly refuses to go away (and allow his mother to live with Tianqing), the experience and the traumas of the Cultural Revolution continue to haunt directors and the Chinese people to this very day.

In *Raise the Red Lantern,* the blot is materialized on the level of the sound track as a quasi *voix acousmatique,* or a feminine voice agent that constantly disrupts the film's narrative at the diegetic level.[27] While the more common definition of the *voix acousmatique* requires the absence of the voice bearer to bring its ideological functioning as a blot into full cycle, its conceptual implications are still applicable to the passionate singing of the third concubine, Meishan, a former Beijing opera star, as well as the soft and gentle sound of Feipu's flute, both of which seem not only to disrupt but also to perpetuate the patriarchal narrative of love and sex. Although both voice bearers are present in the film, their physicality is extremely tenuous: Feipu, for example, is always absent, a son who lives far away and who is literally not fully present to himself in his effeminacy, which perhaps suggests a latent homosexual tendency. Yet, he is the one who plays the flute, the phallic object par excellence, that attracts Songlian. As for the third concubine Meishan, she lives more in her singing, executed in the ghostly early hours every morning from the roofs of the house, and in the memories of her successful career as a Beijing opera star than in her mundane existence as an emotionally and sexually unfulfilled mistress. Her subsequent murder, enforced by the patriarch as a fitting punishment for the ultimate crime of adultery, literally removes her from the scene at a time when Songlian needs her emotional support most as she struggles to maintain her sanity.

Whenever the sound track is interrupted by the flute and Meishan's singing, the camera shows Songlian as the sole listener to these sounds as they insinuate to her that something is lacking in her present existence as a married woman. But her belief in the power of the phallus is too strong for her to be able to realize that heterosexual love is an impossibility, especially in the context of her objective existence as an oppressed female in a patriarchal household. Not surprisingly, her attraction to Feipu and his effeminacy (he gives her a gift that a woman normally offers her male lover) and the spiritual bond she builds with the exquisitely feminine Meishan are not acknowledged by Songlian as a form of attraction to same-sex love, albeit possibly the result of patriarchal aggression toward women. In the final instance, it is the corporeality of the *voix acousmatique,* that is, the phallic appearance of an instrument and a woman's body, that allows Songlian to avoid her traumatic encounter with the Real as it is embodied in the erotic sound of Meishan's voice and Feipu's flute.

In *The Story of Qiuju,* the blot cannot be found on the film's diegetic level because it is *structural* in nature. Interestingly enough, the blot here can be considered to be *meta*diegetic: it is the *film* itself that unnaturally "sticks out" among Zhang Yimou's films. Within the familiar knowledge of Zhang's obsession with strong erotic images, *The Story of Qiuju* is a structural aberration in the scopic, as well as affective, regime of his fantasy objects. Before the release of the film, Zhang's reputation as a "true" Chinese director was seriously doubted by Chinese officials because his Westernized films failed to capture the attention of Chinese audiences. Rumor has it that Zhang made this film only to ward off increasing government criticism of his tendency to "sell out to the foreigners" and to "be different."[28] In any case, this certainly explains why, of all the films Zhang has made so far, only *The Story of Qiuju* has won a prestigious prize in China and has politically satisfied the Communist hard-liners' dogmatic call for movies to deal with the "real China."[29] By the same token, the domestic success of *The Story of Qiuju* clearly bears witness to the fact that Zhang's attempt to be different is not simply a matter of affirming otherness but also one of escaping repetition, that is, of avoiding the same "Thing."

But how does the act of repetition produce the Thing as the Real? In his perceptive reading of Freud's notion of repetition (*Wiederholung*), Lacan points out that *Wiederholen* is not so much related to the idea of reproduction as to the concept of *Erinnerung* (remembering): "The subject himself, the recalling of his biography, all this goes only to a certain limit, which is known as the real."[30] This limit of knowing is structured by the Real that gives rise to *jouissance,* which for Lacan is "an adequate thought, *qua* thought, at the level at which we are, [which] always avoids—if only to find itself again later in everything—the same thing."[31] In this sense, repetition always brings back the real at the symbolic level, or, to use Lacan's phrase, "the real is that which always comes back to the same place—to the place where the subject in so far as he thinks, where the *res cognitans,* does not meet it."[32]

With regard to *The Story of Qiuju,* the Chinese government's urgent call for a return to the "real China" as a prerequisite for Chinese cinema production in the 1990s may now be read as the return of the Lacanian Real inscribed in the dogmas of socialist realism and the celebration of the people. As such, *The Story of Qiuju* embodies a traumatic leftover from the Cultural Revolution that simply refuses to go away—a blot or stain in the field of vision that cannot be symbolized. But why, we could ask, does this socialist leftover resist symbolization at a time when economic trends in China point in the opposite direction? In Žižek's words, what is at stake might perhaps best be described as the attempt to "level all social differences, the production of the citizen, the subject of democracy,... through the allegiance to some particular national Cause."[33]

Lacan was among the first to understand that this Cause materializes enjoyment and serves societies in a crucial way to organize their collective enjoyment through the perpetuation of national myths. In the context of China in the era of global capitalism, the national Cause here is the stubborn insistence on equating Chineseness with the Communist state at a time when state Communism has already collapsed throughout the rest of the world. In the United States, on the other hand, it is multiculturalism's perverted tolerance for the "real difference" of the Other. Here, then, is the key to the success of *The Story of Qiuju* in China and the popularity of Zhang's other films in the

West: the Thing is always conceived of as something inaccessible to the other but simultaneously threatened by him. To borrow a phrase from Žižek, what we are witnessing here is the "Nation-Thing," the sublime object as the "ethnic Cause" and "pathological stain" in the field of desire, which, in the final instance, procures our jouis-sense, our senseless enjoyment-in-meaning.[34]

Notes

An earlier version of this paper was presented at the Association of Asian Studies conference in Boston in March 1994.

1. Lawrence Chua, "Making Movies (or Trying to) in China," *Premiere*, March 1992, pp. 29–30. See also Chris Berry, "Market Forces: China's 'Fifth Generation' Faces the Bottom Line," in *Perspectives on Chinese Cinema*, ed. Chris Berry (London: British Film Institute, 1991), pp. 114–40.

2. Bérénice Reynaud, "China on the Set with Zhang Yimou," *Sight and Sound* 1, no. 3 (1991): 26–28.

3. Ibid.

4. For a discussion on this issue, see Arif Dirlik, "The Postcolonial Aura: Third World Criticism in the Age of Global Capitalism," *Cultural Critique*, Spring 1993.

5. In an interview, Zhang Yimou responded to the interviewer's remark, "You make your tragedies very beautiful," by saying, "When Tragedy is 'made aesthetic,' then it is all the more overpowering." See Mayfair Mei-hui Yang, "Of Gender, State Censorship and Overseas Capital: An Interview with Director Zhang Yimou," in *Public Culture*, vol. 5 (Chicago: University of Chicago Press, 1993).

6. Jacques Lacan, "The Split between the Eye and the Gaze," in *Four Fundamental Concepts of Psycho-Analysis*, ed. Jacques-Alain Miller, trans. Alan Sheridan (New York: Norton, 1981), pp. 67–123.

7. This quote is taken from Slavoj Žižek, who is one of the most avid readers and proponents of Lacanian theory today: Slavoj Žižek, *Looking Awry: An Introduction to Lacan through Popular Culture* (Cambridge: MIT Press, 1991), p. 125.

8. Ibid.

9. Ibid., p. 103.

10. Ibid., p. 84.

11. Slavoj Žižek, *The Sublime Object of Ideology* (London: Verso Books, 1989), pp. 30, 47.

12. Ibid., p. 104.

13. See Lawrence Chua, "Making Movies (or Trying to) in China," *Premiere*, March 1992, p. 29.

14. The writer Dai Qing has commented on Zhang's rather careless attention to details in this film. See Dai Qing, "Raised Eyebrows for *Raise the Red Lantern*," *Public Culture* 5 (1993): 333–37.

15. In the original novel on which the film is based, the character Feipu occupies a more important narrative space. There are also explicit references to his impotence and homosexuality. See Su Tong, *Wives and Concubines* (*Fu yu qie*).

16. For an illuminating discussion of this idea, see Rey Chow, "Modernity and Narration—in Feminine Detail," in *Woman and Chinese Modernity: The Politics of*

Reading between West and East (Minneapolis: University of Minnesota Press, 1991), pp. 84–120.

17. See Mayfair Yang, "Of Gender," pp. 308–9.

18. Jianying Zha, "Beijing Notebooks," *Utne Reader,* September/October 1994, pp. 98–105.

19. See ibid. and Žižek, *Sublime Object,* p. 104.

20. David Chute, "Golden Hours," *Film Comment* 27, no. 2 (March/April 1991): 64–66.

21. Bérénice Reynaud, "Ghosts of the Future," *Sight and Sound,* festival coverage of the *Manchester Guardian,* 1992, p. 17.

22. Ibid.

23. Slavoj Žižek, *Looking Awry,* pp. 114–16.

24. Ibid., p. 114.

25. Ibid.

26. Ibid., p. 93.

27. For a discussion of *voix acousmatique,* see Žižek, *Looking Awry,* pp. 125–27.

28. See Chris Berry, "Market Forces," pp. 127–28.

29. See Xiao Bo, "*Qiuju da guansi* he *Gao peng man zuo* ronghuo guoji dajiang," *Dazhong dianying* (Popular cinema) (Beijing), April 1993, no. 478.

30. Jacques Lacan, *The Fundamental Concepts of Psycho-Analysis,* ed. Jacques-Alain Miller, trans. Alan Sheridan (New York: Norton, 1978), p. 49.

31. Ibid.

32. Ibid.

33. Slavoj Žižek, "Formal Democracy and Its Discontents," in *Looking Awry,* p. 162.

34. Ibid. See also Žižek, "Eastern Europe's Republics of Gilead," in *Dimensions of Radical Democracy: Pluralism, Citizenship, Community,* ed. Chantal Mouffe (London: Verso, 1992), pp. 193–210.

4 / Contesting and Contested Identities: Mathura's Chaubes

Owen M. Lynch

Mathura City lies about one hundred miles south of New Delhi, India. It is famous for the ancient Buddhist and Jain cultures buried in its soil and displayed in its museum; it is even more renowned among Hindus as the birthplace of India's beloved god, Lord Krishna, and as a sin-cleansing bathing spot, Vishram Ghat, on the banks of the holy river Jamuna. The city is one of the *saptamahātīrtha*s, Hinduism's seven great pilgrimage centers. Pilgrims come to Mathura throughout the year for a day or so to bathe in Jamuna's waters and visit temples, including that erected over the site of Krishna's birth. Others come for the annual *Braj Caurāsī Kos Parikramā* (160-mile circumambulation around the land of Braj), a forty-day pilgrimage visiting many of the places where Krishna, as a child, performed his miraculous *līlā*s (sports, play).

Mathura is equally renowned for its Chaubes, a community of priests of the high-ranking Hindu category (*varṇa*) of Brahmans. Chaubes act as guides and ritual specialists (*paṇḍā*s) performing necessary rites for pilgrims at various holy stations. In Mathura a Chaube is hard to miss, for they often have hefty, husky wrestlers' bodies and unfailingly confront unwary pilgrims with demanding offers of their ritual services.

The Chaubes densely inhabit an elevated part of Mathura known as Chaubiya Para, whence they look down upon the river Jamuna. In

74

1882 Growse (1979:9) estimated their population to be 6,000, although Chaubes today say that their population is about 4,000. My own rough estimate puts their population resident in Mathura at 11,300 in 1978.[1] I, too, needed a *paṇḍā* for my study of Mathura as a pilgrimage center, and that need led me to ask them about themselves and who they were. I quickly learned that there was no simple answer enabling me to locate them in time and social space; all their answers were open to interpretation, and were sometimes seemingly contradictory, and as often contested. Such answers led me to abandon an approach of determining who the Mathura Chaubes "really" were as a socially distinct, bounded group or caste and to concentrate instead on the narratives of their contesting and contested identities and what they might reveal. This chapter, then, first asks what a narrative perspective reveals about self-identity and social order in India.

My concern is narrative*s*, rather than narrative, because in daily life the self is not experienced or displayed in one totalized whole; rather, it is constituted through narratives of multiple identities in social situations, as Mead (1934) long ago argued. Self-identity, therefore, "is not a fixed 'thing,' it is negotiated, open, shifting, ambiguous, the result of culturally available meanings and the open-ended, power-laden enactments of those meanings in everyday situations" (Kondo 1990:24; see also Carrithers 1985:255). Thus, selves, as agents, in any society are constituted and experienced through multiple identities in the process of daily life.

Such a perspective of narrative as constitutive necessitates an appropriate theory of self as agent. I draw, then, upon Charles Taylor's (1985a, 1985b) theory of the self and only briefly and inadequately outline it here. Taylor understands an agent as one who can make life plans, hold values, and make choices. An important characteristic of such an agent is not consciousness, although that is involved; rather it is significances intrinsic to the agent. Intrinsic significances are constitutive in that the things humans experience, such as their identities, their feelings, and their emotions, are inseparable from their understanding of them (see also Lynch 1990b); they are not, then, pure representations in consciousness of objects separate from the self as subject. Such significances are human beings' own and not the derivative ones of machines or artifacts whose purposes are ultimately given to them by human beings.

A second characteristic of such an agent is that significances involve the agent's awareness of self-definition and self-transformation, not merely awareness of purposes that can be sought. For that reason the significances agents seek are such that "our not choosing them reflects on us rather than undermining their status as ends" (Taylor 1985b:266); they are strong evaluations "concerned with the *qualitative* worth of our desires" (Taylor 1985a:16). Thus, if I choose not to eat ice cream, it merely ceases to be an end for me, but if I choose to go to Hawaii rather than attend my daughter's wedding, my choice reflects poorly on my paternal identity on that occasion.

Finally, agency is characteristically connected with language or discourse, through which agents focus on significances, bring them into view, disclose them, acquire, and even change them and thereby their selves. Such focusing involves not just self but *other* in communication or conversation and, therefore, some *public space* for the disclosure of significances:

> We learn language in conversation, and hence the original acquisition of articulacy is something *we* do, rather than *I* do. Later we learn to do it to some extent on our own. But we do so in a language which is ours, and hence in principle our formulations should always be capable of being common formulations. That is why they are all in principle addressed to others, and open to criticism by others. And for certain key matters, the human significances among them, *the connection between the attainment of clarity and continuing conversation is never relaxed very far.* (Taylor 1985b:275; emphasis added)

I shall make use of Taylor's theoretical notion of a public or social space of disclosure through language, or discourse, in this chapter. Theoretical space, when manifested in specific cultural form, I shall call place. My second question, then, is, What does a narrative perspective through a space of disclosure reveal about how self is experienced and understood among the Chaubes of India?

The importance of Taylor's theory for purposes of this essay is threefold.[2] First, it is not representationist or internalist and, therefore, does not assume a culturally specific metaphor of an interiorized consciousness making agents self-evidently aware of themselves and their significances. That assumption involves "a total suppression of any recognition of a space of disclosure" (Taylor 1985b:280). The appeal of Taylor's theory is its decentering the subject/agent without eliminating it; agency remains. Because the subject/agent is not located in an interiorized consciousness, it is not phonocentrically self-present to itself, logocentrically aware of all meaning, and culturally limited by one language's metaphor for its conception. Rather, the subject/agent is theoretically located in the open-ended public and social space given through language.

Second, agents become selves as interlocutors; they are "self-interpreting animals" (Taylor 1985a:226) whose identities involve significances, those strong evaluations fundamental to who selves are. Yet, because those identities are culturally contingent and articulated in the public space of language, the self is not a coherent, unique object or essence clearly known to agents.[3] The search for clarity and the conversation about the self are unending and expressed most often in narratives of self-identity.

Third, numerous studies (for example, Hardgrave 1969; Lynch 1969; Barnett 1973; Rao 1979) of Indian castes in the process of change, particularly that of Sanskritization (Srinivas 1966), have emphasized change of identity. Yet they all implicitly assume that a caste is a bounded, coherent entity of individuals sharing some essence. Berreman (1972) does not share that assumption, but he shares with those studies the additional assumption of the interiorized self, such that change in the myths of caste identity is something epiphenomenal to or, like a mask, on the surface of the real interiorized self. Thus, language is not constitutive, but merely a medium for reference to things purportedly more basic. In taking a narrative approach, this essay argues against those assumptions.

Narrative, as a linguistic phenomenon, is characterized by *différance* (Derrida 1973, 1976), such that self-identity bears the presence of absent other meanings, other identities. Derrida notes three aspects of *différance*: difference, deferral, and dissemination. Difference refers to a signifier having a space between it and its signified; the two are not identical. Therefore, there is always some play allowing a difference between signifier and signified; a signifier is not tied to only one signified or referential meaning. Deferral concerns a temporal space between a signifier's present signified and its other possible signifieds at other points in time. Finally, dissemination refers to a signifier's taking on new, as well as losing old, signified meanings. A signifier, then, is characterized by the presence of an absence, the *trace* of other things it can mean. It is not that signifiers have no meaning; rather, they have contingent meaning; otherwise, there would be nothing to deconstruct.

Narratives composed of signifiers are caught in what Derrida calls "the play of difference"; as intertexts, they carry the possibilities of multiple interpretations. Narratives of self-identity, then, are "strategic assertions which inevitably suppress differences, tensions and contradictions" (Kondo 1990:10); they can be socially contesting and contested.

Narratives form part of a discursive field—that is, a range of competing narratives focused on an institution or central organizing concept, such as self. Discourses, such as those of law, medicine, rhetoric, or scripture, are social frameworks of intelligibility enabling or constraining ways of thinking within a discursive field. Their use makes narratives seem natural and culturally appropriate (see Duncan 1990: 16; Foucault 1972).

This chapter is itself one more narrative resulting from a dialogue with individuals and their writings in answer to my incessant questions and puzzled attempts to make sense of their narrative answers (see Daniel 1984). My questions, then and now, are, What is your name, where do you live, and who are you? The answers received had more to do with self-identity in the Hindu world of *saṃsāra*, the world of desire, attachment, change, and the everyday, than with self-identities in the world of the individual soul (*jīva*) as identical to the ultimate soul of the universe (*ātma*). Thus, my concern is with self-identities in the world of *saṃsāra*, which, I believe, tends to be overlooked in studies of the Hindu self. The narratives of self-identity that I heard are also "we" rather than "I" narratives; their narrators speak as though similarly named others identified and agreed with them. Unfortunately, they are also male narratives, because I had restricted access to females.

Scriptural Identities

When I first began asking them about themselves, Chaubes adamantly asserted that their ancestors had been present in Mathura since its very foundation. They advised me to go to Mathura's museum, renowned for its collection of Buddhist and Jain sculptures, and to look at its stone sacrificial pillar (*yupa*) from the time of Raja Huviska (second century), upon which are inscribed the following words: "In the twenty-fourth year of Vashishka on the thirtieth day of the fourth month of summer, Dronal, son of Rudral, a Bharadvaj Mathur Samvedi Brahman, after making a twelve-night sacrifice, placed this sacrificial pillar here" (V. K. Caturvedī n.d.:14).[4] V. K. Caturvedī asserts, as do other Chaubes, that Dronal, the Mathur Brahman mentioned in the inscription, was their ancestor. Dronal metonymically stands for all Chaubes today. The sacrificial pillar is for them, then, material proof of their ancestry and grounds them in the soil of Mathura itself; the pillar is proof of their identity as continuous with that of their Mathur ancestor. It *is* their past in the present; myth "transforms history into nature" (Barthes 1972:129).

Some learned Chaube scholars (B. M. Caturvedī 1986; V. K. Caturvedī n.d.; Y. K. Caturvedī 1968; R. P. Caturvedī 1981) trace their ancestry at least as far back as the *Satya* or *Krita yuga,* the first of the Hindu mythological ages when, in one version, it is said that they came from the sweat of Lord Vishnu in his incarnation (*avatāra*) as Varah (*Vārāha*), the boar (Y. K. Caturvedī 1968:25; see also R. P. Caturvedī 1981). Varah settled the Chaubes in Mathura. An idol (*mūrti*) of Varah said to be from that age is today installed in a Chaubiya Para temple, once again giving concrete proof of their ancestral roots in Mathura. Vishnu Chaube told me another narrative from the Varah Purana that makes the same point:

> *Hiranyaksh [a demon] did *tap* [austerities giving magical powers] and through this got the power to take all of Prithvi [the earthly world] to hell, except for Mathura. Everyone was in great fear, so they asked God to help. He took the form of Varah [the boar], killed Hiranyaksh, took Prithvi, and put it on his tusk. Mathura had remained, because it is *tīn lok se nyārī* [separate from the three worlds of heaven, earth and hell]. Varah put Prithvi down behind Vishram Ghat and said to Prithvi:
>
>> There is no god equal to Keshav
>> There is no Brahman equal to Mathur Brahman [Chaube][5]
>> There is no pilgrimage place equal to Vishram Ghat
>> O Earth! This is the essence of truth.[6]

Chaturvedi Brahmans were, then, in Mathura even before Varah's time. That proves, say many Chaubes, that they, the Mathur Brahmans, resided in Mathura during the *Satya yuga.* Thus, when they say that the name Mathur in the text refers to themselves, the Mathur Chaubes, they strategically use an ancient, yet living, Hindu scriptural discourse to locate themselves in a place of disclosure, Mathura itself continuous with and identical to the Mathura of the Varah Purana.

In the *Treta yuga* during which Lord Rama reigned, the Chaubes find proof not only of their residence in Mathura, but also of their honored status and place in it. In the scriptural epic, the Valmiki Ramayana, it is said:

> "A resident on the bank of the Jamuna, Nar Singh, was a happy person."
>
> The above verse mentions the Mathurs by calling them Jamuna people, because it was unnatural for them to be unhappy while living on the banks of the Jamuna near Madhuvan [Mathura]. (V. K. Caturvedī n.d.:13)

In quoting that verse the author identifies himself and other Chaubes with the holy river Jamuna, whom Chaubes consider a goddess (see Lynch 1988). Chaubes say that they are *"Jamunā ke putra,"* children of the Goddess Jamuna; she is, among other things, one source of their livelihood, as well as of their constantly renewed purity from daily lustrations in her holy waters. How, then, when living on her banks, could they have been unhappy, even while the rest of Mathura was under duress from the demon Lavanasur? Mukund Chaube narrated to me:

> *Madhu's son was Lavanasur. He fought with the Chaubes because when his father died, he asked them to come and do *srāddh* [ritual of remembrance of ancestors] for his father. But they refused, because at the same time Durbasa *muni* [sage] ... asked them to give him food. They went and gave him [Durbasa] food.... Lavan began to attack the Chaubes in anger for what they had done. Seven of them went from here [to Ayodhya] and spoke to Rama and asked his help. He sent his younger brother, Shatrughna, back with them and Shatrughna killed Lavan and founded [resettled] Mathura.

Thus, the Chaubes again locate themselves in Mathura during the time of the great god-king Lord Rama.

In the *Dvāpara yuga* of Vishnu's manifestation (*avatāra*) as Lord Krishna, Chaubes' narratives of identity become more complex and more implicated in current concerns. Krishna was born in Mathura but was raised outside of it by foster parents. While still a young boy,

Krishna returned to Mathura to slay demons sent by his wicked and oppressive uncle, King Kans of Mathura, whom, it had been prophesied, Krishna would destroy. Krishna prevailed over the demons, slew Kans, and liberated the city. Chaubes say that, as Krishna's friends, their ancestors assisted him in purging the world of one of its most ancient tyrants, Kans. They are, then, a brave and courageous people, a theme of their character iterated in other narratives of identity to follow.

Annually in Mathura on the tenth day of the bright half of the Hindu month of Kartik (early November) Chaubes celebrate *Kams Vadh kā Melā* (festival of Kans's destruction) by a victory parade through the Chhata Bazaar section of the city. Chaubes monopolize and control the entire festival.

On that day an image (*putlā*) of Kans about two stories high is constructed using an inner frame of cane covered with a face and garments of brightly colored paper. In the evening it is brought to Kans Tila, a Chaube hilltop garden (*bagīcā*) (Lynch 1990a) where menacing Chaube young men wielding *sauntā* (heavy wooden staffs) surround it. Then, two specially chosen Chaube young men dressed as Krishna and his brother, Balram, both mounted upon an elephant, march toward the hill. At an appointed moment in their approach, Kans is decapitated, his head impaled upon a staff, and his body destroyed, its battered remains tossed over the hill. The Chaube warriors followed by Krishna and Balram on the elephant then begin their victory procession through the Chhata bazaar section of the city. Carrying aloft Kans's impaled head, as well as other symbolic loot from his castle, they gleefully dance around the hapless head and sing the following song of victory:

> Ram was brave among Krishna and Baldev's friends.
> To Madhupuri [Mathura] marched slayers of Kans
> And trembled with fear his kin in castle.
> Parading to thunder of *lāṭhī* [wooden staff] and dust-storm swirl
> They hoist aloft the impotent mustache.[7]
> Incense and sandalwood perfume the walls
> And fresh, green cowdung purifies courtyard floors.
> Friends embrace and chant auspicious songs
> Under victory canopy bedecked with elephant pearl and
>   banana.
> Chajju dances with the looted bed.

Then, before arriving at Vishram Ghat on Jamuna's river banks, they halt at Kans Khar, where they lower Kans's head to the ground and triumphantly pulverize it into confetti. Thereafter, they march to Vishram Ghat, where the youths dressed as Krishna and Balram, each sitting in the lap of a Chaube elder, are worshipped and fed. All, thereafter, enter Jamuna's waters to purify themselves from the sin of killing Kans.

The festival of *Kaṃs Vadh kā Melā*, a celebration of Mathura's victory over a wicked ruler, is also a performative narrative that produces and reproduces Chaube identity; its participants metonymically stand for their ancestors' participation in the original event. Moreover, their agonistic display is not lost upon the non-Chaube audience, for whom Mathura's Chaubes are a dominant and contentious presence to be dealt with cautiously, if not feared.

Recently Chaubes' domination of the festival has been contested. In 1980 the All India Yadav Conference was held in Mathura. The Yadavs are traditionally cowherders, as was Lord Krishna, who is said to have sprung from the Yadav clan. At their meeting, I was told, the Yadavs asked how the Chaubes were able to get control of the *Kaṃs Melā* when the Yadavs were in Mathura long before the Chaubes. The implied Yadav narrative is that they, as Krishna's clan brothers, are the original and real heroes of the festival and that the Chaubes are poseurs and usurpers. The Yadavs also vowed that the following year's festival would be in Yadav hands. It was not.

Chaubes over and over again narrated to me their version of episode 10.32 from the Bhagavata Purana wherein they again identify themselves:

> Once Lord Krishna's helpers Subal, Satok, Shridan, and others felt very hungry. Lord Krishna sent them to the Mathurs [in search of sustenance]. A Mathur Brahman named Angiras was engaged in a ritual, but for fear of breaking the Vedic rules he did not give them food even while knowing about the *avatāra* [divine manifestation, here Krishna]. After the cowherds returned, Lord Krishna sent them to the Brahman women, who recognized Lord Krishna as a god beyond Vedic rules. They brought many things, soup, rice, and so forth, and fed Lord Krishna and his good friends. Thus, they brought home his blessings. (V. K. Caturvedī n.d.:15)

In gratitude, it is said, Krishna promised that from that day forward the Chaube women would be renowned for their fair-skinned beauty, as indeed they are today, and the Chaube men would control pilgrimage in the area of Braj, as they do today. Also said is that on that day Krishna bestowed upon them knowledge of all four Vedas rather than one, two, or three, as among other Brahmans, and also gave them their name, Chaube or Chaturvedi, knower of the four Vedas. In narrating the episode, Chaubes proudly tell how no one other than a cheeky Chaube would ignore Krishna's hunger and thirst.

Communities of Brahmans in India are many. The narratives of self-identity related thus far are signifiers of difference that constitute, as unique and separate from other Brahmans, all Chaturvedi Brahmans owing their origin to Mathura. Just as one cannot change one's blood, so too one cannot change one's place of origin. An original place of disclosure in the sacred soil of India permanently marks and constitutes the self through discourse. Thus, for the Chaubes these narratives, somewhat like social charters (Malinowski 1948:101), are of strategic, vital importance. They assert an autochthonous identity as high-status Brahmans; they discursively constitute their self-identities as different from others through location in a place of disclosure; and they claim social honor and political power through prestige of primordial origin in holy Mathura.[8]

The narratives to this point also hint at another essential characteristic of Chaube self-identity; they are happy-go-lucky, even in adversity, and are warriors on behalf of their holy city and its soil. In short, they are *mast* (happy, carefree, intoxicated, lusty), an emotion they say is *sāttvik* (good, pure, virtuous) in moral significance (Lynch 1990a).

Historical Identities

We come, then, to the *Kali yuga*, the present age of decay and moral decadence, as well as of more conventional history. Muslim conquerors and invaders, beginning with Mahmud of Ghazni (997–1030), who in A.D. 1018 saw Mathura's opulent temples and bejeweled Hindu idols as abominations, sacked the city repeatedly. Although the Moghul emperor Akbar (1556–1605) had friendly and supportive relations with Mathura and its Hindus, they bitterly remember his great-grandson Aurangzeb (1658–1707) as the city's worst despoiler.

Chaube narratives of self-identities for this age involve two important figures: the emperor Akbar and the saint Vallabhacharya, founder of the Pushti Marg Sect. Mukund Chaube told me the following version of the Akbar narrative:

*Only for four hundred years have we been doing this *jajmānī* system [priests holding individual pilgrims as patrons]. Before this all money was put in a common alms box (*dān pātr*) and distributed to all by a headman. It was shared equally. Akbar used to go to Agra from Delhi by boat. When he passed by Mathura he asked, "What is this place, who are these people, what are they doing?" [concerning Chaubes on Vishram Ghat]. He summoned them to him, but the Chaubes did not go because of fear. One Chaube, Ujagar Chaube, got into a boat and went to see Akbar.[9] He told Akbar that this is the place of Krishna and it is filled with his history. "The box into which you see people putting money is for charity, alms [*khairāt*]. We take [*dan*] religious donations. Whether a person gives a cowrie shell [worth much less than a penny] or a *lākh* [100,000] of rupees, it is the same." Akbar gave Ujagar a [worthless] broken cowrie [*kāni kaurī*] into his hand. Ujagar returned to Vishram Ghat. The Chaubes on the Ghat asked him to put what Akbar had given him in the alms box, but he refused and said, "No, because Muslims are not of our religion and I did not take it on the Ghat." They started to fight with him and he fled. Akbar sent his servant and called back Ujagar. Akbar asked what the fight was about. Ujagar told Akbar,... "That is our custom." Akbar asked why he didn't give the cowrie. Ujagar said, "I kept it in my fist so no one could see it. In this fist is your and my honor [*ijjat*]." [That is, if he should show the worthless cowrie people would wonder what kind of emperor would give such a worthless thing. The emperor would be dishonored.] Akbar then said, "What do you want?" Ujagar asked to be made the priest [*purohit*] of the four [Hindu] sects and the fifty-two kingdoms around Mathura. Akbar gave a *pharmān* [royal decree] in which this was done.

Chaube association with the saint Vallabhacharya is different. It begins with Vallabhacharya's arrival in Braj to make a pilgrimage. He tried to do so, but, lacking a guide, he was unsuccessful. Arvind Chaube narrates one version of what Vallabhacharya then did:

*He asked Jumunaji (the river goddess, Jamuna) what he must do to have success. He was told that it was important to have a guru from the Chaubes and to get their blessing. So he went to [Ujagar], got his blessing, and took him as a guru. After that he got success in his pilgrimages. Until today followers of Vallabhacharya must come to descendants of [Ujagar] to begin pilgrimage.[10]

From that day forward, all followers of Pushti Marg take one or another Chaube as their pilgrimage priest, and even today Vallabhacharya's descendants take their pilgrimage vows from Ujagar's descendants. It is important to note that Harirayji (1905) and other hallowed Pushti Marg hagiographers (see Caube 1967) have narratively inscribed that event, in essence although not in detail, in Pushti Marg scriptural discourse. The event was decisive for the Chaubes; the wealth of Vallabhacharya's followers has been a major source of their income and has supported many of them in a prosperous style of life.

What do these two narratives have to do with Chaube self-identity? First of all, the narrative of Vallabhacharya, an authoritative figure, has him recognize Ujagar, his descendants, and synecdochically all Chaubes as Brahmans and as *paṇḍās* (pilgrimage priests). Today Vallabhacharya's descendants and the followers of his sect revalidate those identities whenever they utilize Chaubes' ritual services on pilgrimage. Second, that identity is confirmed by its appearance in the scriptural discourse of Pushti Marg. Third, the emperor Akbar, a Muslim, ironically and not without ambiguous consequences for the Chaubes, did likewise when he gave to Ujagar the *pharmān* granting to him rights to the four sects and fifty-two kingdoms. Although I was never allowed to see it, the *pharmān* has inserted, as we shall see, Chaubes' claim into a legal discourse and added legal authority to their strategic assertions of identity and rights.

In Hindu India, one of the traditional sources of valid knowledge (*pramāṇ*) is verbal authority (*sabda*), as in the scriptures or the words of some learned or holy person, such as Harirayji. Thus, by continuously finding their narrative identities in scriptural discourse and by asserting them in daily life, Chaubes implicitly and strategically base many of their identities on this taken-for-granted criterion of proof. Their narratives of self-identity are, then, implicated in power through constitutive scriptural discourse.

Moreover, as Appadurai (1981) has noted, the past is a scarce resource not only in political debate but also in problems of identity itself (see also Lynch 1969). Such debate proceeds in India according to five cultural norms:

1. that *textual evidence* for the authority of any charter is superior to any other kind; 2. that the evidence for a charter ought to involve the ratification of a credible *external authoritative figure* (whether sacred or secular) in the past; 3. that the charter should

be based on an authoritative document that encodes (in addition to the claims of the group in question) the *privileges of a maximum number* of other relevant groups; 4. that the evidence for the charter in question should be reflected, as far as possible, *continuously* in the documented past, and 5. that the greater the *antiquity* of the referents of the charter in question, the better the case for the rights in question. (Appadurai 1981:204)

Chaubes in written and spoken narratives constitute their identity as "the" autochthonous Mathur Brahmans by using the discourse of *ancient scriptural texts,* including that of the museum's sacrificial pillar. The *Kaṃs Melā* is a performative narrative text that recreates, or better re-realizes, another identity in which Chaubes actually become Krishna's friends and allies, as well as Mathura's ancient citizens. When the two youths portraying Krishna and Balram are crowned, they do not merely portray, rather they *become* the two divine brothers and are worshipped as such. The *Kaṃs Melā* is more than a festival; it is a ritual event that grounds its truth and Chaube identity in actual experience.

When the Yadav's contest Chaubes' control of the festival by asserting that it is theirs, they implicitly acknowledge the power of the *Kaṃs Melā* as a performative narrative socially producing and reproducing a Chaube identity in the present. Likewise, the ritual wherein Vallabhacharya's descendants take pilgrimage vows from the Chaubes is a performative narrative text producing and reproducing their identity as Brahman pilgrimage priests. The same is true whenever they act as pilgrimage priests for other pilgrims and members of the sects, as granted in Akbar's *pharmān.*

Chaubes cite Varah, Krishna, Rama, Vallabhacharya, Harirayji, Akbar, and British government officials as *external authoritative* figures ratifying their identities and their claims to be the pilgrimage priests of Mathura in Braj. In 1901, British census officials listed the Chaubes in the third and last category among all Brahmans. The British, then, became another external secular authority recognizing a new Chaube census identity and privileging them among others, even though Chaubes rejected classification in the third category and submitted such proofs, as I have already presented, to claim classification in the first and highest category (Māthur Maṇḍlī 1964). In more recent days, as I describe later, some of their privileges, as pilgrimage priests versus other claimants, have been validated by judges in courts of justice.

Thus, Chaubes today construct their identities using three recognized discourses: scripture, performance, and secular law, including governmental classification. Each narrative using one of those discourses implicitly asserts the absent presences of all other Chaube identities.

The evidence, as Chaubes see and present it, is continuously documented in the past, and its antiquity stretches back to the beginning of the *Satya yuga*. Thus, the *Kaṃs Melā* victory song crucially emphasizes the continuity of blood relationship between today's Chaubes and their ancestors. No clearer illustration of their metonymical turn of thought could be given.

My own narrative conceals the audiences, the others, for the Chaube narratives of self-identity: Hindu pilgrims, occasional interested anthropologists, and, in particular, other Brahmans for whom Chaube narratives strategically assert a charter constituting them as Brahmans; as autochthonous offspring of Mathura, its soil and holy river Jamuna; and as legitimate priests for the pilgrimage sites in the area, especially Vishram Ghat. More important, their discourses—scriptural, legal, and performative—are not merely political, they are also constitutive of Chaube self-identities, of the selves they know themselves to be.

Contesting Identities

Chaubes' vehemence and certainty in constructing their narratives of self also obscure and conceal the ambiguities, tensions, and uncertainties with which their self-identities are fraught; "their [Chaubes'] origin and history is riddled with controversy [*vivādgrast*]" (Bhagvāndatt Caturvedī 1958:487). I came upon this when Chaubes began telling me about the Karua (*kaṛuā*—bitter, astringent) and the Mitha (*mīṭhā*—sweet), which are names summarizing contesting narratives of identity within the Mathur Chaturvedi community more than they are units or groups of social structure. Yet, the names and the narratives they imply are felt deeply and contested bitterly because their significance involves honor (*ijjat*). *Kaṛuā*, bitter, is a trope for bravery, courage, and truth, while *mīṭhā*, sweet, is a trope for cowardice, evasiveness, and duplicity.

During the centuries of various Muslim invasions and atrocities in Mathura there were different migrations of Chaubes to nearby villages, cities, and states.[11] Marriage relations were broken off and a number of different subcommunities of Chaturvedis were established, one of which is the Mitha. From the Mathura Chaubes' point of view, those who remained in the city are the true Karua because they tasted the bitter fruit of persecution and fought for the preservation of their religion and its holy relics. They talk as though *all* who left Mathura under threat of Muslim persecution are Mitha who fled like cowards, diluted their pure blood by intermarriage with other communities, and even took up polluting habits, such as smoking cigarettes. Most Mathura Chaubes date the Mithas' flight to the reign of Aurangzeb.

But ask many of those to whom the Mathura Chaubes give the name Mitha, and they reverse the name, saying that they are the Karua and the Mathura Chaubes are really the Mitha. Gopal Chaturvedi, an emigrant's descendant now resident in Mathura, told me:

> *We are the Karua because *karuā* means to speak straightforwardly with truth. In the time of Aurangzeb some of his soldiers came here and took some of our women during a marriage. Some Chaube men resisted them and killed those attacking them and abducting the women. After this, they were forced to flee Mathura. They did not want to become slaves of the Muslims and to be affected by their teachings. They settled in the villages of Madhya Pradesh and the Chambal valley.... Even today we celebrate the interruption of the wedding.

Thus, they are courageous because they did flee and thereby preserved their Hindu faith in its pristine purity without taint of Islamic association and religious doctrine, and especially without becoming slaves to Muslims. The thrust of the narrative is that by remaining in the city the Mathura Chaubes degraded the purity of their blood by association with Muslims, sullied the orthodoxy of their Hindu faith with Islamic influence, and dishonored themselves by becoming slaves to Muslims.

Mathura's Chaubes themselves will occasionally tell the narrative of the gravediggers in which only a few will dare to name as the protagonists Ali Datt and Kuli Datt, two Mathura Chaube ancestors. Mohan Chaube narrated the following version to me:[12]

> *Ali Datt and Kuli Datt were two famous Chaube wrestlers. One day Akbar [in almost all other versions it is Aurangzeb] came to Brindaban and he saw two fat [*mote*] Chaubes. He asked how they got so fat. They said, "Because we eat till our bellies are full

[*bharpet*]." He said, "I eat and am not as healthy as you two." So he said, "Come and show me," and he took both of them to his camp, but then he forgot about them. Birbal [friend of Akbar] was partial to the Chaubes, so he got them out of prison, but they were told to dig graves. They then proceeded to dig many, but made two very big ones. The emperor saw these and asked what they were doing. They said, "We are digging these two graves for you." The emperor then took fright because he thought he might die. So he dismissed Ali Datt and Kuli Datt immediately.

Most often the names of Ali Datt and Kuli Datt are not given in versions of this narrative, and mention of them is hard to come by. Mohan Chaube's narrative asserts not that some of those Chaubes who remained behind in Mathura were forced into slavery and grave-digging for the Muslims, but rather that the Chaubes cleverly outwitted even the emperor's attempt to enslave them. Yet, some Chaubes were and are known as *gulmatā,* who, according to Govind Chaube, were "*those who stayed in Mathura and converted to Islam—at least openly so, if not in their hearts." For that they were outcasted, although they have now been accepted back into the community. Moreover, some Chaubes now live in a place called Gol Para, said to have been a burial ground for Muslims.

The factual historicity of these events and persons is not at issue here. In Mohan Chaube's narrative, Ali Datt and Kuli Datt are clever, defiant heros standing for all their Karua descendants in present-day Mathura. Indeed, one narrative asserts that Ali Datt was a renowned and powerful wrestler during Emperor Akbar's reign, when that sport was more popular and more patronized than in the present (Jīvanlāl Caturvedī 1972:33). All such narratives are strategic assertions claiming an unblemished self-identity and heroic status. To some extent in the present, and I'm told in the past also, marriage relations occur between Mathura Chaubes and different Chaturvedi emigrant communities, but not with the real Mitha. Thus, the actual "group" is not at issue; the name Karua, and its constitutive narrative of self-identity, is. The identifying names disclose the significances, the moral evaluations, that the narratives are about, namely honor (*ijjat*) for the Karua and shame (*śaram*) for the Mitha.

Many Chaturvedis who emigrated from Mathura became prosperous village agriculturalists, and others became highly educated and well placed throughout northern India. Some of them are called *kulīn* (see

Y. K. Caturvedī 1968), a name that Mathura Chaubes often use for all emigrants, particularly those with western-style educations. *Kulīn* means "of noble ancestry, educated." That name is opposed to the name *paṇḍā*, identifying those in Mathura who work as pilgrimage priests. From the Mathura Chaubes' point of view, the Mitha Chaturvedis were and are *kulīn* also, and the words are often used interchangeably. Thus, some will stigmatize *kulīn* identity, saying that *kulīn* means "*kul hīn*," of low caste, without proper ancestry. From the point of view of those labeled *kulīn* and who claim to be true Karua, the *paṇḍā*s practice a demeaned and demeaning profession. Mukesh Chaturvedi, a *kulīn* whose community emigrated many years ago, said to me, "*We hate that profession [*peśā* — of *paṇḍā*]."

What is the *paṇḍā*'s profession and why do the *kulīn* hate it? The role of *paṇḍā* as ritual mediator between gods and humans is as ancient as Hinduism itself and is restricted to Brahmans by birth. *Paṇḍā*s perform required rituals at pilgrimage places, as do Mathura's Chaubes. *Paṇḍā*s appear daily at Vishram Ghat where they dun pilgrims for alms (*dān*) and badger them to use their ritual services. Others go to Mathura railroad station in search of old clients scheduled to arrive or new arrivals to whom they can offer ritual services.[13] Patrons most often have hereditary *paṇḍā*s with whose family their own family has been linked for generations. Records of patrons are kept in registers (*bahi*), and a proud *paṇḍā* is one who can show a young person of today an ancestor's signature or thumbprint in his register.

If, as Marx says, humanity makes itself through work as *homo faber* and if work and identity are intrinsically linked, then the Chaubes' daily praxis constitutes one of their identities in performing *paṇḍāgīrī* (*paṇḍā*'s work). It must also be remembered that the right to do this work is rooted deeply in religious tradition whereby it is inherited through their bloodline; purity of lineage is, therefore, crucial. But Brahmans who do that work, because they depend upon the goodwill and alms of others, have always suffered an ambiguous reputation, because dependence is demeaning. Indian folklore is filled with stories ridiculing greedy and pusillanimous Brahmans (Srinivas 1976:1), and *paṇḍā*s at pilgrimage places are reputed to be especially greedy.

Anand Chaube admitted to me, "*Hamārā kām bhīkh māṅgnā hai*" (our work is to beg). Another *paṇḍā* said as we were walking along on the 160-mile pilgrimage, "*Ham lenevālā hai, denevālā nahīṃ*"

(I'm a taker, not a giver). No clearer assertion of self-identity than that could be given; it sums up the significances, the moral identity, that Chaube *paṇḍā*s conceive themselves to have and a purpose (*dhyey*) for which they exist. As a taker, a *paṇḍā*'s entire livelihood and ancestral profession involves taking *dān* (religious donations), which *kulīn*s look down upon and *paṇḍā*s themselves fear because it carries with it inauspiciousness and even moral peril (see Parry 1989:66–77; Raheja 1988). According to Vishnu Chaube: "*By giving me *dān* one gets *prāyascitt* [expiation] but it gives me your sins [*pāp*]. If I have power [*śakti*], then I can digest it [*hajam kar saktā huṃ*], it won't harm me. If I don't have power, then my mind [*buddhi*] will be destroyed because I have done bad things." For that reason, whenever Chaubes intone for a pilgrim the *saṅkalp* (dedication) of an offering at a hallowed place, they end it with the incantation "*Śrī kṛṣṇa arpaṇ*" (an offering to Krishna), whereupon the offering is handed over to Krishna, who hopefully takes the responsibility for the money and its dangerous inauspiciousness, while the *paṇḍā* avoids the liability but keeps the money. Yet, one is never certain, for, as Vishnu Chaube also said, "Dàn lenā āsān hai, magar uskā hajam karnā kathin ... cīj ek magar uskā bhāv alag" (to take *dān* is easy, but to digest it is difficult ... it [the money] looks like money, but it's really different).

Thus, in following their religiously ordained, patrilineally inherited, and socially sanctioned occupation, Chaubes, as *paṇḍā*s, paradoxically produce and reproduce their somewhat demeaned but high-status Brahman self-identity while perilously risking their very moral destiny. The contesting narratives of *paṇḍā* and *kulīn* are about the significance of *dān* and go deeply into the very pith of the Chaube self, its moral value in society, and its ultimate destiny. Mahesh Chaturvedi, who identified himself as *kulīn*, succinctly summarized the essence of those conflicting narratives of identity when he said, "*None of us does *paṇḍāgīrī* [the work of *paṇḍā*] ... The main thing is that we do not take *dān*."

The situation of conflicting narrative identities is fraught with ambivalence for the *paṇḍā*s today. Not only have some emigrant *kulīn* returned to Mathura where they operate shops and engage in other professions — thus, no longer keeping at bay, outside the city, an other self of the Mathura Chaubes — but also a goodly number of their own sons are increasingly turning to secular education and professions, particularly commerce and accounting. Thus, those sons bring the contesting identity *kulīn* right into their own homes and bloodlines. *Paṇḍā* self-identity is in danger of becoming *kulīn* other-identity.

The contrast between the two identities is vividly symbolized in the spatial separation of a father praying alongside other *paṇḍā*s at Vishram Ghat and a son bargaining alongside other merchants in a Chhata Bazaar store. It is also symbolized in the *Kaṃs Melā* procession, wherein old *paṇḍā* families sponsor Krishna and Balram on the elephant, while the Chaturvedi Students Association and the Bombay Chaturvedi Progressive Association sponsor two of the colorfully decorated floats introduced in recent years. Many of those who have a modern education, some with Ph.D. and chartered accountancy degrees, are themselves migrants to Bombay, Delhi, Ahmedabad, and other cities of India. Marriages between members of new and old *kulīn* families create for Mathura's Chaubes further confusion, tension, and ambivalence about their identities.

In the past, patrons, particularly those of the Pushti Marg sect, for whom it was meritorious to give to Brahmans and to keep them well fed, took generous care of their Chaube *paṇḍā*s. They gave Chaubes alms of gold, endowed them with religious guest houses (*dharmśālā*s), and even gifted them with dowries to marry off their daughters. In return Chaubes provided patrons with ritual services, religious advice, visits during the year, and, in the case of Pushti Marg devotees, forty days of guidance and assistance over unknown forest, field, and fen during the 160-mile annual pilgrimage (*Braj Caurāsī Kos Parikramā*).

In the present, however, the occupation is not as rewarding as it is reputed to have been in the past. Instead of visiting for a few days and staying at their *paṇḍā*s' own homes, some pilgrims stay at a hotel or guest house or leave by car within a day or so. Pious, generous pilgrims seem fewer and less generous, and the traditional cords tying priest to patron are wearing thin. Sukdev Chaube, an educated young man who frequented the religious guest house where I lived said, "*In my grandfather's time things were different. People came for a pilgrimage, now they come just to tour around [*ghūmne ke liye*]." It is no wonder, then, that educated young Chaube men tend to evaluate the significance of *paṇḍā* identity as would a *kulīn*. Sukdev Chaube again said to me, "*I don't like this work of begging. Even now if there is a family register [*bahi*], on a man's death it is divided among sons and so on over the generations, until almost no patrons are left. Who can live from that?" Another, Narendra Chaube, once confidentially told me, "*In the Arthashastra does it say there is any place for *sādhu*s [holy men who live off the alms of others]? They can get food by begging, but there is need for more things than that, such as food and medicine. If you have money, then you will always have food."

Contested Identities

The Chaubes' contesting narratives of self-identity are matched by other narratives, some quite vicious, of contested self-identities told by non-Chaube enemies and detractors who go so far as to say that the Chaubes are really Muslims masquerading as Brahmans. Most significant among Chaubes' detractors are the Sanadhya Brahmans, who themselves are the most numerous *paṇḍā*s controlling many of the sacred places throughout the Braj area except for Mathura City (Entwistle 1987:6).

Concerning Mathura's Chaubes, a Yadav told me, "*They were Lodhi Muslims. They were pushed out of their kingdom and came to Mathura. Their children began to show pilgrims around and slowly they took over that profession and became Hindus." A non-Chaube Brahmani (female Brahman) spit out, "*The Chaubes are not real Brahmans. They came here with Akbar and were gravediggers. They were known as *pāī māngnā* [beggars for *pāī*, an old copper coin of which there were about four in a *paisā*, an Indian penny]. We don't have marriage relations with them." Finally, another non-Chaube Brahman narrated to me the following, which in different versions others repeated:

*The Chaubes are not real Brahmans. They came here from a city in Afghanistan called Chauba. Up until about 100 years ago they still had marriage relations with people there. They came from Afghanistan.... Babur brought them here to India, where they were slaves of Muslims. Even today there is a group among them known as *gulmate* [plural of *gulmatā*], which is the same as *gulāmte* [*gulām*, slave]. There is a part of Chaubiya Para known as Taj Pura, which at first only Muslims occupied. They were the gravediggers for Muslims.... During Akbar's time they moved to Chaubiya Para....

Before this time, all was in control of other Brahmans. About 150 years ago there was a war over Vishram Ghat. The other

> Brahmans surrendered, and the Chaubes took over.... After the
> battle for Vishram Ghat, Sanadhya Brahmans sold their *bahi*s
> [register of pilgrims] to the Chaubes.

This narrative takes up the theme of Chaubes and the Muslims and
strategically asserts not only that some of them were slaves and
gravediggers for the Muslims, but worse, that they *were* Muslims. That
assertion implies that because one is a Brahman only by birth, then
Chaubes still *are* Muslim by birth. It implicates, therefore, all Chaubes,
not merely the *gulmatā*, and strikes at the very heart of Chaube scriptural identities: Hindu, Mathur Brahman, *paṇḍā*, companion of Krishna, and slayer of Kans. If they are not Brahmans connected by birth to
ancestral autochthons in Mathura, then the rituals they perform as
*paṇḍā*s for pilgrims lack efficacy and are a travesty. Such narratives
contest the vital, constitutive significance of Chaube narratives of
identity framed in scriptural discourse. As well, they seek to invali-
date Chaubes' claims to alms gathered at Vishram Ghat and elsewhere for performance of pilgrimage services.

Worth noting here, however, is that scriptural discourse, especially
in modern times, has great capacity for meeting new and unexpected
situations, although that is of little comfort to the Chaubes. Brooks
(1989:106–41) has shown that in the pilgrimage town of Brindaban,
six miles from Mathura, American Hare Krishnas have been accepted
as real Brahmans. One reason pilgrims gave was that "if the deities
accepted the foreigners, then so should they [the pilgrims]" (Brooks
1989).

The narrative disclosure of Chaube origin in Afghanistan attempts
to undermine every one of the narratives of self-identity dependent
upon Chaubes' autochthonous origin in Mathura, the place of ultimate disclosure for their identities. Yet, Mathura Chaubes themselves,
as well as some *kulīn*, hint at relationships with Afghanistan up until
the recent past that only muddle the issue. Mohan Chaube told me
one such narrative:

> *In Moghul times two boys were forcefully taken away to Afghan-
> istan. One died. The other was very beautiful, and he fell into
> the favor of a woman there. She arranged to send him back and
> gave him two camels for his journey. He finally arrived back here,
> but no one would accept him as a Chaube. He had been out-
> casted. Finally [a] ... headman [*sardār*] said that he would ac-

cept him back and, after expiation [*prāyascitt*] ..., publicly accepted him back into his family.

Moreover, the narrative of Chaubes as Muslims from Afghanistan is not unmotivated and tastes of sour grapes. The Sanadhya Brahmans in the past controlled more pilgrimage stations and temples in Mathura City than they do today. Chaubes, such as Binod Chaube, tell a counternarrative of Chaube identity and of rights flowing from it:

> *When the Muslims came to Mathura, the Chaubes retreated to Tila Chaubiyana near Amresh Tila. They would come to Vishram Ghat only in the morning and evening. Thus, the Sanadhyas took over the Ghat for the rest of the time and began to monopolize it. This place where I live was inhabited by Muslims and was a burial ground [*kabristān*]. The Sanadhyas live in Mandi Ram Das. When Muslim pressure died out in British times, quarrels began to arise between Sanadhyas and Chaubes about the Ghats and money given there. At that time all contributions were put in a common pot, and one-third went to the Sanadhyas and two-thirds went to the Chaubes. The Sanadhyas wanted more, and we wanted to cast them out. A court case arose that went all the way to Allahabad [location of the High Court], and the Chaubes won because they had papers and *pharmān*s as proof.

Another narrative relates that the court's decision mentioned one of those *pharmān*s as the very one given by Akbar to Ujagar Chaube (Caube 1967). That case is part of the continuous record Chaubes have established for their own strategic assertions of identity, their use of legal discourse to do so, and their capturing the past as a scarce resource in constructing their identities.

In winning their case and the bitter enmity of the Sanadhyas, the Chaubes not only gained complete control of Vishram Ghat, but also strengthened their claim to be pilgrimage priests as given by their control over Vishram Ghat, with all its religiously constituted associations and their place in them.

In introducing this section, "Contested Identities," I explicitly inserted myself into my own narrative about the Chaubes when I said that some of their detractors' narratives are "quite vicious." In so doing, I revealed my own opiniated sentiments. Here I will deepen them by inserting an argument that Chaubes never explicitly made to me, but that is, I think, implicit in what they told me. Once again, actual historical events are not at issue; interpretation for strategic deployment in the present is. Some detractors of Chaubes say that Chaubes are not real Brahmans because they were not included in the categories of the Five Northern and Five Southern Brahman castes recognized by the great Hindu philosopher Shankaracharya (A.D. 728?–820). According to Guru Sharma, "*Shankaracharya did not recognize them [Chaubes] as Brahmans because of mixed blood. He specifically excluded Brahmans of Mathura and Magadh from the Five Northern Brahmans [*pañch gaur*]." That, however, contradicts the argument that the Chaubes came into India with the Muslims. It unwittingly asserts Chaubes' presence in Mathura long before the Muslim arrival and posits their Brahmanical status. In any case, Chaubes themselves retort that they were excluded only because they did not have to do penance for being tainted by Buddhist influence; they had always remained pure and orthodox, while other Brahman castes had not.[14] V. K. Caturvedī put it well: "Two hundred preachers of the Buddhist Dharma lived here but no Mathur Brahman converted to that religion and none were caught up by political enticements. That is proven by Shankaracharya's not requiring the Brahmans of this place to do penance" (V. K. Caturvedī n.d.:14).

Conclusion

1. There is more than rings in the ear to the assertion that Chaubes originated in Afghanistan or elsewhere outside of Mathura. Space is never neutral; it is always defined culturally as place. India itself is more than a politically defined, geographically bounded nation-state; it is also a sacred place cosmologically constituted in Hindu belief. Almost all Mathur Chaturvedi Brahmans, resident in Mathura or not, agree that they are the Mathur Brahmans whose ultimate origin or place of disclosure is in Mathura. In that, they are like most other Indians who trace themselves back to some ancestral village or place, because ancestral place is a metaphor for self-identity, if not a metonym for it (see Daniel 1984). Thus, when Chaubes assert their autochthonous origin in Mathura, they simultaneously posit their self-identity not as man-made, but as cosmologically given; they and Mathura are one. Mathura, as the place of fullest and most salient public disclosure of Chaube self-identity, grounds that identity in a primeval place of ontological significance. As a counterplace of disclosure, the narrative of Afghanistan seeks to totally deny to Chaubes their identity,

with all its constitutive importance for the significances of their social worth. The same can be said for the narratives of Karua, who remain resident in Mathura, and Mitha, who now have an alternative place of disclosure outside of Mathura, as well as for the narratives of the *paṇḍās* who locate themselves at Vishram Ghat and the *kulīns* who locate themselves in the stores of Chhata Bazaar and Bombay.

Self, then, is culturally disclosed not by an interior place of conscious self-awareness, but by an external place of revelation. "What is relevant is not the capacity to have some inner sense of the human significances—this is a typically 'internalist' way of understanding it—but rather access to some force or to some region which lies outside of us" (Taylor 1985b:279). As self-defining agents, Chaubes narratively constitute both that place and its temporal location not through biological constants of development or so-called material forces, but rather through their involvement in the conversation or argument given through language.

2. My own narrative tends to conceal in its chronological ordering that Chaube self-identities are many, not one. Each narrative was told to me at different times, in different places, and by different Chaubes. Each was about a different identity in the *present,* for which the past was a politically strategic resource. For example, the *Kaṃs Melā* asserts: I am a descendant of Kans's slayers, a warrior and a force to be reckoned with in Mathura, if not elsewhere. The food-for-Krishna narrative asserts: I am a *mast* Chaube who can even refuse Krishna while doing sacrifice, therefore, I am to be respected as a Brahman. The narrative of Ujagar and Vallabhacharya asserts: I am a descendant of Ujagar's people and therefore am one of those who alone act as pilgrimage priests for the Pushti Marg sect. And the narrative of the Karua Chaubes asserts: I am a defender of my Hindu religion and a speaker of the bitter truth.

Narratives of self-identity, then, concern two things of fundamental importance to the social order: identity and interests. In terms of identity they are concerned *about* significances, those strong evaluations that constitute the self's qualitative worth vis-à-vis others and ontologically locate it through language in some place of disclosure. That location is made culturally intelligible and salient through deployment of scriptural, legal, and performative discourses, which as forms of knowledge are implicated in power. In terms of interests, narratives are concerned *with* strategic assertions and claims. For the

Mathura Chaubes, those interests involve claims to political dominance over others in Mathura and control over the *Kaṃs Vadh kā
Melā,* claims of economic control over Vishram Ghat and the *Braj
Caurāsī Kos Parikramā* (the 160-mile pilgrimage), and claims to social honor greater than that due to the Mitha or Kulin Chaturvedis
or to the Sanadhyas.

3. From a narrative point of view Karua, Mitha, *paṇḍā, kulīn,* and
gulmatā are not subgroups of some larger group or caste; rather they
are conceptually and strategically deployed names, not merely categories, asserting self-identities.[15] The "authentic" Chaube narrative
self of scriptural discourse is not coherent, essential, and univocal.
Rather, it is contingent, semiotically constituted, and equivocal; it is
historically and situationally refracted into the multiple, contesting
narratives of Karua and Mitha, *paṇḍā* and *kulīn.* As well, it is contested in the narratives of Chaubes as Muslims that are told by their
enemies and detractors, just as it is reactively reproduced in Chaubes'
own counternarratives of heroes outwitting Muslim emperors and
fearless warriors commandeering rights over Vishram Ghat. Authentic caste self-identity and status, then, have always been in flux, multiple, and changing in ways other than that of Sanskritization (Srinivas
1966), which importantly revealed change of *varṇa* categorization even
as it concealed stasis of a bounded, essentialized caste group (*jāti*).

From such a perspective, a caste, like the eighteenth-century Rajput
state (Peabody 1991), is not a rigid, bounded, essentialist group, but
rather a fluctuating, fluid (Marriott 1990; Shah 1988a, 1988b), un-
bounded collectivity of agents who deploy narratives of self-identities
to deal with historical and situational contingencies. Today's *paṇḍās*
are tomorrow's *kulīn,* and sometimes one is both. Orthodox Hindu
and hegemonic academic theories conceal those fluctuating, contingent, and open boundaries, as well as the multiple self-identities constituted through language. A narrative, processual, and nonessentialist
perspective, then, offers a revealing understanding of caste in India different from that of a totalizing, essentialist perspective.

4. Detractors' narratives assert that Chaubes were Muslim. Yet, pilgrims today do not concern themselves with such narratives and defer instead to praxis, as in the case of the American Hare Krishnas in
India who claim Brahmanical status (Brooks 1989). Those who achieve
public recognition for their occupation are who they claim to be. Important, too, is that it is conceivable among some Hindus that Chaubes

were at one time Muslims but today are Brahmans.[16] Chaubes' detractors implicitly reveal such ironic possibilities whenever they tell
their narratives. The line, therefore, between the dynamic semiotics
of Hindu mythological thought, in which beings transform and trans-
migrate from one state into another, and a narrative semiotics of the
dynamics of the social organization of castes is and was porous.[17] It
is so in a way that remains merely the presence of an absence, a trace,
in an essentialized and totalized theory. Even the concept of Sanskritization (Srinivas 1966) did not suggest the possibility of non-Brah-
mans, let alone Muslims, moving into the Brahman category (*varṇa*).

5. Like sticks and stones, names in some cultures can hurt because
they matter—they have moral value. Names—Karua, Mitha, *paṇḍā*,
kulīn—are important as summaries of the narrative self-identities that
imply significances, strong evaluations constitutive of the self. Self-
identities cannot, then, be reduced to material or political factors without depriving them of what is most humanly significant about them.
Because self is constituted in and through public narratives, it is never
totally known as a unique coherent thing; it can only be known and
experienced by focusing on contingent identities through a space of
disclosure in language. Thus, change in caste or other identities is neither changing an essential self nor putting on or off identities masking
a more basic self.

Notes

This essay is the result of fieldwork carried out in Mathura from September to December 1980, from August 1981 to August 1982, and from mid-June to mid-August
1985. The research from 1980 to 1982 was generously supported by a Senior Faculty
Research Grant from the American Institute of Indian Studies. The essay has greatly
profited from comments by Vijay Mishra, Sudhir Kakar, Mattison Mines, William
Kelly, and other participants in the August 1991 Conference on Self and Social Order
held at the Institute for Culture and Communication in Honolulu, Hawaii. My thanks
to Wimal Dissanayake for inviting me to the conference and encouraging me to investigate this topic. I am grateful to Doranne Jacobson for her fine-grained reading and
incisive comments; to Joan Lehn for her edits and penetrating questions; to Arvind
Shah, Jack Hawley, and Alan Entwistle for sending me to sources I might otherwise
have missed and for sharing with me their deep knowledge of Braj culture; to Diana
Wells for her suggested improvements and comments; to Constance Sutton for her encouragement; and to Enid Lang for opening the way for me.

1. This figure is based upon a register book for a distribution of food (called *dainī*)
which is given to all male Chaubes in Chaubiya Para. The distribution was done in
1978 in celebration of a young man's sacred thread ceremony. The register lists 1,165
families with 5,574 male members. I have simply doubled that figure for a total of

approximately 11,300. My reason for doubling the figure is that in the state of Uttar Pradesh the sex ratio is biased in favor of males. Chaubes say that in their community today females outnumber males, although in the past it was the opposite. Because I believe there is some truth to their assertion about the present, I have split the difference and evened the sex ratio.

My figure is remarkably similar to that of Bhagvāndatt Caturvedī (1958:487) who says, "The population of the Karuas today is ten or eleven thousand and of these only about six hundred live in different places in the country, while the rest live in Mathura City. The population of the Mitha Chaubes is many times that of the Karuas. The vast majority of Mathura's Chaubes live by alms for Brahmans."

2. A fourth reason for the theory's importance is its presentation of a strong argument for a nonreductionist understanding of human significances, whether they be vital, in terms of survival, or sentient, in terms of physiological processes. Such motives are in themselves not significant. They become so only by contextualization in terms of human significances, such that being a martyr to a cause can be judged either heroism or contemptible self-promotion. Thus, finding motivation in terms of so-called material economic gain, or drive to power, cannot really be explained without contextualization in culturally defined human significances. In this chapter I am particularly concerned with human significances and their relationship to self-identity.

3. "The subject of radical choice is another avatar of that recurrent figure which our civilization aspires to realize, the disembodied ego, the subject who can objectify all being, including his own, and choose in radical freedom" (Taylor 1985a:35).

4. One line of the inscription ends with the syllable *ma*; the next line begins with the word *ṇacchondoga*. But, according to Lüders (1961:126), "The meaning of *māṇacchandoga* has not yet been ascertained," and in footnote 4 of the same page he says, "There seems to have been no more writing after *mā*." Chaubes are not so uncertain about the inscription's meaning and about a missing syllable after *mā*: they believe the word was Mathur. About this disagreement I heard nothing while in Mathura and, therefore, I have not discussed it as contested. I am very grateful to Alan Entwistle for directing me to Lüders's work and to its possible implications for the Chaubes.

5. Growse (1979:129) translates this line from the Varah Purana as "No god like Kesava, and no Brahman like a Mathuriya Chaube."

6. Narratives beginning with an asterisk are from my notes and are my transcriptions of what I heard or remembered hearing on a particular day. Otherwise the narratives are verbatim.

7. The mustache is a sign of virility, courage, and honor. The mustache standing for the whole severed head is the defeated Kans castrated of his honor even in his death.

8. Alter's (1992) book on the discourses and practices of the gymnasium (*akhāṛā*) and the body is an excellent example of how Indian wrestlers constitute their self-identity through the metonymically related places of disclosure: the wrestling floor and the body. The somatic self-identity of the wrestler has much to do with ethical and moral beliefs, or significances, in the world of *saṃsāra*.

9. Information about Ujagar and especially his cousin Udhav, including their birth and death dates, is given by Bāl Mukund Caturvedī (n.d.).

10. I have given the name Ujagar in brackets because I recorded Ujagar's name as that of his nephew, Udhav, with whom he is very closely associated and often paired. This was perhaps an error of memory during my first days of fieldwork with the Chaubes. The narrative itself was confirmed in other versions.

11. See note 1 for the number of Chaubes said to be living outside of Mathura in 1958. That number is probably much greater today. See also Mītal (1966:75) for a cultural historian's description of the impact of these events on the Chaubes.

12. For another version see Lynch (1990a:97).

13. See Lynch (1990a) for the way in which Mathura's Chaubes categorize those seeking patrons in these two ways.

14. In 1980–81 Chaubes mentioned the need to regain the site of Krishna's birth, which is supposed to be underneath a mosque now at that site. When I visited them in 1987, this topic was more in the air, and I had the impression that the Chaubes saw themselves at the forefront of this movement, part of the long-term strategy of the Hindu nationalist movement propagated by the Vishva Hindu Parishad and the Bharatiya Janata Party. That movement in 1993 brought about the destruction of the Babri Masjid in Ayodhya and its violent aftermath. Chaube self-identification is anything but Muslim.

15. Although not taking a narrative perspective, Shah (1988a, 1988b) has insightfully and with a wealth of rich data written about the multiple levels of identity in castes.

16. From an essentialist perspective one is a Hindu by birth in, and ancestry from, a particular caste. Yet even within Hinduism there are competing perspectives on this question. In Arya Samaji teaching one is a Brahman by action, not by birth. A group of South Indian untouchables who recently converted to Islam has now converted back into Hinduism. If that is possible, then most Indian Muslims who are descendants of Hindus could technically return to Hinduism and their former caste. There are untouchable and upper-caste versions on whether Ravi Das was really a Brahman because of a previous birth or really an untouchable (Khare 1984:40–50).

17. The space of disclosure, as public and social, may paradoxically make change easier than when it is that of the interiorized, coherent, and unified self. An externalized space of disclosure in a scripturally authenticated place opens up to Chaubes all the possibilities of India's vast corpus of myth that can be used to devise solutions for present-day problems (Kakar 1989), while the self of the interiorized place of disclosure is left to work it out from personal resources.

References

Alter, Joseph. 1992. *The Wrestler's Body: Identity and Ideology in North India.* Berkeley: University of California Press.

Appadurai, Arjun. 1981. "The Past as a Scarce Resource." *Man.* n.s., 16:201–19.

Barnett, Steve. 1973. "Urban Is as Urban Does: Two Incidents on One Street in Madras City, South India." *Urban Anthropology* 2(2):129–60.

Barthes, Roland. 1972. *Mythologies.* New York: Noonday Press.

Berreman, Gerald D. 1972. "Social Categories and Social Interaction in Urban India." *American Anthropologist* 74:567–86.

Brooks, Charles. 1989. *The Hare Krishnas in India.* Princeton, N.J.: Princeton University Press.

Carrithers, Michael. 1985. "An Alternative Social History of the Self." In *The Category of the Person,* edited by Michael Carrithers, Steven Collins, and Steven Lukes, pp. 234–56. Cambridge: Cambridge University Press.

Caturvedī, Bāl Mukund. N.d. "Brajbhāsa ke Śaiśav-yug ke Mahāmanoso Śrīuddhav Jī Ujāgar Jī." In *Brij Bhāratī,* edited by Rādheśyām Jośī, pp. 27–34. Mathura: n.p.

———. 1986. *Māthur Caturvedī Brāhmaṇoṃ kā Itihās.* Mathura: Palival Press.

Caturvedī, Bhagvāndatt. 1958. "Mathurā ke Caube." In *Braj kā Itihās,* edited by Śrī Kṛṣṇadatt Vājpeyī, pp. 487–89. Mathura: Akhil Bhāratiya Braj Sāhitya Maṇḍal.

Caturvedī, Jīvanlāl. 1972. *Braj ke Pramukh Mall. Mathurā Patrikā (Brajāṅk).* Mathura: Campa Agraval Inter College.

Caturvedī, Raghunāth Prasād. 1981. "Ek Niścit Satya." *Māthur Pradīp* 2(7–8):6–16.

Caturvedī, Vāsudev Kṛṣṇa. N.d. *Mathurā evam Māthur Caturvedī Saṅkṣipt Paricāy.* Mathura: Śrī Māthur Caturvedī Sabhā.

Caturvedī, Yugal Kiśor. 1968. *Māthur Caturvedī Brāhmaṇ Paricāy.* Jaipur: Agraval Printing Press.

Caube, Vijay Cand Bare. 1967. "Māthur Kul Divākar, Dharm Mūrti, Vednidhi Tapasvī Śrī Ujāgar-jī Māthur Caturved." *Māthur Pradīp* 2(1–2):5–6.

Daniel, E. Valentine. 1984. *Fluid Signs: Being a Person in the Tamil Way.* Berkeley: University of California Press.

Derrida, Jacques. 1973. "Différance." In *Speech and Phenomena and Other Essays on Husserl's Theory of Signs,* translated by David B. Allison, pp. 129–60. Evanston, Ill.: Northwestern University Press.

———. 1976. *Of Grammatology.* Translated by Gayatri Chakravorty Spivak. Baltimore, Md.: Johns Hopkins University Press.

Duncan, James S. 1990. *The City as Text: The Politics of Landscape Interpretation in the Kandyan Kingdom.* Cambridge: Cambridge University Press.

Entwistle, A. W. 1987. *Braj Centre of Krishna Pilgrimage.* Groningen: Egbert Forsten.

Foucault, Michel. 1972. *The Archaeology of Knowledge and the Discourse on Language.* New York: Pantheon.

Growse, F. S. 1979. [1882]. *Mathurā: A District Memoir.* New Delhi: Asian Educational Services.

Hardgrave, Robert L. 1969. *The Nadars of Tamilnad: The Political Culture of a Community in Change.* Berkeley: University of California Press.

Harirāyjī, Gosvāmī. 1905. *Śrī Govarddhannāthjī ke Prākatya kī Vārtā.* Edited by Paṇḍit Mohanlāl Viṣṇulāl Paṇḍya. Bombay: Śrī Veṅkateśvar Yantralāya.

Kakar, Sudhir. 1989. *Intimate Relations: Exploring Indian Sexuality.* Chicago: University of Chicago Press.

Khare, R. S. 1984. *The Untouchable as Himself.* Cambridge: Cambridge University Press.

Kondo, Dorinne. 1990. *Crafting Selves.* Chicago: University of Chicago Press.

Lüders, Heinrich. 1961. *Mathurā Inscriptions: Unpublished Papers.* Edited by Klaus L. Janert. Gottingen: Vandenhoeck and Ruprecht.

Lynch, Owen M. 1969. *The Politics of Untouchability: Social Mobility and Social Change in a City of India.* New York: Columbia University Press.

———. 1988. "Pilgrimage with Krishna, Sovereign of the Emotions." *Contributions to Indian Sociology* 22(2):171–95.

———. 1990a. "The Mastram: Emotion and Person among Mathura's Chaubes." In *Divine Passions: The Social Construction of Emotion in India,* edited by Owen M. Lynch, pp. 91–115. Berkeley: University of California Press.

———. 1990b. "The Social Construction of Emotion in India." In *Divine Passions: The Social Construction of Emotion in India,* edited by Owen M. Lynch, pp. 3–34. Berkeley: University of California Press.

Malinowski, Bronislaw. 1948. *Magic, Science, and Religion and Other Essays.* Garden City, N.Y.: Doubleday.

Marriott, McKim. 1990. "Constructing an Indian Sociology." In *India through Hindu Categories,* edited by McKim Marriott, pp. 1–40. New Delhi: Sage.

Māthur Maṇḍlī. 1969 [1901]. *Kārravāī Māthur Caturvedī Maṇḍlī Mathurā.* Mathura: Māthur Maṇḍlī.

Mauss, Marcel. 1985. "A Category of the Human Mind: The Notion of Person, the Notion of Self." Translated by W. D. Halls. In *The Category of the Person,* edited by Michael Carrithers, Steven Collins, and Steven Lukes, pp. 1–25. Cambridge: Cambridge University Press.

Mead, George Herbert. 1934. *Mind, Self, and Society.* Chicago: University of Chicago Press.

Mītal, Prabhudayāl. 1966. *Braj kā Saṃskṛtik Itihās.* Delhi: Rājkamal Prakāśan.

Parry, Jonathan. 1989. "On the Moral Perils of Exchange." In *Money and the Morality of Exchange,* edited by Jonathan Parry and Maurice Bloch, pp. 64–93. Cambridge: Cambridge University Press.

Peabody, Norbert. 1991. "*Kotā Mahājagat,* or the Great Universe of Kota: Sovereignty and Territory in Eighteenth Century Rajasthan." *Contributions to Indian Sociology,* n.s., 25(1):28–56.

Raheja, Gloria. 1988. *The Poison in the Gift.* Chicago: University of Chicago Press.

Rao, M. S. A. 1979. *Social Movements and Social Transformation.* Delhi: Macmillan.

Shah, A. M. 1988a. "Division and Hierarchy: An Overview of Caste in Gujarat." In *Division and Hierarchy: An Overview of Caste in Gujarat,* edited by A. M. Shah and I. P. Desai, pp. 1–39. Delhi: Hindustan.

———. 1988b. "A Response to the Critique on 'Division and Hierarchy.'" In *Division and Hierarchy: An Overview of Caste in Gujarat,* edited by A. M. Shah and I. P. Desai, pp. 92–133. Delhi: Hindustan.

Srinivas, M. N. 1966. *Social Change in Modern India.* Berkeley: University of California Press.

———. 1976. *The Remembered Village.* Berkeley: University of California Press.

Taylor, Charles. 1985a. *Human Agency and Language: Philosophical Papers I.* Cambridge: Cambridge: Cambridge University Press.

———. 1985b. "The Person." In *The Category of the Person,* edited by Michael Carrithers, Steven Collins, and Steven Lukes, pp. 257–81. Cambridge: Cambridge University Press.

5 / Self-Made

Richard G. Fox

Clifford Geertz (1983:59) tells us that "the Western conception of the person as bounded, unique, more or less integrated motivational and cognitive universe ... organized into a distinctive whole and set contrastively both against other such wholes and against its social and natural background is ... a rather peculiar idea." Geertz is hardly alone in recognizing this supposedly singular Western conception. For example, the psychiatrist Alan Roland (1988), under heavy influence from South Asian anthropologists, contrasts the "prevailing psychological maps and norms" of "Western man" (we must assume he also means to include Western woman)—the Western universalizing mode of thinking, as he labels it—with an Indian contextualizing mode (Roland 1988:xvii). Another distinguished anthropologist, Louis Dumont, calculates that modern Western individualism "took at least seventeen centuries of Christian history to be completed" (Dumont 1985:94).

For Geertz, Roland, and Dumont, the Western conception of the person is singular because it is culturally distinctive, perhaps even somewhat odd (especially if it took all of seventeen centuries to develop). They assume, implicitly however, another singularity—that there is *a* Western conception of the person, that there is a unique, weighty, and encompassing tradition of Western self-identity, either timeless or time-lost.

When cultures begin to cheat on their ostensible traditions, anthropologists are often the last to know, even scholars as astute as Geertz and Dumont. Americans (and the French, too?) in everyday life have increasingly begun to fool around with "our" singular conception of the person. Increasingly, that is, American cultural practice allows for radical or revolutionary transformations in the individual self, as if there can be several selves, not just one. Perhaps in keeping with American serial polygamy, these several selves are also commonly serial. Some Americans are born again. Others find new selves in Oriental mysteries or Occidental therapies. Likely as not, they will say, "I came out a different person." Drugs, too, we say, can wipe "you" out as they turn you on. Our very concept of the human person seems under reconsideration: in hospital beds, for example, where we see individual selves undergo revolutionary transformation into vegetables — and where the dignity of the former self, some Americans have come to believe, can only be guaranteed by allowing the vegetable to die.

What are we to make of these anomalies? Geertz's bounded and more or less integrated person seems to shatter into several serial selves. Will seventeen centuries of Christian endeavor at building this-worldly individualism now self-destruct into nonworldly "multividualism"?

I put these anomalies to you as suggestive anecdotes, not conclusive proofs. They suggest that our scholarly analysis of personhoods, in this culture and any other, may need to be reformed, that we ought to rethink the very notion of the person or self we employ, whether as a reflex of Western tradition or not. This suggestion I will not pursue in this paper (but have done so elsewhere: see Fox 1988, 1989 on "revolutionary selfhoods"). The anomalies also suggest that perhaps no single or singular conception of the person need exist in American culture or any other and that our descriptions of such conceptions have to be more contingent and historical. This suggestion is the focus of my chapter.

I understand "self" to mean "self-identity" and, even more specifically, consciousness, which is, obviously, only one understanding of this concept. Marcel Mauss (1985 [1938]:3), in a pioneering essay, sharply distinguished his study of (cross)cultural conceptions of the self (the social self) from research on the psychological sense of self (the inner self). Mauss, however, did not heed his own distinction, and in his essay, he presents the modern sense of self as almost entirely an artifact of a particular cultural conception of self (see Carrithers 1985: 235–36). The relationship between a cultural conception of personhood or selfhood and an individual's perception of self is much more problematic than Mauss allowed. Nevertheless, in this essay, I emphasize, as Mauss did, the compelling force of cultural conceptions of self over individual self-identity and self-perceptions: the "predicament of personhood," in Steven Collins's apt phrase, is that it can only be completed in a particular cultural setting (Collins 1985:74).

I wish to argue that our accounts of cultural conceptions of the self must begin to be more open-ended, contingent, and disintegrated. They must allow for rapid changes in self-identity and consciousness. Mauss and Durkheim did recognize a slow evolution in a culture's conception of self (and so, too, does Dumont), but that does not go far or fast enough.

One new beginning might be the question Mariko Fujita (1991: 21) asks: how do notions of selves change over the course of the life cycle? Mattison Mines answers that question for India when he suggests that over the course of the life cycle Indians increasingly take responsibility for their actions (Mines 1988:568). Another is the question Wimal Dissanayake poses about the Indian writer Raja Rao: how does an individual author a self-identity using the language of the colonial masters? These questions disintegrate individual self-identity from cultural conceptions of self and give them a contingent relationship. Whereas most South Asian scholars argue that individual identity is fused with the social group (family, caste, and community), Mines (1988) and others remind us that this fusion is neither as unproblematic nor as complete as Dumont, Marriott-Inden, and other Indianists assume — in other words, that even if the Indian cultural conception of the person is based on the effacement of individuality, it is not wholly constitutive of all self-identities.

I want to pursue a related disintegration by trying to problematize the very cultural conception of self said to be Indian or Hindu (too often treated as equivalent in this literature).

The first step in this disintegration is to become wary of the idea that it is normal or expectable for a culture to have a singular conception of the self. If there is or ever was a singular conception of self in South Asia, then that condition needs explanation; we have only taken it for granted because we work with a unitary, integrated, erector-set conception of culture. Should we adopt a multiple, disintegrated, and plastic conception, then we might better see how a singular conception of self develops in a culture (if it ever does). The second step (logically following from the first) is to look for the historical and social processes by which cultural conceptions of self come to constitute inner senses of self rather than assuming that they automatically and completely do. We need to expand the argument beyond whether India has individualism or not to encompass a wider range of inner self-identities — sexual and somatic, family and political identities — and better link them to cultural conceptions and social identities located in specific times, places, and contexts of power. Otherwise we run the risk of replacing a corporatist essentialism of the Indian Self with an individualist essentialism.[1]

To this end, we might ask these questions: how do historical contingencies (I do not mean the evolutionary stages of Durkheim, but real historical events) disorder cultural conceptions of self? How do cultural conceptions of self and self-identities arise — get invented — out of struggles for power in society? How do conceptions of self unravel and then perhaps get tied together again, but in new ways, as people labor "with minds and hands" to meet the conditions of their everyday existence? Finally, how can we historicize conceptions of self — that is, can we find the history of their production? I take the last question up initially in this essay and then move on to engage the others, although much too briefly.

My premises are as follows: (1) The conception of the conception of the Indian self as fused with social groups, as nonindividualistic, and as the very opposite of the West is constructed in the colonial situation, in the imperial embrace between British masters and Indian subjects. (2) Later, this conception of the conception of the Indian self passes for a sociological theory, under the aegis of Louis Dumont. Finally, the conception of the conception begins to be a lived condition, when Hindu nationalists present it as a constituting national ideology and live it out in everyday life (which also sometimes brings everyday death to those who do not agree).

Before proceeding, let me make very clear exactly what sort of contingency, open-endedness, and disintegration I am calling for. After all, open-endedness and contingency have been the vogue in recent anthropological writing, commonly labeled "postmodern" or "reflexive."

Reflexive anthropology has been good at uncovering the literary conventions — what reflexivists sometimes call the tropes — used by anthropologists to authorize their fieldwork. Reflexive anthropology has not been equally good at showing its own tropes. In keeping with the much larger world of modern "regret," reflexivists commonly employ two tropes: the End of Ideology and the God That Failed. The trope of the end of ideology becomes for reflexivists the desuetude of Grand Theory. The trope of the Failed God is for them the impossible fiction of the realist ethnography.

George Marcus and Dick Cushman (1982:45) see a Failed God in realist social science. A realist ethnography requires a tidy package of the Other. It must provide an account with all the ends neatly tied. Marcus and Cushman contrast this failed genre with a new experimental approach, which recognizes "that meanings are contingent upon ever-changing contexts of interaction, [therefore] ... impossible to express as determinant knowledge, nailed down." Such an account "leaves the world observed as open-ended, ambiguous, and in flux," because, presumably, the ethnographic encounter is that way. That, at least, is what Steve Tyler (1986:131) believes, when he writes, "A post-modern ethnography is fragmentary because it cannot be otherwise. Life in the field is itself fragmentary, not at all organized around familiar ethnological categories." James Clifford (1986:109) agrees: "Much of our knowledge about other cultures must now be seen as contingent, the problematic outcome of intersubjective dialogue, translation, and projection." Tyler (1986:126) tells us, similarly, that postmodern ethnography rejects the realist ideology of the observer and the observed — "there being nothing observed and no one who is observer. There is instead the mutual dialogical production of a discourse, of a story of sorts."

The God of realist ethnography having failed, here is the call for an anthropology based on flux and open-endedness — in short, based on accounts nearly as fragmentary as the chicken commonly eaten in India, chopped into so many unidentifiable pieces that we call it "fractured" chicken (or is it preferable to say "postformic"?).

Still, reflexive anthropologists are right: the idea of a neatly tied-up ethnographic package, of a realist ethnography that was temporal, functionalist, and unmindful of inequality and power — that was certainly a god that failed. Knowledge is indeed contingent and changeable. Perceptions are fragmentary and in flux. But not mainly for the reasons reflexive anthropologists give. Contingency and flux do not only reside in the ethnographic encounter, in the interlocutions of ethnographer and indigenes. Loose ends, open ends, and fragmentation are attributes of the cultures we study (and also the ones we live in). For example, I hope to show here that what Dumont took as The Indian Conception of Self is in fact only one of several self-identities involved in ongoing political struggles in India—struggles over (among other things) precisely what (which?) the Indian conception of self was and should be. Our cultural accounts must therefore be contingent, open-ended, and disintegrated because what happens in society is contingent on power and history, and therefore the object of our research is always in flux, permanently open-ended, and constantly in the making.

Ashis Nandy helps get us started by providing a more complex and contingent approach to cultural conceptions of the self, in India and elsewhere. Nandy (1983) believes that a culture has a "dominant" conception of the self, which, however, coexists with "recessive" conceptions. Circumstances in the world, such as colonialism, can alter the balance between the dominant and the recessive. For example, Nandy argues that colonialism perverted English culture by strengthening a dominant masculine conception of self until it became a hypermasculinity and thereby weakened alternative (recessive) bisexual or androgynous conceptions. He also says that early Indian nationalists confronted British domination by trying to build on a masculinity that represented only a recessive self-conception in India. By opposing the British domination with a self-conception dominant among the British, these Indian nationalists only succeeded in greater loss of self (Nandy 1983, chap. 1). Recovery of self was not possible until Gandhi resynthesized the dominant Indian conception and turned it directly against the British.

Nandy's approach is a major improvement in its admission of historical contingency and coexisting dominant and recessive self-conceptions. But is it contingent enough? Although he allows that cultural conceptions of self can change, Nandy also believes that cultures have "authentic" self-conceptions (Nandy 1986:359). Gandhi recaptured the authentic Indian self that had been lost when Indian nationalists self-identified with British selves (Nandy 1983:48ff.). Nandy's terms, "dominant" and "recessive," suggest a cultural gene pool resistant to fundamental mutation. The "authentic" seems to be the same as the "dominant" conception of self (and therefore akin to the "adaptive," if the genetic analogy is pursued?), and it has rather fuzzy historical

and spatial coordinates: Nandy (1986:352) speaks of shared conceptions across "Eastern civilizations," and he seems to treat Indian self-
conceptions as basically unaltered until the advent of the British.

Where did what Nandy calls India's dominant conception of self
come from? That is, where did the conception that India's self-conception was nonindividualistic, corporatist, androgynous, and so forth
come from? Has it always been? We have increasingly evidence, cour-
tesy of Mines and Kakar, that it often is not a lived reality today. Why
not suspect the same for the past? Perhaps we should have a look at
the prodigious efforts in the nineteenth and early twentieth centuries
to construct and then legitimate this conception of India's self-conception. Let me review them briefly.

Elsewhere (Fox 1989) I have distinguished two sorts of cultural essentialisms, or Orientalisms, that India's colonial condition produced.
Pejorative Orientalism, authored in the main by British imperialists and
their toady missionaries (by no means all missionaries), was exactly
the sort that Edward Said would expect and all that Ron Inden has
imagined. It broadcast a stereotypic image of India, with cultural con-
demnation and domination as its intent. But there was another kind
of Orientalism, one that I label "affirmative Orientalism." Its essentialist image of India, equally stereotypic, was, however, positive about India; it was suffused with a "condescending veneration" (to use Raymond Schwab's term) of Indian or, anyway, Hindu culture. Not all
essentialisms or Orientalisms are alike, a fact that Said and Inden do
not recognize. Some Orientalisms, the ones I label "affirmative,"
have the responsibility of generating effective cultural resistance to
domination: such was the context in which the conception of the Indian cultural conception of the self was generated.

Affirmative Orientalism arose — in the West — among the many experimental and countercultural movements that appeared in the United
States and in Europe's core capitalist nations as the nineteenth century ended. For instance, because Unitarians perceived ancient Hinduism as also embracing monism, they looked sympathetically on
India during their battles with Trinitarians. Theosophists and other
Western occultists also believed that India possessed an ancient wisdom. For late-nineteenth-century vegetarian socialists like Henry Salt,
a vegetarian Indian proved that an ancient and great civilization could
be built by humans who neither feasted on their fellow creatures nor

cannibalized their fellow men by capitalist wage labor. The antimodernist Edward Carpenter not only found release from Western materialism in India's ancient Wisdomland, but also escaped (he thought) the aggressive masculinity of the West by embracing India's androgyny.

Stephen Hay (1970:314–15) labels this essentialist construction of India "Orientophilia," and strongly emphasizes its European authorship, as also does Nirad Chaudhuri. Ascribing affirmative Orientalism exclusively or predominantly to Europeans is too simple. So is viewing it entirely as an indigenous response to foreign rule. There was joint effort by Indian nationalists and their European allies. (I give more space here to European affirmative Orientalism to offset Said and Inden.) Both parties worked with an Orientalist stereotype, and that stereotype was just as much at home in India as in Europe; it resided, in fact, in the world system. The result was the production of the conception of India's self-conception, or so I would like to suggest.

To very briefly show the coauthorship and the conception of self so authored, let me take two exemplary figures, the one ostensibly European, the other Indian, although by this time the world system had made such designations much too simple, as if India and Europe were still cultural islands rather than locked in a forced imperial embrace.

The European Theosophist, Annie Besant, thought she had been Indian in another life. She also felt cozy enough in early-twentieth-century India to author a series of textbooks instructing Hindu schoolboys in — what else? — Hinduism, and to admonish Gandhi for using protest methods — nonviolent resistance, what else? — not in character with Indian culture. Crisscrossing the country, Besant broadcast her belief in India's great future — when India would rightfully claim a high place among the world's nations by following its ancient Hindu cultural traditions.

Besant sharply contrasted Western culture with Indian, the starting point of any Orientalism. For the West, Besant (1904:12–14) said, the ideal was the self-reliant, free, and independent individual, whereas India's ideal was based on duty and the recognition of the unity of all beings: "From this naturally followed the view [in India] that each man was but a part of a whole; he was not isolated, he was not independent, he was a portion of a vast interlinked and interdependent order. He was not born free; he was born into numerous obligations, and by the very fact of living he was constantly adding to his debts" (Besant 1904:18–19). It also followed that the respective personalities differed, the Westerner being "aggressive, combative, tend[ing] to separateness" and the Indian "yielding, peaceful, and tend[ing] to unity" (Besant 1904:20).

A consensual, hierarchical, and corporate civilization was another essential heritage of India, according to Besant. In the West, democracy, the rule of the many, evolved over centuries (Dumont could give the exact number: seventeen centuries!) of struggle against state oppression. Ancient India also gave individuals liberty, but in a quite different way: "Liberty was ensured to the individual by the careful ordering of society and the definition of the place and duties of each class by wise men.... This was Aristocracy, the rule of the Best, growing out of the eastern Ideal as Democracy grew out of the Western" (Besant 1904:113). Besant, as Gandhi did, defended the ancient caste system as based on natural occupational divisions, although she disowned its contemporary form as a corruption.

My other exemplary affirmative Orientalist, Mohandas Gandhi, is too well known to require much elucidation from me (although I've tried it; see Fox 1989). Gandhi, too, constructed a conception of the Indian conception of self: (1) he disavowed individual competition because it was not in keeping with the genius of Indian culture; (2) he defended the caste system (in its ancient or ideal state) because it created a consensual, corporate society where each person had a place; he said the same for the ancient Indian village community — his so-called "panchayat raj"; (3) he imagined a future India based on *sarvodaya* or the "welfare of all" rather than the well-being of a few individuals, again in keeping with India's ancient traditions; (4) he recognized individual differences in intelligence, skill, and industry but leveled the effects of these differences (without leveling the differences): the rich, the creative, the entrepreneurial would hold their skills in "trusteeship" for society at large, not themselves individually; (5) he opposed legal or electoral protections for minorities, as, for example, reserved seats for Untouchables, because his corporatist image of society did not admit of the status of "minority"; and (6) in contrast to this vision of an India perfected in the future by resurrecting and then improving on its past, he condemned the individual selfishness and possessiveness of the West. Although Gandhi gave an individual (meaning "personal") twist to this conception, many of his ideas were anticipated or echoed by Swami Vivekananda, Sri Aurobindo, Tilak, and others, as was also the case for Besant's.

The next step is when early-twentieth-century affirmative Orientalism becomes mid-twentieth-century sociological theory. For Louis Dumont, India consists of a hierarchical caste system. It is a system, not a collection of castes, because the identity of each caste is dependent on an encompassing hierarchy. The hierarchy rests on a basic contradiction between purity and pollution, and each self within a caste finds its separate identity within the constitutive hierarchy by reference to the overarching purity-pollution system (Dumont 1970: 44–47). The caste system is a unity, but within that unity there is great diversity. Individual castes and the selves they contain (and constitute) have very different practices, beliefs, and degrees of pollution. There is thus "unity in diversity" in the very special sense that unity, based on hierarchy, is primary and diversity exists only secondarily. Human individuals do not exist in Dumont's version of the Indian Conception of Self; only Homo hierarchicus does. Besant, Gandhi, and several generations of Indian nationalists would agree. I suspect that if Dumont had been writing three-quarters of a century earlier, he would have ended up in the list of authorities at the end of Gandhi's *Hind Swaraj*.

The final step (so far) is when mid-twentieth-century sociological theory gets lived out (and died over) in India's streets late in the twentieth century.

In India today, there is great flux in self-conceptions. Dumont is not simply in academic competition with Marriott and Inden or with Nandy. Their models are fought over in Indian politics and even in India's streets. Different political groups, ethnic communities, and social movements put them forward as constituting and legitimating ideologies, that is, they put forward self-conceptions and identities that fit with one or another of these models, although they do not cite Dumont, Marriott-Inden, or Nandy (activist movements usually do not observe the niceties of academic citation). Each model pretends to a national hegemony it has not yet achieved. These would-be models of the Indian conception of self have come into direct and sometimes violent competition only recently, within the twentieth century at the earliest. They reflect open-ended and contingent struggles in the social and political flux of the society. People are living—and, unfortunately, dying—for these contingencies and in this flux. I will briefly show that Hindu nationalists champion a Dumontian model of "unity in diversity" against Sikhs, Muslims, Dalits, and others who obviously do not ascribe to it.

Hindu nationalists struggle for a stronger and better Indian-ness with a Dumontian model of self-identity. For them, unity in diversity has always been India's distinctive tradition. For example, M. S. Golwalkar, former head of the Rastriya Swayamsevak Sangh (RSS), perhaps the premier Hindu nationalist association, believed the term Hindu covered Muslims, Christians, Parsis, and Sikhs. They all shared a similar dharma, or duty, based on the "age-old" traditions of India. This underlying similarity made sectarian differences secondary. Hindu nationalists fight with determination, and often with violence, for a national self-identity based on *bharatiya,* that is, "Hindianness." I have proposed the term "Hindian" to represent the Hindu nationalist belief that India embodies "the harmony of disparates." Like Dumont, Hindu nationalists say that Indian unity is paramount and diversity is epiphenomenal (I discuss Hindu nationalism at length in Fox 1989 and 1990).

For Hindu nationalists, Sikhs are Sikhs superficially but basically they are Hindus. For many members of the RSS today, Sikhs are just a sect of Hindus suffering from "self-inflicted alienation," as one RSS leader put it. At one mass Hindu unity meeting (organized by the Vishwa Hindu Parishad), the audience chanted, "Hindus are all one; one tree, numberless branches." They too are willing to do battle for what in effect is Dumont's view but of course is much more. Witness the many Hindu nationalist protest marches against Sikh terrorism, the several mighty Hindu unity campaigns, including the giant Ekatmata Yajna of 1983, and the resurgence of Shiv Senas, regional paramilitary forces mobilized by an encompassing Hindu identity.

Hindu nationalism goes back to the early twentieth century only. It is another example of affirmative Orientalism, only one that has long ceased to mount cultural resistance and, instead, marshals cultural defensiveness (if culture truly changes, then what was once progressive can become reactionary). Veer Savarkar, Bhai Parmanand, and others in the 1920s and 1930s promoted a nationalism based on the concept of *Hindutva* or *bharat(iya)*. These terms refer to India at once as a geographical region and a cultural realm with deep-rooted traditions and thus combine the English terms "India" and "Hindu" (in a cultural, not sectarian sense). To capture this dual sense, I have suggested the translations "Hindia" and "Hindian" to get at the national conception of self that Hindu nationalism promotes.

With Hindu nationalism are we finally seeing enforced in the streets and in the polling stations a conception of the Indian cultural conception of self that began as an affirmative Orientalism, then became a sociological theory, and only now is being turned into a cultural practice for Indians, sometimes over their dead bodies?

Note

1. The argument that individualism and individual responsibility do exist in India is important as a critique. However, we have to be certain that this argument does not get reduced to the opposite but equally categorical assertion, namely, that individuality and individualism do exist in India for all times and everywhere. If this happens, what was an important critique gets reduced to a counterassertion with the same disabilities as the original.

References

Besant, Annie. 1904. *Hindu Ideals for the Use of Hindu Students in the Schools of India.* Benares and London: Theosophical Publishing Society.

———. 1913. "India's Mission among Nations." Article contributed to the *National Educator,* n.d. Reprinted in *India,* vol. 4 of *Essays and Addresses.* London: Theosophical Publishing Society.

Carrithers, Michael. 1985. "An Alternative Social History of the Self." In *The Category of the Person,* pp. 234–56, edited by Michael Carrithers, Steven Collins, and Steven Lukes. Cambridge: Cambridge University Press.

Clifford, James. 1986. "On Ethnographic Allegory." In *Writing Culture: The Poetics and Politics of Ethnography,* edited by James Clifford and George E. Marcus, pp. 98–121. Berkeley and Los Angeles: University of California Press.

Collins, Steven. 1985. "Categories, Concepts, or Predicaments? Remarks on Mauss's *Use of Philosophical Terminology.*" In *The Category of the Person,* edited by Michael Carrithers, Steven Collins, and Steven Lukes, pp. 46–83. Cambridge: Cambridge University Press.

Dumont, Louis. 1970. *Homo Hierarchicus: The Caste System and Its Implications.* Translated by Mark Sainsbury. Chicago: University of Chicago Press.

———. 1985. "A Modified View of Our Origins: The Christian Beginnings of Modern Individualism." In *The Category of the Person,* edited by Michael Carrithers, Steven Collins, and Steven Lukes, pp. 93–122. Cambridge: Cambridge University Press.

Fox, Richard G. 1988. "Revolutionary Selfhoods as Belief and Practice." Paper prepared for a conference at the University of California, Santa Barbara.

————. 1989. *Gandhian Utopia: Experiments with Culture.* Boston: Beacon Press.

————. 1991. "Hindu Nationalism in the Making, or the Rise of Hindian Identity." In *Nationalist Ideologies and the Production of National Culture,* edited by Richard G. Fox. American Ethnological Society monograph no. 2. Washington, D.C.

Fujita, Mariko. 1991. "The Diversity of Concepts of Self and Its Implication for Conducting Cross–Cultural Research." *Anthropology and Humanism Quarterly* 16: 20–22.

Geertz, Clifford. 1983. " 'From the Native's Point of View': On the Nature of Anthropological Understanding." In *Local Knowledge,* pp. 55–70. New York: Basic Books.

Hay, Stephen N. 1970. *Asian Ideas of East and West: Tagore and His Critics in Japan, China, and India.* Cambridge, Mass.: Harvard University Press.

Marcus, George E., and Dick Cushman. 1982. "Ethnographies as Texts." In *Annual Review of Anthropology* 11: 25–69.

Mauss, Marcel. 1985. "A Category of the Human Mind: The Notion of Person, the Notion of Self." In *The Category of the Person,* edited by Michael Carrithers, Steven Collins, and Steven Lukes, pp. 1–25. Cambridge: Cambridge University Press.

Mines, Mattison. 1988. "Conceptualizing the Person: Hierarchical Society and Individual Autonomy in India." *American Anthropologist* 90: 568–79.

Nandy, Ashis. 1983. *The Intimate Enemy: Loss and Recovery of Self under Colonialism.* Delhi: Oxford University Press.

————. 1986. "Oppression and Human Liberation: Towards a Post-Gandhian Utopia." In *Political Thought in Modern India,* edited by Thomas Pantham and Kenneth L. Deutsch, pp. 347–359. New Delhi: Sage.

Roland, Alan. 1988. *In Search of Self in India and Japan.* Princeton, N.J.: Princeton University Press.

Tyler, Stephen A. 1986. "Post-Modern Ethnography: From Document of the Occult to Occult Document." In *Writing Culture: The Poetics and Politics of Ethnography,* edited by James Clifford and George E. Marcus, pp. 122–40. Berkeley and Los Angeles: University of California Press.

6 / Defining the Self in Indian Literary and Filmic Texts

Vijay Mishra

No comparable civilization has argued over definitions of selfhood as much as the Indian. Throughout its long and august history almost every branch of knowledge (including philosophy, literature, religion, and linguistics) has grappled with this extremely elusive concept. There is, however, one point on which all the commentators agree: the self is other than what our faculties persuade us it is. In other words, the construction of the self through social processes (which would require a social other to begin with) is overtaken by a principle in which the "real" or the "true" self comes into being only when it can become identical with an abstraction beyond its own self. Once such a principle is postulated as the ground for the definition of the self, a culture must then give this principle a frame of reference. The Brahmanical orthodoxy, traditionally the arbiter on questions of knowledge, put a mechanism in place that stipulated that the self came already karmically formed (an earlier life explained the present human condition), and self-representation was therefore no more than a mode of being linked to a series of stages that one went through in life. In all this theorizing the final signified of the "other" became a higher principle designated by the word Brahman (neuter). In our discussion of the ways in which selves get structured in a number of literary and filmic texts (which is not to be confused with the sociology of the self), this pervasiveness of the Brahmanical conceptualization of the self must be kept in mind. The conceptualization itself, then, functions as a metatext or a metanarrative in the culture. Theories about the self become meaningful only if their relationships to the metatext are kept firmly in mind. There is a prior system that acts as a template, as a sanctioned pattern, for the realization of the self.

The discussion that follows speaks about the manner in which selves are artificially constructed agencies in works of the imagination. That these selves will seem so alien to "real" Indian social beings reflects both the nature of the generic principles that govern the portrayal of the self in art and the limitations of a civilization to grapple, interrogatively, with the issues surrounding the problematic of the concept of self in society. The dangers of such an approach are obvious. A transsocial formulation linked to a Hindu epistemology would exclude large sections of the Indian community. It would also work with essentially mystified categories that have little to do with real-life contemporary experience. My aim, however, is not to offer a definition of a "true" Indian self (if that is possible) but to suggest ways in which classical definitions of the Hindu self impinge upon our reading of works of the imagination. The principles of exclusion implicit in this classical articulation of the self are clear from the definitions of *self* we find in a dictionary.

Defining "Self" and "I-ness"

Dictionary definitions give us one body of information because the source texts of dictionaries are the written word. This is especially true of a dead language like Sanskrit, the source texts of which came to an end around four hundred years ago. The constant upgrading of a dictionary with reference to contemporary use is therefore not available to Sanskrit. Thus to defer to the authority of the lexicon in this instance is to employ one kind of "semantic" taxonomy. There are clearly other taxonomies, such as those found in vernacular dictionaries, that one could use with better results. However, I go to Monier-Williams's *Sanskrit Dictionary* because what I am interested in is the manner in which received definitions of the Hindu/Indian self govern the construction of selves in the texts that I will examine. There are two words for the self that I would want to look at. The first word is *ātman*, which functions largely as a substantive in the language, although it may be used (especially in the reflexive) as a pronoun. The other is the word for the grammatical "I"—*aham* (*asmad*)—through which the self is articulated in discourse. The *Sanskrit Dictionary* (Monier-Williams 1976:135–36) devotes three and one-half columns to the word *ātman.* Variously derived from root forms to mean "breath," "movement," or "the act of blowing," it has the not necessarily complementary meanings of "the soul, the principle of life and sensation," and "the individual soul, self, abstract individual." As a word for the self its most common occurrence is as a reflexive pronoun (in the singular) for all three persons (first, second, third) and all three genders (masculine, neuter, feminine). Hence *ātmanam sā hanti,* "she strikes herself." Often the word is used to mean "essence," "nature," or "character," and when not used as a reflexive pronoun it signifies the corporeality of the body as distinct from its individual parts. In some instances the word is transferred to "understanding, intellect, mind" and by extension to Brahman, the highest principle of life: the compound *āatma-brahman* means the self is Brahman. The unusual semantic range of the word *ātman,* self, thus establishes connections between the individual self and the first principle that subsumes the universe. Such a conjunction tells the Hindu that there is always another self, larger and much more permanent, than that which exists as a marker of a socialized "I." So that even when the word *ātman* is used for the self as a social being, it is already coded (as something more than just an agent). A range of compounds—from *ātma-karman,* "one's own act," and *ātma-ghāta* or *ātma-hatyā,* "suicide," to *ātma-prabodha,* "cognition of soul or supreme spirit," and *ātma-vidyā,* "knowledge of the soul or the supreme spirit,"—makes the usage clear enough.

The common grammatical marker for the self is, however, *aham,* "I," the subject of enunciation. This Sanskrit word, too, enters into compounds, although not quite so extensively as *ātman.* Of particular interest to us here is the compound *aham-kāra,* "conception of one's individuality, self-consciousness," "the making of self; thinking of self; egotism, pride, haughtiness." In Sāṃkhya philosophy *aham-kāra* is the third of the eight sources of creation, defined as the conceit or conception of individuality, where it clearly has the meaning of "I-ness." Perhaps the best-known occurrences of the pronoun *aham* are to be found in phrases such as *so [a]ham,* "I myself," and *aham brahman asmi,* "I am Brahman."

In the literature the proliferation of *ātman-* and *aham-* compounds tends to indicate two specific kinds of problems. *Ātman* compounds invariably relate to questions of self-knowledge: what is *ātma-vidyā*, what is *ātma-brahman*, and how does one find both oneself and Brahman? In these uses of the word, what we get is a dehistoricized "sanctioned pattern" (Kakar 1981:15), into which a relatively passive ego situates itself. There is no essential incompatibility here, although one might feel uneasy about any theory of individual development that also stipulates right from the start the necessity of an ideal process to maturity. In other words, the Indian emphasis on the four stages of the individual (*brahmacārya,* the student stage; *grhastha,* the stage of the family man; *vānaprastha,* the stage of retreat into the forest; and *samnyāsa,* final renunciation of the world) is a metanarrative that frames the development of the self. The artificiality of the four stages may be seen in the largely fictitious status given to the third stage of *vānaprastha* (O'Flaherty, Biardeau, in Sullivan 1990:43). The Indian self, in this version, is thus a subject that already has an itinerary that stipulates a kind of primal history locked into a compulsion to repeat an already sanctioned narrative. Individuality or subjectivity thus becomes not so much a question of a free-floating signifier or of socialized individuality; on the contrary the self is already framed, if not already constituted. The second compound (the *aham-* compound), while still speaking of self-knowledge, emphasizes the ideology of self-denial through not so much a metaphysics as a psychology. What must be denied is *ahamkāra* or sense of I-ness, and Indian culture constantly constructs its social and spiritual values with reference to the need for this self-denial. Again the need is so persistent that one begins to wonder if the excessive insistence is not an overcompensation for a personality defect in the Indian character itself. The self-ideal in this system of denial is of course the figure of the renouncer. Why does this figure have such immense value and mystique in Indian culture? I think these are important issues that must be taken up in any materialist critique of the construction of the self in Indian culture. Such a reading would require us to adopt a different kind of strategy in which the emphasis would shift from abstract knowledge to the authorization of such knowledge by the priestly caste. Valuable as this strategy will be for a thoroughgoing materialist critique of the construction of the self in Indian culture, the nature of this essay (a limited account of the uses of the mystified definitions of the self that permeate Indian culture) would preclude any systematic examination of that aspect of the construction of the subject. Before we move on, however, a word or two must be said about terms that function as limits within which the foregoing definitions of the self operate.

Let Me Take You Down ... to Mokṣa Fields, Nothing Is Real

"The world is unreal, Brahma alone is real, the self is none other than Brahman" ("Brahma satyaṃ jagan mithyā jīvo brahmaiva nāparah"), Śaṅkara, that fiercely nondualistic thinker, never fails to remind us (Masson 1980:68). The growth of the self in this cryptic formulation is toward an abstract principle into which the self finally dissolves. But like all other aspirations toward such abstractions, the implied state of bliss remains a goal, a fact that served the aims of the priestly caste very well indeed. The difficulties posed by this very desire for union become evident when we examine Krishna's own attempts at defining three key concepts that underlie Hindu definitions of the self: *brahman, (adhy)ātma,* and *karman* (*Bhagavadgītā,* VIII). In defining the *adhyātma,* Krishna introduces another term, *svabhāva,* and describes the *adhyātma* in terms of this *svabhāva*: "svabhāvo [a]dhyātmam ucyate" ("the *adhyātma* is the inherent nature of the individual self"). Literally translated as self-being (or the state of being that defines one's own self), the *svabhāva* introduces (the prefix *sva* implies ownership, as in *svadharma*) a term through which the *adhyātma* (which is also Brahman) is given expression in the world we inhabit. In this portion of the *Gītā,* Krishna's unease with this definition (Arjuna's question in fact begins with: "kim tad brahma kim adhyātmam") is obvious as he continues to make further distinctions by introducing the perishable part of being (*adhibhuta*), the divine agent within (*puruṣa*), and perhaps even a god lower than Brahman to whom sacrifices are offered (*adhiyajña*). The use of a technical Sāṃkhya terminology to make precise distinctions between the various states of the self demonstrates both an unease with narrow definitions of the concept of the self and its irrelevance in the greater cosmic design, which takes us back to Śaṅkara's dictum about the ideal of nondifferentiation so central to classical Hindu thought.

The experience of oneness is captured in the word *mokṣa*. In psycho-analytic parlance *mokṣa* is the principle of death, the feeling state desig-nated by the term "oceanic sublime" (*ozeanisches Gefühl*) used by Freud in *Civilization and Its Discontents* (1930). J. Moussaieff Masson has traced the origin of the "oceanic sublime" (which Freud borrowed from Romain Rolland) to an uncompromisingly *advaitavedāntic* (non-dualistic) text called *Aṣṭāvakrasaṃhitā,* which "denies the reality of all phenomena of the outer and inner world in favour of the one re-ality that is Brahman, and which is also the same as the innermost self, the Ātman" (Masson 1980:37). "You are an infinite ocean" ("tvayy anantamahambhodhau"), begins one of the relevant verses from this text. In examining it further, Masson discovers recurring themes of disgust with the world, the world's transience, and the de-sire for a long sleep in death, which are also, as we know, the themes that proliferate in Indian philosophical thinking, as well. If the world is in fact maya, illusion, a construction of Viṣṇu's power, then the re-turn of the self to the undifferentiated moment of the oceanic sub-lime in *mokṣa* is also a desire to return to the place where we have been before.

Mokṣa is clearly going to be a difficult concept to handle, but such is its centrality in Indian culture that it must be negotiated, "however difficult or professionally disconcerting the attempt may be" (Kakar 1981:17). Sudhir Kakar's work is helpful here because he grounds the experience of *mokṣa* in the "common" mystical experience called *samādhi*. In discussing the *samādhi* state he makes a useful distinc-tion between self and ego. With some help from Freud, Kakar distin-guishes between the unconscious states of the ego, "the primitive id and the constraining superego" (Kakar 1981:19). Because the ego is unconscious, one can only be conscious of its work but not of *it*. Let me quote his definitions of ego and self at this point.

> By ego I mean the inner agency of the psyche which screens and synthesizes the impulses, needs, emotions and memories from within and the impressions, ideas, expectations and opportuni-ties from outside, both of which become part of our conscious-ness and call for some kind of action ... The individual ego is in a state of constant flux, mediation and exchange between inner and outer, past and present, unconscious and self-conscious, self and society, between the instinctual and the institutional in hu-

man life.... The self, on the other hand,... is preconscious in the sense that it becomes conscious when "I" reflects upon it, or rather upon the various selves—body, personality, social roles—which make up the composite, or whole self. The counter-players of the self are "others," or more precisely, the selves of others. (Kakar 1981:19)

Kakar, then, takes up the thorny question of the "I," which can neither be the self (since it, the self, is the object of the "I") nor the ego, the psychic agency. It must be stressed that Kakar adopts the traditional Hindu definition of "I" (*aham brahman asmi*) as found in the Upanishads, where the "I" is pure consciousness, that is, Brahman. The state of *mokṣa* may be considered as that moment when the "I" is no longer objectified into the self and retreats into its own being as pure consciousness. The narrative of the self in the culture is thus predicated upon a principle that would, finally, lead to its own death, since without the "I" the self ceases to be. But before this happens, the "I" has been in play constantly and to its fullest capacity. It has been the "centre of awareness and existence in all experienced situations" (Kakar 1981:19). Kakar then attempts a socialization of the "I" that I do not think is evidenced in the texts. His claim that before *mokṣa* is attained the "I" should have experienced the material conditions of being—sexual life, work, play, and so on—implies that the four stages of Hindu life are fully theorized along material lines. This is not the case. What the metanarrative endorses is precisely the essentialism of the self, not its constitution through discourse. The self is not a product of the processes of change; it is contained within and moves unproblematically through the narrative. What I am suggesting here is that the larger pattern, the system, is more important than individual beings. The absence of boundaries between inner and outer, self and other, and the absence of any apparatus by which reality might be tested (since at one level reality is maya, unreal) certainly makes the self as social subject a difficult proposition to defend, and it would be best, at least for the purposes of this essay, that we do not mount that defense here. Nevertheless, it must be conceded that definitions of the self as part of social order in the age of late capital would require us to go outside Hindu metanarratives. Caste and class, the role of fanzines and films, and the politics of difference and ethnicity are probably more legitimate ways in which the idea of the self in modern India may be approached. For the construction of the self in terms of the framework developed here, the difficulty, however, arises from another quarter. I have in mind the law of dharma, and the nature of action, karma.

The Genres of Dharma and Karma

If *mokṣa* is the goal of life, then dharma is what life itself is all about. The texts spell out clearly how *mokṣa* may be realized; they also lay down rules for the proper conduct of the individual. The self as social being is therefore not a subject that constructs its own actions but follows prescriptive rules that are constitutive of the subject's dharma. From the Sanskrit root *dhṛ* ("sustain"), its basic meaning is "that which sustains." In Barbara Stoler Miller's words, dharma is therefore "the moral order that sustains the individual, the society, and the cosmos" (Miller 1986:164). Such is the power of dharma in Hindu thought that, as van Buitenen has so brilliantly mapped out, even the entry of God into the Hindu worldview does not lead to the establishment of the law (because dharma is already given) or a new code of justice but to the final positing of a category of being who in its self-sufficiency "knew the bliss of wanting nothing" (van Buitenen 1981:27).

In actual practice the type of dharma that a person follows is based upon a number of things, including the period in which he or she lives and, more important, the caste to which he or she belongs. Sudhir Kakar does not spell this out clearly, referring instead to *guṇās*, traits transmitted through one's past life. It is clear that at the macro level, at the level of general dharma, one's caste allegiance defines the type of dharma one must follow. There is, however, a micro-dharma as well, which is the dharma of the individual. As in the word for the individual self (*svabhāva*), the prefix *sva-* is used to define a self-dharma (one's *svadharma*). This *svadharma* is what unites the dharma of the various castes, since at the level of *svadharma* a uniform code of morality certainly operates. But since occupation is by and large a function of caste, the dharma of an individual is indistinguishable from the work that he or she does. It is here that the related concept of karma comes in. Since karma is action or activity it implies that a person's proper dharmic conduct subsumes his or her karmic role. One's actions therefore are part of one's dharma, and both are connected at a deeper level with the function of one's caste. At this level the Hindu social order is an organic whole marked by levels of inter-dependencies. But it is an order, like the definitions of the self, that is locked into an essentialist conception of society. Dharma is immutable and, by extension, so too is the social order. In Kakar's words again:

> Hindus share the belief that the legitimacy of social institutions lies in the *dharma* they incorporate rather than in utilitarian con-tractual agreements and obligations ... Moreover, it is generally believed that social conflict, oppression and unrest do not stem from the organization of social relations, but originate in the *adharma* (not *dharma*) of those in positions of power. (Kakar 1981:40)

Thus Viṣṇu reincarnates himself whenever dharma is challenged, since any perversion of power ultimately corrupts dharma: "yadā yadā hi dharmasya glānir bhavati bhārata," says the *Bhagavadgītā* (IV.7). It does mean, however, that revolutionary change in Indian society is possible only within the parameters of the law of dharma. As a generic system it lays down structural imperatives that must be followed. And since this is an ahistorical generic system, its permutations are ex-tremely limited. Like shifts in genre itself—one recalls the rise of the bourgeois novel from the ruins of the epic form, for instance—dharma can change only if there is a radical change in the definitions of the self in Hindu culture, and that won't be possible unless there is, as Kakar says, a *"totalistic rejection of the personal-cultural past"* (Kakar 1981:42). The "personal-cultural" past, however, needs to be histori-cized. To understand Hindu time, destiny, and history one needs to return to the crucial category of karma.

Since the individual soul (*jīva*) is immortal, the Hindu worldview sees present life as a moment in a much longer journey, whose very longevity transforms its linearity into a cycle. Time is cyclical and subject to return like the uncanny. History, therefore, gets quickly transformed into an immemorial tradition, and events are either mag-nified or get framed in a prior discourse. Hagiography marginalizes biography; cosmology finally triumphs over history. "The Hindu time sense is more psychological than historical; it has the dream-like qual-ity of timeless time as it exists in the human unconscious," writes Kakar (47). In the absence of concrete time, karma alone enables an individual to translate lived experience into a type of historical event. Since action as karma implies that, whatever the real, material conditions of the subject's existence here and now, nothing is ever wasted; it gives the subject a promise of hope. It is, of course, easy to trivialize karma as fatalism, which is what it is not. On the contrary, of the three crucial determinants of the Hindu collective self (*mokṣa*, dharma, and karma), karma is perhaps the only one that has some room for individual growth through radical action. This is possible if karma is seen not purely as a metaphysical category inextricably linked to dharma but as its parallel, not its obverse side. The emphasis on the propriety of one's action—Krishna spoke about his own karma, his own action that kept the universe going, and had insisted upon the selflessness of the karmic act—redefined leads to the idea of social action and, in the period of late capitalism, to a belated individualism. It is perhaps for this reason that the *Bhagavadgītā* is of such central importance to Indian thought. Not surprisingly, the latter concept—the relationship between action and the proper dharma—is argued at length in the *Bhagavadgītā*. The emphasis here is on the significance of the disinterested action, like Krishna's own as a *karmayogin*, the doer of karma, and the collapse of the mistakenly absolute distinctions between the renouncer and the man-of-the-world. Hence, "he is both the renouncer (sa saṃnyāsī) and the doer (ca yogī) who performs the task set for him (karma karoti yaḥ) without interest in its consequences or fruits (anāśritaḥ karmaphalam)" (van Buitenen 1981:92–93). Earlier Krishna had redefined karma by pointing out that there is no necessary and self-evident connection between karma and action, since there can be karma in inaction, too.

Mokṣa, dharma, and karma are thus part of the cultural unconscious of the Indian race. Any critique of the self in Indian culture must take account of these metanarratives even if, in the final analysis, they are demonstrated to be structures of mystification that kept the Brahman patricians in power.

"Fables," concludes Kakar in his central chapter on the Hindu image, "exquisitely capture the essence of the Hindu image" (Kakar 1981:49). It is the same belief that takes me to my literary and filmic proof texts for an account of how the self may be defined in works of the imagination. Clearly, to read theories of self and representation through imaginative literature is perhaps not as valuable as reading them through actual social practices. It is with this proviso and with this confession that I turn to Paul de Man's influential essay entitled "Ludwig Binswanger and the Sublimation of the Self" (de Man 1983). What I find exciting about this essay is not Binswanger's ideas on Ibsen but Paul de Man's larger, essentially literary, concerns about the centrality of the idea of consciousness in debates about the self. De Man's entry point here is Michel Foucault's *Les Mots et les choses* (*The Order of Things*, 1974), in which Foucault distinguished between the history of ideas and the archaeology of ideas. The distinctions drawn in this important work had far-reaching consequences on subsequent theories of self and subjectivity in that Foucault emphasized the significance of outward signs and transformations in dealing with "the constitutive power of consciousness." Discursive formations—politics, economics, and sociology in particular—came to occupy an important space in any reading of the self, which, for Foucault, was not a matter of self-reflection or representation through consciousness but of effects of discourse. Not surprisingly Foucault rejected a reading of consciousness in terms of its own history through self-knowledge or understanding. At one level this was an important act of demystification in that Foucault relegated the humanist reading of self and understanding to the level of ideology. As de Man summarizes, for Foucault "the past can only be studied as a network of surface structures, without any attempt to understand the movements of consciousness from the inside in an act of self-reflection." If one reads Indian discourses one is struck immediately by the persistence of the acts of understanding from within the movement of consciousness. The self comes into being only through acts of intense contemplation in which the thinking consciousness establishes through reflection the ground of its own being. In Foucault's terms a study of such reflections is not an archaeology but a history of ideas. It is clear that Foucault's emphasis on the discursive domain arose out of a very real unease with the hidden essentialism of all prior definitions of the self. But what Foucault is less careful about is the degree to which this very essentialism had been subjected to radical scrutiny, especially in recent German thought. Phenomenology, in particular, had attempted a redefinition of the self by placing on hold all empirical definitions of the self and by constantly reflecting upon the ways in which being is constituted.

At one level all arguments about definitions of the self are basically ethnographic: are selves culturally constituted or is there a universality about selfhood in terms of a bourgeois reading of it as autonomous individuality? Although the question of the self is not explicitly raised, this basic ethnographic dichotomy is also at the very heart of current debates surrounding the postmodern condition. One can almost claim that the emphasis upon the grand *récit* by someone like Jürgen Habermas is a variation on the epistemic privilege of the thinking, autonomous consciousness against its psychosocial construction through language, social formation, and the unconscious. Those who distrust the grand narrative and would proffer instead multiplicities and small *récits* (like Lyotard and Foucault, for instance) are deemed to be free-floating relativists whose ideological agenda can be so easily appropriated by the forces of conservatism. Hence Habermas's designation of the French postmodernists as neoconservatives. What is at issue here are the conflicting positions of the tradition of the Enlightenment in which there is an insistence both on a community of thinkers and on reason, against the proposition that any argument, or point of view, is valid only insofar as it "convinces a given audience at a given time" (Rorty 1985:162). It is easy enough to see that Habermas's use of "neoconservatism" is meant to suggest a criticism of purely "context-dependent" forms of social thought. The argument of the Enlightenment project is based upon a reading of humanity as a more or less regularized collectivity seeking its emancipation in history through constant self-examination. For this reason, perhaps, the systematization of the domains of reason, ethics, and aesthetics by Kant continues to have such a powerful influence. It soon becomes obvious to any reader of Indian philosophy that the legitimization of metanarratives that Habermas advances is duplicated, although with greater persistence, in an earlier legitimization of metanarratives in Indian thought. I have used the qualifying phrase "with greater persistence," because communicative intelligibility is superseded by the hegemony of transcendental philosophy and a continued neglect of what Habermas senses was a flaw in Hegel's philosophy of the subject, as well. In Hegel a "sense of rationality as *social*" is missing (Rorty 1985:167) in exactly the same way in which a similar absence may be found in Indian theories of the self.

There is one important qualification that I must make — once again with reference to Paul de Man's essay — and this is that while the phenomenological tradition did emphasize the importance of the self for purposes of reflection and self-analysis, it did not fall into the humanist anthropology of a Dilthey or a J. G. Frazer by resorting to a preconceived concept of the category "man." I am going to have difficulty with this concept in Indian thought later on in this essay. But I am getting ahead of myself here and must establish my groundwork more fully to begin with. In this "philosophical anthropology" (the phrase is de Man's) there is a tendency to relapse into a basically empirical definition of the self through categories of mind (reason, imagination, judgment, and so on), which in turn offer formulaic definitions of the self. "Man is a thinking animal" is one such definition. The question we need to foreshadow is whether Indian definitions of the self are similarly framed or whether they anticipate a more fully articulated phenomenology of being. In this latter conception of self the interest shifts from fixed categories to a continuous definition of the self through a radical critique of being.

In the artistic world "the problem of the self is particularly delicate," writes de Man, since in "the study of literature, the question of the self appears in a bewildering network of often contradictory relationships among a plurality of subjects" (de Man 1983:39). There are four basic ways in which the self appears in literature:

1. the self that judges the aesthetic product;
2. the self constructed through the intersubjective relationships between the author and the reader;
3. the self as the subject of an intentional act between the author and the self that writes; and
4. the self as the author who is changed (and interpreted) by his or her own work.

More succinctly de Man calls these four more or less distinct types "the self that judges, the self that reads, the self that writes, and the self that reads itself." The last of these is arguably the most complex form of self-presence in Indian texts, since it implies a degree of self-transcendence in which the authorial self contains, in the words of Georg Lukács, "within itself the fullness of experience that makes up the totality of the human species" (de Man 1983:42).

Although there is an important fifth type of the self—the self that performs—I shall restrict myself to these four types of selves when reading my proof texts. What follows is a very limited, and somewhat schematic, account of "four selves" as seen in a range of Indian literary and filmic texts.

The Self that Judges: Jayadeva's *Gītagovinda*

Jayadeva's *Gītagovinda* is a twelfth-century love poem composed in reasonably straightforward classical Sanskrit. The name Jayadeva occurs in the text itself in many of its signature verses (*bhaṇita*) and may not be identical with a real, historical personality of that name. The poem is divided into twelve cantos, each one of which is made up of from one to four songs. These songs are composed as a series of stanzas in rhyming couplets, with a particular moric meter (a meter based on the number of beats in a line) and set to an appropriate *rāga*. In terms of its structure Sanskrit aestheticians would call this poem a *citrakāvya*, literally a "picture poem," or an "unacted" anecdotal narrative. So Bhoja writes in his thirteenth-century theoretical treatise, *Śṛngāra Prakāśa* (The light of love): "to the cultured soul of the Sahṛdaya, there is no difference between un-acted drama and poem. When a drama is not acted but yet can be relished as keenly by mere reading ..." (Bhoja in Raghavan 1978:80). The poem thus has a kind of "stilled" dramatic structure, a set of monologues articulated by Krishna, the *sakhī* (the *sahṛdaya* or friend), and Rādhā. It begins in an anecdotal fashion with a pastoral narrative that ends in a presumed sexual tryst on the banks of the Jamuna river. As the poem advances—and we never forget that it is all about the pastoral god Krishna and his consort Rādhā—there is a gradual intensification of the sexual relationship of the lovers, so much so that the passion of the lovers threatens to destroy the harmony of the pastoral, a mode that has traditionally either eschewed sexual desire or at best sublimated it. Desire reaches a high point in Krishna's own burning passion:

> kṣamayatām aparam kadāpi tavedṛśam na karomi
> dehi sundari darśanam mama manamathena dunomi

> Forgive me now!
> I won't do this to you again!
> Give me a vision, beautiful Rādhā!
> I burn with passion of love. (Miller 1977:83)

Krishna and Rādhā's eroticism has clear voyeuristic possibilities, and the self that is drawn into it could easily adopt that position. The judging self, however, is given ways in which such an unmediated reading might be avoided. In terms of *rasa* theory — in terms of Sanskrit theory of reception — the poem is pure *śṛngāra*, infused with the *rasa*, the relish, of the erotic: śṛngāra sakhī ... harīḥ krīdati ("Harī plays the erotic"). But how can one circumvent this, how does one transform the erotic into an experience that transcends sexuality? What definition of the self is implicit here? If the aim of life is *mokṣa* and if both dharma and karma are part of that aim, then what is this poem about the dark lord doing to the judging self? The system is clearly aware of this and offers at least three levels of sublimation or displaced identification. In the first instance the figure of the poet Jayadeva constantly enters the text and indicates the didactic nature of the poem. This is clearly a pretty forced intervention, since the general poetic discourse is at odds with Jayadeva's moralizing tone. The second level is perhaps much more intriguing, since it signals the mediated nature of the aesthetic experience for the Hindu self. Here we return to what Bhoja himself had detected as the "cultured soul of the Sahṛdaya." Now the Sahṛdaya ("the kindred heart") functions as the dispassionate observer of the sexual trysts; she is the friend, situated in the text itself, who brings the lovers together and is in fact the first reader of the text. Since the self therefore judges through the categories posited by the Sahṛdaya (who emphasizes Krishna's cosmic game and the allegorical nature of the creative process), its actions are locked into a formal structure of response. At one level *rasa* theory itself stipulates some such structuring of response on the part of the self. The point here, however, is that the nature of the self that judges in Indian culture is radically different from its Western counterpart in that he or she never has unmediated access to the text itself. In this respect one can see the strength of a theory of discourse that relates self to discursive regimes of power. The difference, in the Hindu context, however, arises from the fact that the self accepts the mediating power of the Sahṛdaya as crucial to the act of judgment itself. Once this is accepted, the self then judges at the third, dharmic level. In terms of a theory of reader-response, the category of reader we may advance may be called the *infra reader*.

The self, finally, judges the text, as Jayadeva and the Sahṛdaya have also done, in terms of an aesthetic paradigm that transforms the profane into the sacred. One of the features of this paradigm was its insistence upon the efficacy of love-in-separation in the work of art. What is meant here is that the participants in the text as *nāyaka* and *nāyika* (male and female actor) symbolically play out the desire for union with the transcendental other (Krishna) in an economy of desire where the goal is *mokṣa*. This was possible for a text like the *Gītagovinda* because prior to its composition an entire tradition of Puranic literature had already "homologized the sacred and the profane dimensions of love, explicitly theologized sexual love, reconciled human passions as exemplified in the love of the cow-herdesses for Krishna with bhakti, religious devotion valued as the highest means and the highest goal" (Siegel 1978:38). The nature of sexual love as a paradigm for heavenly love ("Never ever chaste except you ravish me," wrote John Donne in his *Divine Meditations*) was formulated as the dramatic oscillation between *vipralambha* (love-in-separation) and *sambhoga* (love-in-union). In short what we find is the representation of a parallel text through the self's identity with the Sahṛdaya, and by extension with Jayadeva. It is for this reason that an Indian reader can claim quite unproblematically that

> this eternal *līlā* is the eternal truth, and, therefore, it is this eternal *līlā*—the playful love-making of Rādhā and Kṛṣṇa, which the Vaiṣṇava poets desired to enjoy. If we analyse the *Gītagovinda* of Jayadeva we shall find not even a single statement which shows the poet's desire to have union with Kṛṣṇa as Rādhā had,—he only sings praises of the *līlā* of Rādhā and Kṛṣṇa and hankers after a chance just to have a peep into the divine *līlā*, and this peep into the divine *līlā* is the highest spiritual gain which these poets could think of. (Dasgupta 1976:125–26)

The self that judges the literary text—at the level of both the reader and the author (the self in this paper is always both)—comes close to being socially constructed. The aesthetic order is also a structured system that connects, finally, with the ontology of self as designated by the Hindu world order. What the literary citation, however, signifies more clearly is the manipulative nature of that definition and its grounding in an entire epistemology of self and other endorsed by Hinduism. But the literary evidence also supports the massive continuity of the tradition and endorses the often-cited view that all Indian culture, past and present, is in fact one grand narrative. When we move, for heuristic reasons, to the other three selves, we will find that there is going to be a strong overlap of de Man's distinctions.

The Hindu self very quickly collapses the various selves into one composite self, canceling out distinctions of inner and outer, presence and nonpresence, being and becoming.

The Self that Writes: The *Mahābhārata*

The *Mahābhārata* (hereinafter referred to as *Mbh*) is the grandest text of humankind, if by the term "grandest" we mean that text which is a complete compendium of all known genres and to which additions can be continually made. Composed orally from around the fifth century B.C. onward (some would make its earliest version almost contemporary with Homer) until it reached its present form a century or two after the birth of Christ, it is, for Indians, the source text of their civilization. "What is not here is nowhere else to be found [yad na iha asti na tat kvacit]," claims the *Mbh* (I, 56, 34). Any study of the self in India will have to either read this text or use material from it that has made its way into other texts. Clearly an enormous text like the *Mbh* cannot be discussed in a few pages, so we will have to use it selectively. One of the most exciting parts of this epic deals with the nature of writing and the ways in which the narratorial self functions as a stand-in for the "author(s)" of the text. Furthermore, in an implicit theorization about the self as writer, the epic tradition also establishes a complex dialectic between the reader and the narrator. Since the *Mbh* has been most effectively disseminated in modern times through the medium of cinema and drama, no account of the self as writer or reader can be complete without adequate reference to these other semiotic systems. We shall therefore be referring to literary as well as filmic and dramatic versions without necessarily stating as a matter of course the precise version we are using at every point in our commentary.

We observed in our discussion of the many compounds formed by the personal pronoun *aham* and *ātman* the proliferation of words relating to "I-ness" or "Ego." A word that stood out was *ahaṃkāra*—"self-consciousness, egotism, pride." Now one of the features about the composition of the *Mbh* that strikes us is the degree of self-effacement going on at the level of authorship and authorial responsibility, so much so that specific authors are never cited and the name of Vyāsa (which means "the divider") is offered to fulfill what Foucault called the "author function," in which authorship is really a function of a particular discursive formation that requires the positing of the category "author" as a principle of self-legitimation (Foucault, in Harari, 1980:141–60). The relationship between de Man's self that writes, insofar as that self is a textual construction, a screen for the author himself or herself, is considerably complicated in Indian culture, since the relationship between author and narrator—the self in the text and the self behind it—took such a radically different turn in the culture's founding text(s). Hindu tradition, however, states repeatedly, although probably never categorically, that Krishna Dvaipāyāna Vyāsa composed a number of crucial texts, from the Vedas (which he could have only arranged since these are *śruti* texts, and hence unauthored) to the Purāṇas. The text for which he is famous is the *Mbh*, and it is here, and especially in the vulgate, that we are given an extensive account of Vyāsa's role in its composition. As Vyāsa pondered about the means by which his poetic text may be transmitted, Brahma, the *jagat-guru*, appeared before him and suggested the scribal services of Gaṇeśa, who, when asked, agreed to be his scribe on condition that there should be no constraints on his writing. To this demand Vyāsa acceded, reminding him, however, that he must not write anything he didn't understand, which, of course didn't happen since, as Sauti, one of the reciters tells us, even Gaṇeśa could not possibly understand everything he wrote. Such fantastic accounts of the writer-narrator are clearly contrary to the concept of an epic consciousness in total control of the subject. Not surprisingly, empirical textualists like Hopkins, Winternitz, and Oldenberg were contemptuous of the *Mbh*'s implicit definition of authorship and used this to confirm yet again their criticism of India as a "land without historical sense" (Sullivan 1990:15). Yet there is nothing particularly strange here, because the idea of redistributing the center (presented either as a consciousness or a voice) through other nodal points is not uncommon in the Indian narrative tradition. It could be argued that both the nature of "authorship" and the variety of names used for the epic personages are part of this cultural decentering. Arjuna, for instance, is called by at least ten names and about fifty epithets—for example, Phalguṇa, Jiṣṇu, Kiritin, Dhanamjaya, Indrasuta, Pārtha, Bhimanuja, and Bṛhannaṭa (Katz 1989:277–89).

Vyāsa's function is therefore not so much poetic or authorial, in the Western sense of the word, as it is karmic in the sense that the tradition has already refined the role of the "author." Like the Vedic *ṛṣī* the artist was not regarded as the creator of his work but as "the means by which the eternal forms were made manifest" (Sullivan 1990:117). To make proprietorial claims would have led us back to the terrible condition of *ahaṃkāra*, I-ness. There are clearly two levels of reading that I am simultaneously engaged in here. The first is the idea of "author" as symbolic representation of the class "author"; the second is the way in which this representation collapses self and individuality into a much wider category. In the latter respect the author function that Foucault had in mind (which, incidentally, is a historically constituted phenomenon for him — the idea of the author is a relatively late bourgeois idea connected with laws of copyright and so on) takes on a distinctly different inflection, since composition is all about self-knowledge. As Bruce M. Sullivan reminds us, "Vyāsa is the one whose way of life most corresponds to the orthodox ideal which was then being formulated; he is the epic's most dharmic brahmin" (Sullivan 1990:27). At the same time the important category of authorial or narratorial voice is almost completely missing from the text. It is difficult to hear a voice behind Krishna's lengthy dialogue with Arjuna, for instance. But Vyāsa, the "author," participates in the narrative since he is responsible for the real, lived genealogical transmission necessary for the continuity of his text. Without Vyāsa the race of Saṃtānu (and hence of Bharata) itself would have come to an end. As the omniscient sage who moves through the temporal categories of past, present, and future with ease, he signifies, finally, the ideal definition of self as *ātma-brahman* (the self as Brahman). But since he internalizes history, without in fact finding the need to historicize his text, the Brahman ascetic Vyāsa (whose own Brahmanical lineage was not impeccable; his mother was from the fisherman class) actually opts for the path of *pravṛtti* (action), not *nivṛtti* (renunciation), although, as Sullivan points out, his dharmic role is actually "liminal, neither fully in nor out of society" (Sullivan 1990:43). Later, Puranic texts added Vyāsa to the higher pantheon by claiming that he was an avatar of Nārāyaṇa/Viṣṇu, and hence another Krishna in the *Mbh*.

The "ludic" possibilities of the nature of the self that writes are what Peter Brook found so exciting about the *Mbh*. Peter Brook's spectacular ten-hour version of the *Mbh* was based on Jean-Claude Carrière's dramatic reconstruction of the epic. In this version Brook is fascinated by the extremely postmodern nature of the construction of the self in the epic. He, therefore, gives considerable space to those sections from the vulgate that deal with the narrator(s), since these problematize the whole question of the nature of the self that writes. Thus the play emphasizes the implicit radicalization of the role of the writer insofar as he or she questions the functions of linearity, logic, and temporal order in art. Vyāsa-as-writer becomes the most important character in the epic as a consequence. Others question him about his intention: "Why have you created us if you are going to kill us sooner or later?" or "Are you still in charge of the plot since noble kings are also dying?" Since Vyāsa has also invented Krishna, we get interesting reversals whose logic comes straight out of the helix-like structure of Hindu thought. "Vyāsa, which one of us has invented the other?... What role have you in store for me now?" are the kinds of questions that Krishna asks. Not surprisingly he gets the predictable reply, "You know well." The role of the writer as teller of the tale, as "author" (the mind that constructs the text) and as participant in the text's actions—a procedure that complicates the whole Western tradition of mask or persona—necessitates, finally, questions about the kind of definitions of "self" that would produce writer-positions of this order. Since the idea of the self has no intrinsic core, since the self is by itself unstable or decentered, oscillating between a range of subject positions in themselves inadequate for the achievement of authenticity or the establishment of the ground of being, one gets the distinct impression that the self in India, in terms of classical metaphysics, is a congealed longing for a mysterious unity rather than a social reality. It is for this reason that I do not find the absence of the tragic sense in the literature unusual. Perhaps only once in the markedly uncomfortable figure of Karṇa, the antihero of the *Mbh*, we come across a character whose moral universe is locked into meaning and whose actions are dictated by the constraints of dharma as personal morality and responsibility. Of all the characters in the *Mbh* (Krishna included), Karṇa alone keeps his word throughout.

Where Brook emphasized the self that writes because he was intrigued by the postmodern claims about narrative made by the *Mbh*, Indian theatrical and filmic transformations of the great epic have been less interested in this. If we go to a well-known film version, that of 1965, we get a text that shifts quite radically from the self that writes (Vyāsa) to Krishna, the self as the cosmic author. While the film version is not really very productive in respect of self and writer, it nevertheless positions the whole concept of self in ways that demonstrate the immense continuity of the Hindu worldview. In this film version Vyāsa is completely missing from the text, either as narrator or as participant. Instead the self that writes is clearly identified with the figure of Krishna, who knows what has been written and therefore plays the divine clown, teasing his way through the highly complex narrative and connecting all the strands together. In the end the *Mbh* ceases to be an Indo-European epic but becomes an affirmation, finally, of the ideal world order that Krishna endorses. In this world all action is Brahma action, all *ātman* is *ātma-brahman.* The spectator therefore identifies with Krishna as the cosmic author or puppeteer who manipulates the text since the entire narrative is already known to him. This Krishna is, however, not the hero of the epic; he is instead vested with characteristics he has acquired over the next two millennia: the cowherd stealer of butter, the lover of Rādhā, the flute player, and so on. Beyond identification one suspects there is a kind of coauthorship going on since the film endorses the spectator's knowledge of the material practices of Bombay cinema. This includes the citation of song and dance sequences, a conservative politics, a subtext through which the spectator writes another text based upon the collective adulation of the wrestler-turned-actor Dara Singh, who, as Bhima, is all martial action (this after all is the year of the 1965 war with Pakistan) and an overall reinscription of the discourse into the *Mbh* as a text that has been read through the poetics of devotion. But even the section dealing with the *Bhagavadgītā,* which occupies some ten minutes, is meant to establish precisely this latter-day Hindu devotional ideology. Also, since the *Mbh* is seen as a collective text, other texts and their values constantly invade it: a *bhakta* such as Hanumāna (the ideal devotee of the *Rāmāyaṇa*) makes his way into the text through his connection with his half brother Bhima. A notable instance of such discursive intrusion occurs in the context of the Draupadī *svayaṃvara.* When it becomes clear that no warrior has the necessary skills to perform the difficult feat of archery to win Draupadī's hand in marriage, her father says, "I am now convinced that my daughter will be a spinster for life." What in fact he is paraphrasing is more immediately from the Avadhi/Hindi *Rāmacaritamānasa* of Tulasīdāsa, the devotional "Bible" of the Hindi-belt: "likhā na vidhi vaidehi bibāhu" ("For it is written that my daughter will remain unmarried"). Gestures of this kind certainly take us back to what

Roland Barthes said was the ideal of the writerly text—a galaxy of signifiers with an open-ended plenitude of meaning (Barthes 1975: 3–16). Two other features should be noted here. The first is the extent to which this film version reflects the Indian spectator's own definition of cinema as the spectacle of the Imaginary. The hallucinatory power of this spectacle not only derails the intrinsically challenging nature of the narrative of the *Mbh* but also disfigures historical reality by parodying it. Thus in the Pāṇḍava palace of illusions we get examples of modern-day television, a grotesque dance sequence, and dialogue that belongs to the semiotics of Bombay cinema. The second feature that requires a gloss is the positing of the *Bhagavadgītā* in its quasi-monotheistic form as the interpretive text for the rest of the *Mbh*. This is signaled by the isolation of the *Bhagavadgītā* in the theme song of the film: "jis ne dī bhārat ko gītā vo mahābhārat kathā" ("I speak of the text that gave India the *Bhagavadgītā*"). In the ten-minute *Gītā* sequence the emphasis is on the idea of proper action insofar as that action befits a person's caste. Arjuna, the Kṣatriya, must therefore fight. But the extended argument of the *Gītā* proper is now rechanneled through Shakespeare's "Cowards die many times before their deaths, / The valiant never taste of death but once" (*Julius Caesar*, I, ii, 33–34). A version of postcolonial packaging is at work here. The Vedānta is now reread through the high texts of imperialism, and both, in the Indian film, feed upon one another. When such quasi-parodistic refashioning takes place, the self as writer becomes a strange amalgam of contradictory forces.

The Self That Reads: R. K. Narayan's *The Guide*

The distinctions that we continue to make between the four selves in the Indian context become more and more tenuous as we proceed. My insistence upon them is aimed at clarifying, however tangentially, the nature of the self in Indian culture by drawing attention, wherever possible, to differences, even though collapse and identity are the norm in Indian culture. I would now like to examine the self that reads with reference to a well-known Indian novel by R. K. Narayan and its filmic transformation by an equally well known popular film star and auteur Devanand. What interests me here are the ways in which the self is read. Although, in the cultural domain, the four selves are interdependent and should not be clearly demarcated (as this essay seems to be doing), I should nevertheless want to isolate the act of reading as a function of the interpreting self in Indian society. Assuming that the positions of the novelist qua novelist and filmmaker qua filmmaker may be deemed to be exemplary, a careful reading of the texts in question would at least draw us closer to the question of self-representation in this culture. How then do the novel and its film version negotiate this problematic?

Whereas the epic reached us in a completed generic form, the novel is a genre in the making. Its origins in bourgeois culture and its enormous plasticity allow materials from diverse discourses to be included within its overall form. This is more or less Bakhtin's argument, which seems to me to be appropriate in the context of the use of this form by the postcolonial Indian. "When the novel becomes the dominant genre, epistemology becomes the dominant discipline," writes Bakhtin (Bakhtin 1981:15). Theorizing about the self is clearly one of the central concerns of this discipline. With the alien form of the novel this theorization, in the Indian context, is now being done in ways that were not available to that culture prior to the entry of this artistic form. "The novel," wrote V. S. Naipaul, "is a form of social inquiry ... outside the Indian tradition" (Naipaul 1977:18–19). What strikes me so forcefully in R. K. Narayan's *The Guide* is the way in which the entire Hindu metanarrative of the self, which we have discussed above, is now redefined or processed through a genre where questions of self are, inevitably, related to radically different notions of selfhood and being. For what the novel introduces is subjectivity linked to a socioeconomic order, ironizing any earlier metanarrative and carving open domains of self not necessarily demonstrable through an age-old essentialism. If anything, this radical genre splits open the frozen domain of history and renders it meaningless in a world where labor has made metaphysics a commodity for which a different space must be found. It is possible then to see Narayan reading the self at two levels: the self as a grand metanarrative and the self as historically and socially constituted.

Let us look at the metanarrative first. Here the hero of the novel, Raju, would be defined as the self seeking *ātma-vidyā* in the course of his life. The narrative is pregiven, since the dharmic stages by which this may be achieved are clearly laid down by the culture itself. We could then map out Raju's attachment to Rosie as a failure on the part of the self to distinguish between maya, the phenomenal world we inhabit, and the real, which in this instance is not any socioeconomic base, as the Marxist "real," but the state of brahman-consciousness that the *Gītā* had defined as the merging of the self into Krishna: "I am the rite, I am the sacrifice ("aham krartur, aham yajñāh"), Krishna had said (van Buitenen 1981:104–5). Maya is then located in the "body" of Rosie the dancer, the *nartaki,* whose finest dance is the "snake dance." "She is a real snake woman," Raju's mother had warned (R. K. Narayan 1988 [1958]:136), suggesting that the dancer is really part of the world of illusion, which is designed to ensnare the self (Mishra 1979). Of course, Raju's self suffers as a consequence of his passion for the dancing girl, and his arrest for forgery (the ulti-mate sign of confusion of the self through writing as self-deception) occurs at precisely the moment Rosie performs her final item, the snake dance. What follows is arrest and imprisonment for two years. Re-lease takes Raju to a remote village where in spite of himself he be-comes a saint, sacrificing his life in the hope that the famine that had devastated the village would come to an end. Raju then transcends the world of unreality and unites with Brahman. As Radhakrishnan has pointed out:

> Works are vain and bind us firmly to this unreal cosmic process (*saṃsāra*), the endless chain of cause and effect. Only the wis-dom that the universal reality and the individual self are identical can bring us redemption. When this wisdom arises, the ego is dis-solved, the wandering ceases and we have perfect joy and blessed-ness. (Radhakrishnan 1963:16–17)

At the second level Narayan reads the metanarrative much more iron-ically, since the subtext here is precisely the ways in which the self is not so much governed by a grand metatext as a being whose conscious-ness is constantly being formed through very precise historical inter-actions. Furthermore, it is the psychosocial complexity of the self—its caste, social, and gendered difference—that makes the prescriptive application of a Brahmanical ideological system with no basis in the real impossible. For it soon becomes clear that Rosie's own past as a woman of the caste of temple dancers and her fascination with the snake dance are all carefully planted themes that self-consciously (for Narayan) invite comparisons with the grand metatext only to make her own radicality and difference so much more decisive. Rosie the low-caste dancer also defies the respectability of marriage to Marco and enters into an illicit relationship with Raju. And when Raju squanders her earnings in drinking and gambling, it is she who makes the break and leaves him, but not to return to Marco, as another definition of the Hindu woman would have demanded. And this is not because she is insensitive or cruel — she so much wanted to see Marco's book on the Malgudi caves — but because her own self, as woman, needed space for a more meaningful femininity. A similar reading of Raju is now available through the novelistic discourse, since the subject here is as much a construction of the very specific social formations of which he is a part. These formations would include the anxieties involved in earning a livelihood in India, the highly repressed nature of Hindu sexuality, the attractiveness of the world of glamour so powerfully endorsed by Indian commercial cinema, and so on. The subject Raju is thus formed by the metatext, as well as those forces that define the self in a capitalist world. Yet the way in which he captures the imagination of Velan, the villager, who reads even his confessional narrative as indicative of discourses that only enlightened individuals know, shows how in the culture the mantle of mahatma is thrust upon an individual in spite of the person's own protestations. The ironic parallels with Gandhi (the Mahatma) are far too obvious throughout the text. Narayan thus deconstructs prior definitions of the self by placing the subject in a novelistic framework. As we have said before, the self that reads here is thus a different self, and may well demonstrate the coexistence of two not necessarily complementary readings of the self. In the end, Narayan does not spell out the precise nature of Raju's spiritual achievement, leaving the efficacy of and need for it ambiguous.

Devanand's film version of *The Guide* was released in 1965, the same year in which *Mahābhārat* was also released. Called *Guide* (Hindi does not possess the definite article), the film's definition of the self is constructed out of two processes that seem to me to be structural invariants in this filmic practice (Mishra 1985). The first is the construction of the self as star, which, of course, necessitates the projection of an image that is extratextual, in the sense that it is constructed through all kinds of social texts and processes. The second is the primacy given to "essentialism" in cinema. Now the idea of essentialism works very effectively on both the personal level of actor and on the artistic level of character. *Guide* the film therefore cannot be prized out of the glamorous definition of self as actor projected by Devanand, the urbane and suave hero of the fifties and sixties. At this level no change takes place in the filmic transformation. Yet the source text, once foregrounded, cannot be ignored, and it is the novel that finally makes the film so very successful. One notes, for instance, the markedly realistic treatment of the scene dealing with the sudden arrival of the uncle from the village and the mother's decision to leave her house. At moments such as these, *Guide* does destabilize the essentialism of son-mother and wife-husband dharma. But not totally, since both the mother and mistress are made to return to the final scene of sainthood to be with the son/lover. The kinds of surplus value granted the mother or the constant mistress are again reinforced in the film. But so too is the confirmation of the final release and the experience of *mokṣa*. Even the gods are shamed by Raju's sacrifice, and there is a thunderous downpour at the moment of his death. Release for Raju is also comfort for mother, mistress, and villagers: their happiness lies in the ultimate endorsement of selfless karma (the karma that seeks no gain) in the person of Raju.

Yet the *ahaṃkāra,* the very I-ness that the novel had eschewed, rears its head in the form of an almost direct equation, through a number of images, of the identity of the hero, Raju/Devanand, with Krishna himself. The text of the *Bhagavadgītā*, in a highly truncated form, surfaces as a dialogue between the two selves of Raju as alternately Krishna and Arjuna. This is an interesting process, since the dialogue itself tells us that *ahaṃkāra* (ego) must be denied. "Only the *ātman* is eternal, only I.... You are *ahaṃkāra,* you must die," says the good angel in the dream sequence. Yet the film fails to distance the two and ends up endorsing *ahaṃkāra* while at the same time renouncing it. As I have said, this contradiction arises from the demands of the star personality, who must also occupy the heroic space that, in this case, really belongs to Krishna. The last words, again spoken by Raju's now spiritual self, are "Only I, only I," suggesting that Raju/Devanand has unproblematically entered the bliss of Brahman. My worry here is not so much with the confirmation of the Hindu spiritual worldview as with the identity of the actor with the enlightened being. I suppose this is largely because Devanand remains, finally, Devanand and does not distance his role from his status as star. Film, the product of mechanical reproduction (and technically antiauratic, since it has no "aura" of the original text because it can be endlessly reproduced), in India finally reads the self in the way in which Brahmanical culture wants it to read it.

The Self That Reads Itself: Gandhi's Autobiography

"Whatever else it may be, autobiography is the least reliable of genres," writes Roger Rosenblatt (in Olney 1980:169). It is also, in the West, a largely self-reflexive discourse that can be both factual and critical: the self criticizes itself in the act of writing, an extremely important fact in itself. As Michael Sprinkler has observed "Autobiography, the inquiry of the self into its own origin and history, is always circumscribed by the limiting conditions of writing" (in Olney 1980:342). When we examine the nature of the Indian self that reads itself (our fourth type of self), autobiography is the natural genre to choose, and in this genre, what better writer than the Mahatma himself? What we will be particularly interested in are the ways in which the writing of an autobiography places in relief the analytical faculties of the Indian mind, especially insofar as that mind must now present to public scrutiny a self that has already come, at least outwardly, fully formed or at least convinced that the route to that complete transformation of the self has been clearly laid out before him or her. The dharmic metatext establishes a particular trajectory of being and insists upon a narrative linearity (as in the narrative that subtends *The Guide*) that is pregiven. Anything that contradicts this totality or this dharma is ruthlessly repressed. And through this repression the self disavows what are quite natural functions of the ego: cheating, sex, envy, power, and so on. We must therefore be willing to read against the grain, to bring to the center that which has been marginalized or deflected, and we must be conscious of the mechanisms employed by Gandhi to write in this seemingly homogeneous discourse.

Gandhi's autobiography, entitled *The Story of My Experiments with Truth*, stresses the key words "my" and "truth." But "my" and "truth" are presented throughout not as culturally constituted subjects (which is what all selves in fact are) but as a valorization of the self through the categories of the Hindu metanarrative. "Truth," an individual's personal endeavor, is quickly written in the code of the stages by which *mokṣa* may be realized. Truth becomes a stand-in for *mokṣa* as the latter effortlessly displaces the former. What V. S. Naipaul detected was a sense of intense absorption, an incapacity to write fiction, to let representation of the outer world color concentration on the inner world, is in fact nothing less than a writing practice that is part of a very Hindu structure of thought. This reading of the autobiography may be readily demonstrated with reference to a passage in the text in which a Sanskrit verse is quoted, followed by a translation and a gloss. The passage occurs at the end of the chapter in which Gandhi takes the vow of *brahmacārya* at the age of thirty-seven in 1906.

> viṣaya vinivartante nirāharasya dehinaḥ
> rasavarja raso[a]pyasya param dṛṣṭvā nivartate

> "The sense-objects turn away from an abstemious soul, leaving the relish behind. The relish also disappears with the realization of the Highest." Therefore His name and His grace are the last resources of the aspirant after *moksha*. The truth came to me only after my return to India. (Gandhi 1959 [1927]:154)

The key word here is *nirāharasya*, literally "who eats no more" (Zaehner 1969:152), but at this point in the *Bhagavadgītā* (from which the passage is taken) the basic Upanishadic theology of the *Gītā* is being radically altered by Buddhist thought. Both Śaṅkara and Rāmānuja, the greatest of the commentators on the *Gītā*, read the noun *āhara* to mean not "food" but "objects of the senses." Gandhi adopts this reading in his translation, but for us the reading and the citation of this particular verse from a host of others demonstrate once again the extent to which the world as representation is overtaken by what may be called, although not in the strict sense in which Schopenhauer used the term, the world as "will." The emphasis is on the denial of sense perceptions for the discovery of the inner principle of being. Hence Naipaul's incisive observation about Gandhi's skeletal text when it comes to describing his experiences as a novelist would: "Gandhi would have had no means of describing what he saw at Southampton on arrival" (Naipaul 1977:103). Here are the sections that Naipaul isolates from the chapter entitled "In London at Last":

> I did not feel at all sea-sick.... I was innocent of the use of knives and forks.... I therefore never took meals at table but always had them in my cabin, and they consisted principally of sweets and fruits I had brought with me.... We entered the Bay of Biscay, but I did not begin to feel the need either of meat or liquor.... However, we reached Southampton, as far as I remember, on a

Saturday. On the boat I had worn a black suit, the white flannel one, which my friends had got me, having been kept especially for wearing when I landed. I had thought that white clothes would suit me better when I stepped ashore, and therefore I did so in white flannels. Those were the last days of September, and I found I was the only person wearing such clothes. (Naipaul 1977:98; Gandhi 1959 [1927]:31–32)

The self that emerges in these lines is framed by an inner contemplation, fueled by vows Gandhi had made to his mother—no sex, no meat, no liquor—and therefore essentially melancholic. But melancholy, as in the literature of sentimentalism, can also undertake realistic representation: the outer world is still described, although distorted by the confusion within. Later in the chapters on London, a similar lack of description is found. The world is meaningful in terms of deeds and actions or in terms of impediments that must be surmounted. The world as it is, with its complex social formations, is of no consequence to the self that reads itself. "It is the Indian way of experiencing," writes Naipaul (1977:101), and I think there is a lot of truth in this.

Throughout the autobiography there is then a willed silence about general ideology. It is personal ideology and intense contemplation about the self, without the kind of constant self-critique the genre requires (both Augustine and Rousseau, the great precursors of this form, emphasized self-reflexivity), that we find in Gandhi. For what the various experiments with truth demonstrate, finally, is not the fractured, searching self, a self conscious of its own massive contradictions, but one that achieves a kind of perfection by reinscribing the self into the metanarrative of the Hindu world order. Hence the lengthy discourses on vegetarianism and fruitarianism, on sexual abstinence and cleanliness, on the correct path to *mokṣa* (the vow of *brahmacārya* was demanded by the genre) are all part of the symbolic system of cultural behavior that defines the self. By a master stroke Gandhi reinscribes his self in the autobiography in the generic system of Brahmanical hagiography (although he himself was not a Brahman) and in doing so becomes quite literally the *mahā ātma,* the enlightened soul who has achieved *mokṣa.* The transformation was also a brilliant political stroke, even one of genius, since his life galvanized an entire Hindu world behind him. But in the process the secularism of autobiography (like the novel, it too has become a highly secular form in modern times) is sacrificed. The immense analytical capacities of the form, too—its incisiveness, its contradictions, its search for the self in the material world—are lost. Almost in spite of his humility and claims to selflessness, the self that returns as a relic of the repressed is in fact *ahaṃkārik.*

It was, however, in South Africa that Gandhi came face to face with the truism that the self is culturally constituted. In the first instance Gandhi's self was fashioned in this highly racist society through a largely Hegelian master-slave dialectic (Hegel 1977:111–19). The social representation of this fact at least made Gandhi aware of the role and function of power in the construction of the self. But the second, even more important insight that Gandhi gained came straight out of his relationship with the indentured Indians of South Africa with whom he spent some twenty years. By the time he left for India in 1914 Gandhi's personality was fully formed. What that relationship led to was a decisive awareness of the self-as-Indian, a definition that was alien to an Indian, for whom the self was framed by caste and religion. For most Indians, being an Indian was largely irrelevant because the word Indian didn't even exist in their everyday discourses. The dharmic code had no way of handling the relationship between the self and ethnicity. But in South Africa all indentured laborers, regardless of their caste or religious affiliations, were Indian coolies. The term "Indian" became identical with a collective self, a self that had to be defended as a kind of a body politic because its defense was also the defense of the self. This definition of the Indian, which is really postcolonial, is what Gandhi inherited, and therein lay his strength. Of all the nationalist leaders in India, Gandhi alone knew what it was like to be an Indian, since he had been one in South Africa for twenty years. But it is a knowledge about which Gandhi remained silent. He does not retheorize the self in terms of either the "Indian" (as a racial group) or in terms of the African other (Africans are conspicuous by their absence throughout his autobiography). The immense absorption into himself led to a form of writing from which extended descriptions of people or landscape are always excised.

"The outer world matters only in so far as it affects the inner" (Naipaul 1977:101). This is Naipaul's judgment on Gandhi's autobiography, because in it the Indian idea of the self always intrudes as a kind of a transcendental principle and constructs a ghostly text alongside the writing itself. To write about the self, to construct the self that reads itself, is to write in the shadow of a metanarrative that lays down its own fantastic categories. It is this that led European thinkers, from Hegel to Oldenberg, to read Indian culture as peculiarly devoid of any historical sense. But what the reading overlooked was precisely the complex constructions of the self in India and the ways in which the self represents itself in the world at large. The case of Gandhi is exemplary in this regard, since any one of the four types of self discussed in this chapter could just as easily be discussed with reference to his autobiography. But in refusing to deconstruct that self through a materialist critique, the Mahatma avoided a more significant form of writing found in contemporaries like R. K. Narayan and before him in the earlier epic poets. The kinds of mediated selves that we have seen in our literary texts—in Vyāsa, Jayadeva, and R. K. Narayan for instance—are clearly missing from the Indian self that reads its own self through the act of autobiographical writing. Instead what triumphs yet again in the example of Gandhi is not the self but the metatext as self.

Conclusion: Fashioned Selves

Let us return to the project of the Enlightenment as the starting point of these concluding remarks. One of the consequences of this project was that the self was fashioned around the concept of autonomous individual growth through categories of reason. Individualism was prized because it led to progress toward an almost universal (the Enlightenment's own) concept of the self. Others—those who had not received the benefits of European civilization, for instance—could only strive toward this goal of intellectual self-sufficiency and autonomy. At the turn of the century, however, a "new ethnographic conception of culture" (Clifford 1988:93) began to show that a plurality of equally valid cultural subjects was just as important a concept. Cultural relativity, in short, began to threaten cultural essentialism. James Clifford cites an important passage from Nietzsche that we could also put to good strategic use: "What then is truth? A mobile army of metaphors, metonyms, and anthropomorphisms—in short, a sum of human relations, which have been enhanced, transposed, and embellished poetically and rhetorically, and which after long use seem firm, canonical, and obligatory to people" (quoted in Clifford 1988:93). Reappropriated toward our own critique we may use this to indicate the manner in which the Hindu self is rhetorically constructed. In Gandhi's autobiography truth as discourse is not countenanced (and therefore not relativized) because the essentialism of the Hindu world order could not survive such an onslaught. This is not a value-judgment about Hindu constructions of the self vis-à-vis that of the European Enlightenment. On the contrary, it is a statement about how even a Gandhi was conscious of the idea of the self as an already formed "metatext" into which the "I" slots its meditations about selfhood. In a significant way this observation is in itself an endorsement of cultural relativity, since we are not suggesting that there is anything unenlightened about the Indian conception of the self. On the contrary, and in a paradoxical manner, this very relativity draws us remorselessly toward the dangers of an Indian self conceived in the uncritical shadows of a Hindu essentialism where the self is pregiven and transdiscursive even though it can manifest itself only through "writing." It is this double bind that must be grasped in any definition of the self so as to avoid its collapse into the European's other (the Oriental), in terms of which the Enlightenment self was constructed in the first instance. And this too is really another version of the postmodern dilemma. Do we accept all selves as being equally validly constructed and equally valuable, or do we, as Habermas would insist, seek out those implicit concerns of reason and intellect that would avoid the kinds of excesses that may feed into fascist or anarchist practices?

The emphasis on the metatexts and our choice of literary and filmic evidence as departure points for an examination of the Indian self should not be seen as an endorsement of selves in India as always "memorially constructed." But the fact remains—and I owe this observation to James Clifford once again—that the reading of another culture and its norms (or more narrowly the culture's representations of the self) is marked by levels of ambiguity and contradiction that make problematic the truism of cultural relativity itself. In other words, this truism is a creation that glosses over fractures that exist both in the collective informants of the culture under investigation (the four types, or informants, discussed in this paper), as well as in the personality of the investigator. I have probably oversimplified the issue, but in very general terms what I am saying is that the complex attitude that the self as critic and ethnographer maintains toward "fashioned selves" is after all a reflection of the discourses on self and identity that are available to him or her. Although ethnographic discourse "portrays other selves as culturally constituted," writes Clifford, "it also fashions an identity authorized to represent, to interpret, even to believe—but always with some irony—the truths of discrepant worlds" (Clifford 1988:94). This fashioning of an authorized self carries with it the imprint of the person who fashions them in the first instance. Any analysis of the self is therefore as much autobiographical as anything else, and this essay is no exception. Like Malinowksi, any theorist of self and culture must await his or her Conrad before he or she can construct a self, like Marlow, "positioned to mediate between discrepant worlds of meaning" (Clifford 1988:113). For those of us who are much less accomplished, we can only map out the contradictions in the culture and leave others to make the definitive statement—if that is at all possible. After all, the starting point of this investigation has been my own self.

References

Bakhtin, Mikhail. 1981. *The Dialogic Imagination*. Translated by Caryl Emerson and Michael Holquist. Austin: University of Texas Press.

Barthes, Roland. 1975. *S/Z*. Translated by Richard Miller. London: Jonathan Cape.

Brook, Peter. 1988. *The Mahābhārata*. Boya Quarry Performance, February 6, 1988, Perth, Western Australia.

Buitenen, J. A. B. van, trans. 1973–78. *The Mahābhārata, Books 1–5*. 3 vols. Chicago: University of Chicago Press.

———. 1981. *The Bhagavadgītā in the Mahābhārata: Text and Translation*. Chicago: University of Chicago Press.

Carrière, Jean-Claude. 1987. *The Mahābhārata: A Play Based upon the Indian Classic Epic*. Translated by Peter Brook. New York: Harper and Row.

Clifford, James. 1988. *The Predicament of Culture*. Cambridge, Mass.: Harvard University Press.

Dasgupta, S. 1976. *Obscure Religious Cults*. Calcutta: Firma KLM Private Limited.

de Man, Paul. 1983. *Blindness and Insight*. London: Methuen.

Foucault, Michel. 1974. *The Order of Things*. London: Tavistock Publications.

———. 1980. "What Is an Author?" In *Textual Strategies*, edited by Josué V. Harari. London: Methuen.

Freud, Sigmund. 1985 [1930]. *Civilization and Its Discontents*. Vol. 12 of *The Pelican Freud Library*. Harmondsworth: Penguin Books.

Gandhi, M. K. 1959 [1927]. *The Story of My Experiments with Truth*. Translated by Mahadev Desai. Ahmedabad: Navajivan Trust.

Habermas, Jürgen. 1987. *The Philosophical Discourse of Modernity*. Translated by Frederick Lawrence. Cambridge: Polity Press.

———. 1988. *Legitimation Crisis*. Translated by Thomas McCarthy. Cambridge: Polity Press.

Harari, Josué, ed. *Textual Strategies*. London: Methuen.

Hegel, G. W. F. 1977. *Phenomenology of Spirit*. Translated by A. V. Miller. Oxford: Clarendon Press.

Hopkins, E. W. 1968 [1915]. *Epic Mythology.* Varanasi: Indological Book House.

Kakar, Sudhir. 1981. *The Inner World.* Delhi: Oxford University Press.

Katz, Ruth Cecily. 1989. *Arjuna in the Mahābhārata.* Columbia: University of South Carolina Press.

Lyotard, Jean-François. 1986. *The Postmodern Condition.* Translated by Geoff Bennington and Brian Massumi. Manchester: Manchester University Press.

Masson, J. Moussaieff. 1980. *The Oceanic Feeling.* Dordrecht: Reidel.

Mehta, Ved. 1977. *Mahatma Gandhi and His Apostles.* Harmondsworth: Penguin Books.

Miller, Barbara Stoler. 1977. *Love Song of the Dark Lord Jayadeva's* Gītagovinda. New York: Columbia University Press.

———. 1986. *The Bhagavadgītā.* New York: Bantam Books.

Mishra, Vijay. 1979. "The Dialectic of Māyā and Principles of Narrative Structure in Indian Literature." *ACLALS Bulletin,* 5th series, 2:47–60.

———. 1985. "Towards a Theoretical Critique of Bombay Cinema." *Screen* 26(3–4):133–46.

———. 1988. "The Great Indian Epic and Peter Brook," *Meanjin* 47(2):343–52.

Monier-Williams, M. 1976 [1899]. *Sanskrit—English Dictionary.* New Delhi: Munshiram Manoharlal.

Naipaul, V. S. 1977. *India: A Wounded Civilization.* London: Andre Deutsch.

———. 1990. *India: A Million Mutinies Now.* London: Heinemann.

Narayan, R. K. 1988 [1958]. *The Guide.* Harmondsworth: Penguin Books.

Olney, James, ed. 1980. *Autobiography: Essays Theoretical and Critical.* Princeton, N.J.: Princeton University Press.

Radhakrishnan, S. 1963. *The Bhagavadgītā.* London: Allen and Unwin.

Raghavan, V. 1978. *Bhoja's* Śṛngāra Prakāśa. Madras: Theosophical Society.

Rorty, Richard. 1985. "Habermas and Lyotard on Postmodernity." In *Habermas and Modernity,* ed. Richard J. Bernstein. Cambridge: Polity Press.

Siegel, Lee. 1978. *Sacred and Profane Dimensions of Love in Indian Traditions as Exemplified in the* Gītagovinda *of Jayadeva.* Delhi: Oxford University Press.

Sukthantar, V. S., et al. 1933–72. *The Mahābhārata* (Poona critical edition). 19 vols. Poona: Bhandarkar Research Institute.

Sullivan, Bruce M. 1990. *Kṛṣṇa Dvaipāyāna Vyāsa and the* Mahābhārata: A New Interpretation. Leiden: Brill.

Zaehner, R. C., trans. 1969. *The Bhagavadgītā.* Oxford: Oxford University Press.

7 / Selves and Others in Japanese Culture in Historical Perspective

Emiko Ohnuki-Tierney

For this volume on the self of China, India and Japan, I have chosen the concept of self (selves) and other (others) of the Japanese[1] and its symbolic expressions through a twin metaphor of rice and rice paddies.[2] I try to show how the construction and the reconstruction of the self of the Japanese have always taken place through their discourse with different peoples, using the metaphors of rice and rice paddies as the vehicles of thought in these processes. I also argue that the collective self of the agrarian Japanese, as expressed in "Rice as Self," has involved a historical process whereby internal others, that is, minorities, have been formed. While the dominant agrarian Japanese were anchored, as it were, in rice paddies, the social groups that were marginalized were *non*settled populations, who after the medieval period were forced to settle in stigmatized "settlements" and "reservations." Indeed, the collective self as expressed in the agrarian cosmology-turned-ideology of "rice as self" is a product of the dialectic between the self and external others, on the one hand, and internal others, on the other.

For this process of dialectic differentiation and representation of self and other, important foods, such as staple foods, often play a powerful role—the wheat-eating people in northern India versus rice-eating south Indians, the dark bread of peasants versus the white bread of upper-class people in past centuries in Europe, and the sorghum of the Pende contrasted with the maize of the Mbuun in nineteenth-century central Africa (Vansina 1978:117). For the Japanese, rice, or more appropriately rices, have played a major role in their deliberations upon their own identity in relation to other peoples.

It is highly significant to note that only after World War II did scholars begin to question the "unquestionable historical fact" that rice had been the staple food, that is, quantitatively the most important food, of the Japanese since its introduction to Japan. "Agrarian Japan" constructed a false picture, as if all Japanese were farmers, thereby writing off the presence throughout history of all nonagrarian populations. These scholars, who consider that a rice diet was limited to the upper class throughout most of Japanese history, nonetheless recognize its crucial symbolic significance for most Japanese—its place in cosmology and its role in rituals and daily life.

The purpose of this article is to show how the Japanese notion of the self has taken a different contour as a different historical other has emerged, and how the Japanese, as *homo significans,* have used rice as the vehicle of their thought in these processes.

While it is easy to understand how people conceptualize themselves as a single collective self in their encounter with other people, it is a far more taxing question to understand how a particular mode of representation has been chosen, since there are a number of contesting modes of representation and multiple voices in any social group. In fact, now that anthropologists have become acutely aware of the multiplicity within any social group, the term "contested" or "contesting" is an adjective that appears in book or article titles with great frequency. Japanese culture and society too have always been heterogeneous, as I delineated in my earlier work (Ohnuki-Tierney 1987). A study of rice as a metaphor of the Japanese self, then, involves a question of *how* rice has become a dominant metaphor of the Japanese, since there has always been a large segment of the population who engaged in occupations other than rice agriculture, and, as noted above, rice has not been a quantitatively important source of food for a large segment of the Japanese population. In a broader framework, it is a question of the development of a powerful representation of self by the people themselves, on the one hand, and of how to reconcile a dominant representation with apparent multiplicity within a culture, on the other hand. How does a certain representation become strategic, and how does it acquire the power to naturalize its significance?

The question then is also the role it has played in the establishment of the synecdochic "we," whereby a part—in this case agrarian sectors of the Japanese—represents the whole, the entirety of Japanese population (Ohnuki-Tierney 1990b).

It is too easy to conclude that it is a case of powerful individuals instituting a certain structure of meaning that the rest of the population blindly adopts. To simply invoke notions such as "false consciousness," "mystification," "hegemony," or even the "naturalization" process is to evade confronting the questions and to ignore culture-specific meanings and particular historical processes. Nor can the answer be found in the reduction of culture into a composite of as many views as there are members of the society; society or culture cannot be reduced to individuals.

In order to have at least some glimpse into the processes whereby rice has served as a metaphor of the self for the Japanese, I have chosen to examine the meanings of rice in Japanese cosmology, as well as day-to-day behaviors. I have done so by considering archaeological, protohistorical, and historical periods, an approach originally advocated by the *Annales* scholar Fernand Braudel, who, however, gave pride of place to ecological and geographical factors. Although the extension of this long-term approach to a study of *mentalités* has not been altogether successful (see Chartier 1982; Hunt 1986), this approach has an extraordinary advantage in enabling us to understand the historical changes as processes and not as a series of snapshots.[3]

The Self and the Other

In anthropology, since the time of Mauss, the concept of self has been a perennial concern. Mauss's (1985 [1938]) own vision was in part evolutionary, with the transformation of the *personnage* (role) in primitive holism into the *personne* (self) characterizing modern individualism, with the *moi* (awareness of self) as a human universal. While rejecting cultural evolution, Dumont (1970, 1977, 1986) posits the great divide between tribal and Western modern societies, and Charles Taylor, as explicated by Owen Lynch in this volume, stresses the agent and significances intrinsic to the agents.

While many anthropologists would espouse neither the Maussian evolutionary approach nor the Dumontian divide between the Western and modern versus the rest of the world, whatever we may call them (for a critique of the label for the latter, see Augé 1982:10–11; Cohn 1980:211), we have a long tradition of attempting to understand the self, personhood, and related conceptions in a given culture. If we accept that the concept of self is culturally construed, it is important to note that, as with all meanings, the concept of self is construed contextually.

Within a social group, the self of the individual is not a replica of the collective self. Thus, "contesting" and "contested" are terms that appear frequently in describing the selves of individuals in a social group whose interests and consciousnesses differ from those of others. In this sense, in anthropology we have rejected a totalizing label of, for example, "we, the Japanese."

On the other hand, it is a commonsensical understanding that when a social group is juxtaposed against another, each group constitutes a collective self. In fact, at the core of ethnicity and nationalism, which have become central concerns in anthropology and related fields, lies the notion of the collective self vis-à-vis the other.[4] Thus various selves of a social group become irrelevant when they conceptualize themselves in relation to other peoples. These two types of approaches to the self must be analytically distinguished. For any social group, as with the Japanese, the conception of self and other is deeply embedded in cosmology.

Deities as the Other

A predominant interpretation of Japanese deities among contemporary scholars is that from the earliest times they have been characterized by a dual nature and power — the peaceful soul (*nigimitama*), which is good and creative, and the violent soul (*aramitama*), which is evil and destructive. These deities, called *marebito*,[5] were gods in ancient Japan who periodically visited the villages from a world located on the other side of the sea where aging and death were unknown, bringing good luck if treated well by villagers and calamities if mistreated.

I propose that from the perspective of reflexivity, the *marebito*, or stranger deities who come from outside a settlement or outside of Japan, constitute the *other* for the Japanese. Objectified as a semiotic sign, it is the *reflexive self*. It is for this reason, I think, that Japanese deities are symbolized as mirrors (Ohnuki-Tierney 1987:135–36, 1993b:54–55; Ishibashi 1914; Nakayama 1976). The dual nature of *marebito* deities is therefore a projection of the dual qualities that the Japanese see in themselves.

Rice as Deities

Japanese deities are embodied in beings of the universe, among which rice occupies a central place. Fundamental to the meanings assigned to rice in Japanese culture and in most other cultures that use rice as a "staple food" is a belief in the soul (*inadama* or *inadamashii*), therefore life, in each grain. Called *Ukano Kami,* the soul of the rice grain is clearly identified as a female deity (*kami*) (Yanagita 1982a) who is closely related to major deities involved in the creation of the Japanese universe (see also Itoh 1979, 1988).

The eighth-century myth-histories of the *Kojiki* and the *Nihongi* are replete with references to rice as deities. In one version in the *Kojiki,* Amaterasu (the Sun Goddess) is the mother of a grain soul whose name bears reference to rice stalks. Thus the legendary Jinmu Emperor, the so-called "first" emperor, is the son of the grain soul and, therefore, the grandson of Amaterasu, who sent him to rule the earth—an episode referred to in the *Kojiki* and the *Nihonshoki* as the descent of the heavenly grandson (*tenson kōrin*).[6] At the time of his descent Amaterasu gives her grandson the original rice grains that she has grown in the two fields in Heaven (Takamagahara) from the seeds of the five types of grains (*gokoku*) given to her by Ukemochi no Kami, the deity in charge of food (Kurano and Takeda 1958; see also Murakami 1977:13). The grandson of Amaterasu transforms a wilderness into a land of rice stalks with succulent ears of rice (*mizuho*) and abundant grains of five types (*gokoku*), thanks to the original seeds given to him by Amaterasu, whose ray nurtures rice and other plants (see Ohnuki-Tierney 1991).

Unlike creation myths that explain how the universe was created, this version of the Japanese creation myth is not about the creation of a universe but about the transformation of wilderness (*ashihara no nakatsu no kuni*) into a land of abundant rice at the command, according to the *Kojiki,* of Amaterasu, whose descendants, the emperors, rule the country by officiating at the rice harvest rituals (Kawasoe 1980:86; Saigō 1984:15–29).

I suggest that the soul of rice grain is not simply equivalent to deities but is identified more specifically as the *nigimitama,* the positive power of divine purity. It is relevant to note here that while most deities have dual qualities and powers, the Deity of the Rice Paddy has only the *nigimitama,* or peaceful soul. In fact, drought and flood, which destroy rice paddies, are acts of the *Mizu no Kami* (Water Deity) rather than expressions of an *aramitama* (violent spirit) in the Deity of the Rice Paddy.

I therefore see the following symbolic equivalents as crucial to an understanding of the cosmological significance of rice: rice = soul = deity = the *nigimitama* (peaceful and positive power of the deity).

Since human life wanes unless the positive principle replenishes its energy, humans and their communities must rejuvenate themselves by harnessing the positive power of the deities. This can be accomplished in two ways: by performing a ritual or by eating rice. Through the consumption of rice, the Japanese internalize the divine power, which then becomes part of the human body and its growth. Alternatively, they must remove their own impurity by creating scapegoats, as we shall see later.

Rice as Food for Commensality in Daily Lives

The cooperative effort required of rice cultivation in general and especially the intense cooperation to produce enough rice for taxes were certainly means whereby the members of a social group — family and community — came to identify themselves with a group. "Rice paddies" were a spatial symbol of group identity. But even more important for this role were rice and rice products. As a source for sacred energy and power, rice, rice cakes, and rice wine have been the single most important food for commensality between humans and deities, on the one hand, and among humans, on the other (Yanagita 1982b). For farmers, agricultural rituals have always been times when relatives residing elsewhere gather to dine and drink together. Today this is often the only occasion when young family members working in cities come back home to rural areas to participate in the ritual and partake of the accompanying commensality. The New Year's celebration in contemporary Japan is a nationwide ritual during which mirror-rice cakes (*kagamimochi*) are offered to the deities, and then shared among humans. Because the mirror represents the deities, these rice cakes embody the souls of rice and thus are thought to give power to those who consume them (Yanagita 1951:94–95). Not only during ritual occasions, but in the day-to-day lives of the Japanese, rice and rice products serve a crucial role in commensal activities.[7] As a mark of commensality between supernaturals and humans, the daily offering to the family ancestral alcove continues to be cooked white rice. Also, rice is the only food shared at meals, served by the female head of the household, while other dishes are placed in individual containers. This important role is symbolically expressed by the wooden spatula used to scoop rice, which in the past, in some "areas of Japan," was transmitted from the older head of the house to the next in a ritual (Nōda 1943:52–56; Yanagita 1951:264–65).

Rice stands for "we," that is, whatever social group one belongs to. But to give one example among many expressions, "To eat from the same rice-cooking pan [*onajikama no meshi o kuu*]" is a common expression for close human relationships and emphasizes a strong sense of fellowship arising from the notion that they share meals. If you eat together, you are members of the same social group; you become "we" as opposed to "they."

Commonly used expressions today, such as "to eat cold rice [*hiya-meshi o kuu*]," and "to eat someone else's rice [*tanin no meshi o kuu*]," refer to the opposite situation. Unless used as sushi or *onigiri* (rice balls), rice must be served hot. Thus, these expressions refer to the ill fortune of having to go through hardships among strangers. This experience is said to strengthen character, especially among males.

While rice and the rice spatula symbolize commensality within the household, wine (sake) is the most important item of commensality in social settings, especially among men. A basic rule of social sake drinking is that one never pours sake for oneself—one pours it for someone else, who in turn pours sake into one's own sake cup in a never-ending series of taking turns. The phrase "drinking alone" (*hi-torizake*) is an expression for loneliness—there is nothing lonelier than having to pour one's own sake. Unlike the case in some Western cultures in which the independent and autonomous self is regarded as the ideal model of personhood, in Japanese culture the *social* self does not exist without the *social* other, and the *social* self is always dialogically defined in relation to the other in a given social context. A lone individual who must pour his or her own sake is on the verge of becoming nonself.

Rice as Nature, Rice as Past, Rice as Primordial Self

There is another important dimension for rice as the source of evocative power—rice and rice paddies representing "Japanese time and space" — that is, "nature" and, ultimately, the primordial Japanese self. Although the valorization of countryside, epitomized in rice paddies, began earlier, we see its systematic development during the Edo period, when Edo (Tokyo) became an urban center. Nowhere is the construction of countryside more vividly depicted than in woodblock prints (*ukiyoe*) of the time, although the masters of these paintings were more likely agents of consumption and dissemination than of the construction of agrarianism.

For example, in the famous illustrations by Hokusai (1760–1849) for *One Hundred Poems by One Hundred Poets*,[8] the most common motif by far relates to rice and rice agriculture, such as rice farmers at work, sheaves of harvested rice, and flooded rice paddies, comprising twenty-six prints out of eighty-nine.[9] Similar motifs of harvested rice fields, flooded rice paddies, bundles of rice (*komedawara*), and rice sheaves appear in the woodblock prints by Andō (Utakawa) Hiroshige (1797–1858) in his *Fifty-Three Stations along the Tōkaidō (Tōkaidō gojū-san tsugi)* (Gotō 1975).[10]

The recurrent motifs of rice and rice agriculture in these prints represent not rice and rice agriculture per se, but something more. At the most obvious level, they signal seasons of the year. Flooded rice fields, like rice-planting songs, are the most familiar sign of spring or early summer; it is the time of birth and growth. Rice harvesting scenes, including sheaves of rice stalks — the most frequently used motif — represent fall and its joyful harvest, the end of the growing season. What is striking from the perspective of representation is that these cycles of rice growth became markers of the seasons for all Japanese. The lives of urbanites, fishermen, and all other nonagrarian people were also marked by rice and its growth.

At a more abstract level, travelers depicted in these woodblocks symbolize the transient and changing Japan epitomized by Edo (Tokyo), where both roads (Tōkaidō and Kisokaidō) lead. In contrast, rice and rice agriculture in the prints stand for Japan in its pristine unchanging form. Far from the "reality" of mud, sweat, and fertilizer, rice agriculture was valorized into aesthetics, in much the same way that rural France and peasants were idealized by Monet, Millet, and other French impressionists (see Brettell and Brettell 1983).

Inherent in the representations of landscape and subsistence activities are temporal representations. In addition to the representation of the seasonal cycle, agriculture symbolizes the past. As in many cultures, the pristine past embodying a distinct and sacred Japanese identity, uninfluenced by foreign influences and modernity, represented by the city, is symbolized in the reconstituted agriculture and the rural. The valorization of the primordial self of the Japanese symbolized in agriculture saw heightened expressions by intellectuals during the late Edo period (Harootunian 1988:23) and through the Meiji period (Gluck 1985:175, 181), and continues today when the Japanese search for *nature* in the countryside, now nostalgically referred to as *furusato* (old homestead; literally, one's home region), just as the English urbanites construct their "English countryside" (Newby 1979; R. Williams 1973).

In sum, involved in this internal historical processes are symbolic expressions of Japanese land — rice paddies, ancestral land for rice cultivation, family farm land, and, ultimately, *pristine nature,* which from a temporal perspective, stands for the *pristine past,* the Japanese time before its purity became contaminated by modernity and Western influences. Rice paddies stand for the ultimate symbol of Japan in its purest form.

Selves and Others in Historical Conjunctures

The above structure of reflexivity offered a model for the Japanese to interpret other peoples they encountered throughout history. Contrary to the anthropological myth, few peoples have lived in isolated pockets insulated from historical flows of peoples and goods. Intensive interaction among peoples through trade, warfare, colonialism, religion, and so on, is a familiar historical picture in any part of the world. An encounter with another people, directly or indirectly through an exchange of cultural artifacts and institutions, often prompts people to think about who they are in relation to other groups.

Contrary to the stereotype of Japan as an isolated country tucked away in the northeast corner of the world, Japan's history is a series of conjunctures during which internal developments were to a large degree responses to flows in world history. These conjunctures have been interpreted through the lens of the Japanese structure of self and other, and they in turn forced the Japanese to repeatedly reconceptualize their notion of self. More specifically, the stranger-deities provided the model to interpret peoples and forces from outside. The

model propelled the Japanese to reach for the *transcendent other*—
to imitate and then surpass the superior qualities of the Chinese and
Westerners, whether a writing system, the arts, or technology and
science.

Of all the conjunctures, the two that sent the most profound and
lasting shock waves throughout the country were Japan's encounter
with the high civilization of Tang China between the fifth and seventh
centuries and the encounter with Western civilization at the end of
the nineteenth century. In both cases, the Japanese were overwhelmed
by the civilizations "out there" and hurriedly and earnestly attempted
to learn about and imitate them. The heretofore illiterate Japanese
adopted en masse the Chinese writing system, even though the two
spoken languages were totally unrelated and thus not transferable
without considerable difficulty. Likewise, metallurgy, city planning,
and a whole range of other features of Chinese civilization were eagerly adopted by the Japanese, who nonetheless strenuously resisted
Chinese civilization in their chauvinistic effort to protect their own
Japanese culture and their self (Pollack 1986).

When the country reopened at the end of the nineteenth century
after three centuries of isolation, it again went through the painful
experience of encountering another "superior" civilization, this time
the West, with its scientific and technological advances. Once more,
the Japanese avidly adopted aspects of this civilization, while again
guarding their own Japanese identity and self. By this time, China had
suffered internal and external conflicts and had declined in international standing. The West thus replaced China as the transcendental
other in whom "Japan sought its own image" (Pollack 1986:53).

In the discourse of self and other, rice has served as a powerful vehicle for the Japanese to think about themselves in relation to other
peoples.

Chinese Rice, Japanese Rice

Despite the eagerness with which the Japanese, beginning in the fifth
century, adopted features of Chinese civilization, the Japanese self
could not simply be merged with that of the Chinese. In an effort to
redefine Japanese identity, in addition to appropriating rice agriculture and other features of Chinese civilization as their own, they distinguished items imported from China by adding the term *kan* (Han),
kara (Tang), or *tō* (Tang), as in *kanji* (Chinese characters).

While the phrase *wakan secchū* meant a combination of Japanese and Chinese ways, a most revealing expression for the relationship between self and other is *wakon kansai*—the Japanese soul and Chinese brilliance. Referring to the best of the two worlds at that time, the phrase represents a Japanese effort to preserve their identity as "the Japanese soul." We recall that in ancient Japan, rice was symbolically equivalent to the soul, which also meant the deity. Note that in the Japanese conception, humans are distinguished from animals not through their rationality, as in the Western conception, but through the capacity for emotion, which is generated by the soul (Ohnuki-Tierney 1994). Therefore, a seemingly simple expression like "Japanese soul and Chinese brilliance" derives from one of the basic conceptual foundations of Japanese culture.

Some intellectuals of the time were particularly threatened and tried to demarcate their own identity. In this climate, the emperor Tenmu (r. 672–86) commissioned a compilation of the myth-histories of the *Kojiki* and the *Nihonshoki* in order to establish a Japanese identity in opposition to Tang China (Kawasoe 1980:253–54).[11] Ironically, however, rice agriculture—introduced from somewhere in Asia around 400 B.C.[12]—was chosen to establish *the* defining feature of a Japanese identity distinct from that of the Chinese. Thus, in order to reconcile this seeming "contradiction" and to appropriate rice agriculture for the Yamato state, the imperial court "selected" (see Vansina 1985:190–92) from competing oral traditions the "myth" that contended that their own deity grew the first crop of rice and compiled the first written texts in the Chinese writing system they had adopted. In addition, they adopted the Chinese designation for Japan, *Nihon*— "the base where the sun rises"; from the Chinese perspective Japan is situated at the point where the sun rises (Amino, personal communication). In short, the Japanese conception of self was born in the encounter with the Chinese, who represented the stranger-deity at a cosmological level and who, therefore, had to be the model for the Japanese self-identity.

As long as the Chinese remained a well-defined other, the Japanese task of defining themselves vis-à-vis the Chinese was relatively easy. It became more difficult, however, when the world of the Japanese no longer consisted solely of the Japanese and the Chinese. By the eighteenth century, the Japanese had become acutely aware of various Western civilizations. Not only did they eagerly adopt the "superior"

Western science and technology, but Western clothing, hairstyles, food, and style of painting and writing—in short, just about every aspect of culture, as epitomized in the emperor and the empress, whose thoroughly Westernized images, with Western-style hair and clothing, in addition to the famous Kaiser mustache of the emperor, appeared in popular prints sold by the thousands (Bolitho 1977:23–41).

To further complicate the matter, the Japanese had to face the fact that, for the West, the Japanese were indiscriminately labeled "Orientals," just as, ironically, the Japanese lumped all Westerners together. This more complex international scene required the Japanese both to differentiate themselves from other Asians or Orientals—especially Chinese and Koreans—on the one hand, and to distinguish themselves from the West, on the other.[13]

While the distinction between Japanese and Westerners can be easily made and expressed as rice versus meat (or bread), as we will see shortly, the distinction between the Japanese and other Asians was much harder. In particular, the distinction cannot be expressed as rice versus some other food item, since other Asians are also rice consumers, so the distinction must take the form of rice grown on Japanese soil versus foreign rice.

Therefore, toward the end of the early modern period, domestic rice (*naichimai*) as a metaphor for the Japanese as contrasted with foreign rice (*gaimai*) as a metaphor for other Asians surfaced, although foreign rice had been introduced for centuries (see Sansom 1961:183 for the practice in the thirteenth century). Championed by the nativist scholars at the time, the Japanese chose to represent "the pristine Japanese way" by Japanese rice and rice agriculture, while degrading Chinese rice as "inferior" and "begun by the mandate of men," and, therefore, "those who eat are weak and enervated" (Harootunian 1988:211–12). The Japanese effort to extricate themselves from other Asians during the Meiji period continued to be seen in the metaphorical uses of rice. For example, in his novel *Kōfu* (The miners), Natsume Sōseki, one of the best-known writers of the period, summarizes life at the coal mine—the lowest type of existence—as "eating Chinese rice [*nankinmai*] and being eaten by Chinese bugs [*nankinmushi*, bed bugs]." The term *nankin* refers to Nanking, thus to China. Chinese rice is depicted as tasting like mud and as too slippery to manage, unlike Japanese rice, which is called "the silver rice" (*ginmai*) (Natsume Sōseki 1984). Thus, the symbolic opposition of silver—domestic rice—and mud—Chinese rice—represents the basic opposition of Japanese self and marginalized external other, which the Chinese have become by this time in the Japanese view.

Western Meat, Japanese Rice

The seemingly contradictory efforts, since the late Tokugawa period and through the Meiji period, of the Japanese to simultaneously "modernize and industrialize" their country while redefining themselves in terms of the rice agriculture of the distant past were articulated in the discourse on the Japanese vis-à-vis Westerners as rice versus meat. Meat was the distinguishing characteristic of the Western diet because shortly after the introduction of Buddhism in the sixth century, the doctrine of mercy for all living beings was translated into a legal prohibition against meat consumption. The "official" diet of the Japanese since then consisted of fish and vegetables.[14]

Some people favored unabashed imitation of the West and advocated the abandonment of rice agriculture and the adoption of animal domestication. They argued that as long as the Japanese continued to eat only rice, fish, and vegetables, their bodies would never become strong enough to compete with the bodies of meat-eating Westerners (Tsukuba 1986:109–12). They also associated a diet dominated by rice with country hicks and uncivilized habits (Tsukuba 1986:113).

Others opposed the imitation of the West and emphasized the importance of rice agriculture and the superiority of a rice diet. All through the modernizing period, the construction of a Japanese national identity by the military government involved the use of foodstuffs, especially rice, as symbols of the national identity. The rising sun flag motif was frequently used, for example, in the well-known *hinomaru bentō* (rising-sun lunch), which consists of a bed of white rice with a red pickled plum in the center. Importantly, the *purity* of white rice (*hakumai*) or "pure rice" (*junmai*) became a powerful metaphor for the purity of the Japanese self. During World War II, white rice—symbolically powerful but nutritionally deficient—had to be saved for the most precious sector of the population, the soldiers. The shortage of Japanese rice motivated the rest of the population to work hard for Japan's victory, which promised a return of good times with plenty of white rice, namely "Japanese rice" rather than foreign rice (*gaimai*).

Just as Japanese versus Chinese objects are distinguished by prefixes, certain prefixes designate objects of Japanese or Western origin: *wa*, *hō*, or *nihon* designate Japanese origin and *yō* signifies Western origin, as in the case of *washoku* (Japanese cuisine) versus *yōshoku* (Western cuisine). At times foreign words are retained to distinguish them from the Japanese counterparts, as in the case of *wain* (wine), referring to Western wines, in contrast to the Japanese *sake*.

Today, we witness a profusion of foreign foods throughout Japan. Not only are Big Macs, pizza, Kentucky Fried Chicken, A & W, and bagels available and eagerly sought, but also haute cuisine from every culture of the world. In addition to, or more precisely because of, the profusion of Western foods, Japanese cuisine, *washoku*, has made a phenomenal comeback. Streetcars and newspapers are full of advertisements by restaurants and inns featuring numerous courses of Japanese dishes.

Japanese cuisine, whose prototype is the cuisine for the tea ceremony (*kaiseki ryōri*) in Kyoto, is a conspicuous contemporary "construction" or "invention" of Japanese culture. From pictures of these colorful and aesthetically arranged dishes, contemporary Japanese "learn" what Japanese cuisine is about, even though they are by no means a faithful reconstruction of the traditional cuisine for the tea ceremony. In fact, there never was a prototypical traditional Japanese cuisine in the first place. Ironically, Japan now imports most of the ingredients for these "Japanese dishes." Amid a flood of Western foods, contemporary Japanese keep reaffirming their self by constructing their own food way.

Rice is the defining feature of "traditional Japanese cuisine," but its amount is usually small. Indeed, the more haute a meal is, the more side dishes there are and the less rice there is. Thus, while rice continues to be referred to as the main food (*shushoku*) or staple food and other dishes as auxiliary (*fukushoku*) or side dishes, the quantitative balance is reversed in haute cuisine, with an emphasis on the side dishes and not on rice. However, what makes any dish a Japanese dish (*washoku*), whether *haute* or not, is the presence of rice, no matter how small. "Japanese style steak" (*washokushiki suteiki*)—a popular menu item in contemporary Japan—means steak served with cooked white rice. Rice that accompanies a Western dish such as steak is often referred to as "*raisu*," as in *raisu-bāgā* (rice-burger), which is a hamburger sandwiched between two layers of bun-shaped rice. Many Western dishes, such as pork cutlets, hamburgers, steaks, and omelets, are served with rice. At restaurants, a waiter or a waitress usually asks, "Would you like *raisu* or *pan* [the Portuguese word for bread, adopted by the Japanese] with it?" when they serve one of these originally Western dishes.

In contemporary Japan, food for the poor continues to be envisioned as a great deal of rice accompanied by a pickled plum (*umeboshi*) or pickles (*takuwan*), just as the poor in bread-eating countries rely on bread, accompanied by soup or salted pork. But regardless of quantity, rice remains "the king-pin of any meal's architecture" in Japan (Dore 1978:86).

Western Short-Grain Rice, Japanese Short-Grain Rice

"Rice versus meat" or "Japanese short-grain rice versus Chinese long-grain rice" as "we versus they" is apparent and easy to understand. But the enormous strength of "Japanese rice" as a metaphor of Japanese self surfaced when the U.S. government, a powerful "other," pressured Japan to import California short-grain rice—seemingly identical to the domestic rice. The Japanese, not just the government and farmers but also consumers, immediately came to the defense of domestic rice and Japanese agriculture, using various expressions to equate Japanese rice and agriculture as the symbols of their self-identity.

Hardly any contemporary Japanese would hold, even as a collective representation without individual belief, that rice has a soul or that rice is a deity. Many contemporary Japanese are unaware of the connection between rice and the emperor system. Note also that Japan has always imported rice, as Sansom (1961:183) describes for the thirteenth-century case. Furthermore, domestic rice, which contemporary Japanese identify as *the* Japanese rice, is in fact an "invention of a tradition," in that the original species of rice was radically different from any cultivated today, including the two most popular types of rice—*koshihikari* and *sasanishiki*—cultivated in the northeastern parts of Japan, the last region to be reached by rice agriculture. Also, no single species of rice ever constituted *the* Japanese rice in the past in the first place.

In contrast to other rice that has been imported to Japan, California rice is unique in that it is "practically" identical with domestic rice. Unlike long-grain rice from China and other rice-consuming countries, short-grain California rice has been cultivated from Japanese seeds and resembles Japanese rice. Yet symbolically it is just as different as any other food representing "the other," or at least is presented as such by Japanese opponents of rice importation.

The argument, then, is the way in which *both* Japanese rice and Japanese rice paddies are crucial to the Japanese. They argue that rice paddies are essential for Japanese land, functioning in flood control by serving as dams, soil conservation, preservation of underground water, purification of air and water, and beautification of the land (Inoue 1988).[15] Rice paddies then are *our land*—the spatial metaphor of the self. California rice, in contrast, is grown in American paddies, thus serving *their* land, and not *ours*. In addition, it contains chemicals used in the processing (Shimogaito 1988:76–78). After a record low production of rice in 1993 and with the closing of the General Agreement of Tariffs and Trade (GATT) negotiations in December of that year, Japanese consumers are prepared to accept the importation of foreign rices. Yet in newspapers they voice their fear in of the treatment of rice in foreign countries and request the government to investigate the processing method (see, for example, *Asahi Shinbun*, October 30, 1993; November 12, 1993).

The controversy over California rice clearly demonstrates that domestic rice serves as a metaphor of self for the Japanese and their land, water, and air. The equation of self-sufficiency (*jikyū jisoku*) with domestic rice is the most frequent expression in the discourse (see also Ōshima 1984:2–4). Other expressions that equate domestic rice with the Japanese self are "lifeblood crop" (Yamaguchi 1987:40); "the lifeline" (*seimeisen*); "the last sacred realm" (*saigo no seiiki*) (*Kōbe Shinbun*, July 6, 1990); "the last citadel" (used by the Ministry of Agriculture and Fishing; *Asahi Shinbun*, evening edition, June 27, 1990); and "self-sufficiency, national life, the prototype of Japanese culture" (*Zenchū Farm News*, no. 5, January 1987:2). The last two phrases express the Japanese fear that if they make concessions on the rice issue, they would have to concede to any other impositions from the United States, such as the introduction of nuclear weapons.

From the perspective of the structure of reflexivity, the emphasis on the functions of domestic rice for purification of air and beautification of land, coupled with the accusation of chemical use on California rice, reinforces the symbolic equation of "self is to other as purity is to impurity." Chemicals symbolize the impurity of foreign rice and thus constitute a threat to the purity of the Japanese self.

While big business organizations have consistently pressed for an open rice market (Calder 1988:231), the voices of these opponents have a far more receptive ear than one would expect among consumers (*Asahi Shinbun*, June 13, 1990), who are willing to pay a several times higher price for the "symbolic value" of domestic rice.

As I have detailed elsewhere (Ohnuki-Tierney 1995), just before the former prime minister Hosokawa formalized rice importation on December 14, 1993, there was an enormous drama to protect *rice as self*. It was followed by rejection of Thai rice and segregation of foreign rice both in sales and in cooking, although a more positive attitude toward rice from other countries, especially California rice, also surfaced. Yet, after the ripples of the "event" have subsided and with abundant domestic rice already available this year, both the government and the Japanese are paying much less attention to the issue, and most Japanese are buying domestic rice as usual.

In one sense the rice importation event was seen by the Japanese through the structure of reflexivity. In some way the event strengthened *rice as self* when it heightened the awareness of the importance of rice for their identity. Through continued segregation of foreign rice from domestic rice, at least, the Japanese managed to retain their purity of self, as expressed by domestic rice. Therefore, while a formal concession to a partial import of foreign rice produced significant changes in the formal structure of reflexivity, the endangered structure almost simultaneously reproduced itself through the retention of the purity of domestic rice cum Japanese self.[16]

Marginalization of the Internal Other

So far my discussion has been confined to the dialectic development between external others and the Japanese self. But this is not the whole story. Rice's link to land gains an even more profound cultural and politicoeconomic significance when we turn our attention to the formation of internal others in Japan. Until the latter part of the medieval period (1185–1603), Japanese society consisted of two social structures: one for residents (*teijūmin*) and one for nonresidents (*hiteijūmin*). The former included farmers, warriors (many of whom also farmed), and aristocrats. The latter included traders, itinerant priests and other religious specialists, and entertainers, many of whom traveled without having a permanent residence. These two structures were juxtaposed with one another, without hierarchical ranking between the two (Amino 1984).

Toward the end of the medieval period and increasingly during the Tokugawa period, the structure for nonresidents came to be placed below the one for residents in a hierarchical manner. This transformation meant the restriction of nonresidents, who used to enjoy freedom of movement across regional boundaries, to marginal areas for the purpose of "census" within Japanese society, which by then was unified under a single hierarchically divided social structure. The areas where they were settled were called "riverbanks," "scattered places," and so on, symbolically expressing their marginalized status within Japanese society (for details, see Ohnuki-Tierney 1987).

Even in the agrarian sector, stratification is closely tied to the notion of land. We noted that rice farmers were not necessarily rice consumers; that is, they produced rice that was taken away as tax and thus could not eat rice as their daily diet. Those who rose to the top in the stratification were landowners, who thereby were able to control the mode of production, the relations of production, and even consumption. The key is the ownership of land.

Thus, the development of the collective identity of the Japanese, as expressed in "Rice as Self" and "Rice Paddies as Japanese Land," represents a historical process whereby those social groups who were not anchored to politically defined space became minorities—*internal others*—whose presence was written off both from history and from the representation of Japan as "Agrarian Japan." Within the agrarian sector, land ownership became critical in the stratification. This, I think, is the other side of the development of an agrarian ideology, which accrued both symbolic and political centrality to the settled population (warriors and wealthy farmers). The process of the naturalization of the agrarian cosmology-turned-ideology was accompanied by the devaluation of the nonsettled and their way of life. "Landlessness" became *transgression*.[17]

To recapitulate, neither rice as food nor rice paddies as land by themselves engender meanings. However, precisely because these symbols are powerful for the reasons presented above, they can also be mobilized effectively for political purposes, including as tools for discrimination and chauvinism.

Contrary to Hobsbawm's (1992:7) claim that "social disorientation" is the key causal agent for the intensification of nationalism and ethnicity in the contemporary world, in the case of Japan, "social disorientation" is a result of the development of an agrarian ideology that became the ideological backbone of Japanese nationalism at a later time.

Summary

The Japanese identity that was born in discourse with the Chinese, the culturally superior other at the time, has since gone through historical transformations as it encountered different others. In all these encounters between selves and others — both internal and external — the multivocal rice and rice paddies have served as the vehicle for deliberation about self-identity as it transformed into selves and as the internal source of purity for the ever-changing self.

Paradoxically, then, the Japanese collective self has both changed and not changed. Rice too has stayed the same, while not only its meaning but its materiality has also changed. Put the other way, rice has been simultaneously univocal and multivocal; that is, it represents the Japanese self, while that self has undergone various historical changes. To invoke Vansina's (1990:251) phrase, "Tradition is a process: it lives only while it changes."

Food as Metaphor of Self

The power of food as a symbol of self-identity derives from the particular nature of the symbolic process involved. An important food as a metaphor of a social group involves two interlocking dimensions. First, each member of the social group consumes the food, which becomes a part of his or her body. The important food becomes *embodied* in each individual. It operates as a *metonym* by being part of the self. Second, the food is consumed by individual members of the social group who eat the food together. The communal consumption of the food leads to rice as a *metaphor* of "we" — his or her social group and, often, the people as a whole.

Whether a food represents an individual self, a social group, or a people as a whole, this symbolic process renders foods powerful symbols not only conceptually but also, we might say, at the gut level. It is for this reason that "our food" versus "their food" become a powerful way to express "we" versus "they." This is so not only for representation of "we" through a food item, but for discriminating the other from "us." Within a social group, food is also symbolically important for class *distinction* and its reproduction, as Bourdieu concludes: "The body is the most indisputable materialization of class taste" (Bourdieu 1984:190).

In sum, the beauty and purity of "we" are *embodied doubly, in the body of the people and in the food that represents them,* and, conversely, the undesirable qualities of the other are embodied in their foods and food ways.

Furthermore, foods are plants and animals, intimately linked to the earth where they grow or roam. We recall that the Japanese creation myth centered on the transformation of wilderness into the land of succulent rice. In short, rice paddies gave birth to "Japanese land." Rice paddies stand for "the ancestral land" at the family level, and seignorial power was expressed through the image of golden ears of rice stretching across the seignior's territory.

This double linkage to the Japanese self—representing its *body* and its *land*—may be a clue to the enormous power and resilience of rice symbolism, which *outlived both the imperial system and agriculture itself* and continues to exercise evocative power in postmodern Japan, where "true farmers" or even "full-time farmers" may have to be enthroned to the status of "human national treasure" (*ningen kokuhō*).[18]

Purity: Self, Ethnicity, and Nationalism

In the above discussion, my focus has been on the self and self-identity, which lie at the core of ethnicity and nationalism—a burgeoning field in anthropology and related fields. The postcolonial era saw the rise of ethnicity and nationalism all over the world, well before the dissolution of the Soviet Union. Findings from these studies show striking parallels to those of the Japanese conception of self and other.

Most important, for ethnicity and nationalism, *purity* of self is at their symbolic core, be it that of linguistic purity for recent Quebec nationalism (Handler 1988), national purity for the Greeks (Herzfeld 1987), "racial purity" in Hitler's Germany, or ethnic "cleansing" in Bosnia today. Yalman (1992) stresses the importance of purity in ethnicity and nationalism in contrast to tolerance of diversity in an imperial system. Brackette Williams (1989) repeatedly emphasizes how "the invention of purity" is entailed in all nation-building. But is it? Like most "inventions"—a lately fashionable notion—it is often embedded in tradition, if only we are willing to look farther back in historical processes. This long-term study has shown that purity is an integral part of the conception of the self, and thus its emergence and presence antedate the modern political movements of ethnicity or nationalism.

Similarly, metaphors of space and time, or more concretely, land (territory) and time (history), are of critical importance for nationalism, as exemplified in the rewriting of their own history by ethnic groups in the United States or the marking and remarking of territorial boundaries in the former Soviet Union.

Note, however, that the intimate involvement of space for the Japanese conception of the self does *not* derive from a need to spatially demarcate Japan, which is surrounded by the sea. This contrasts to many situations in which ethnicity and nationalism of social groups in adjacent areas are physically in need of territorial boundaries, as symbolized in the Berlin Wall.

One of the defining characteristics of Benedict Anderson's well-known thesis of the nation as the "imagined community" is that the nation is "imagined as *limited*" in that it is within the national "boundaries" (Anderson 1991:7). The Japanese case powerfully argues that "space" or "our land" is essential in the self-identity of a people even in the absence of physical or political need.

If "nature" is summoned as a spatial metaphor of self, it also serves as a temporal metaphor of self representing a past that is pure, simple, imbued with pristine beauty, and uncontaminated by foreign influences. Be they rice paddies in Japanese woodblock prints or peasants and farms in European paintings, they embody *our* history. Here we see a striking cross-cultural parallel, in that urbanization created a need for "the rural" in many societies (Berque 1990). In part for the same reason, it is postindustrial societies, such as France and Japan, rather than agricultural societies that place obstacles in the way of trade negotiations on agricultural products, as we see today in the GATT negotiations. Note also that the Koreans protested even more vigorously than the Japanese against the importation of rice, their protests even leading to putting the prime minister out of office.

In sum, a long-term study enables us to place certain sociopolitical phenomena, such as the rise of ethnicity and nationalism, in their historical context, thereby identifying their critical elements in historical perspective. Thus, we come to understand that enduring principles for the self-identity of a people—such as the concept of purity, time, and space—are summoned, but *not* invented, at particular historical times for purely political purposes. The need to demarcate the self, positively or negatively, but always in relation to the other, has been central to any people, and thus we cannot lose sight of these important dimensions of self-identity even at a time when the globalization process acts as a strong counterforce.

Notes

This article, although much transformed, originated as a paper for a conference organized by Wimal Dissanayake. I am most grateful to him for his warm encouragement, as well as to those present at the conference.

1. I use the terms "Japan" and "Japanese" loosely throughout—neither Japan as a nation nor the Japanese as a well-bounded social group have existed throughout history. Other blanket terms are also used. The term "non-Western" defines the rest of the world as a residual category (Cohn 1980:211), while "Western" lumps many cultures with different traditions into one blanket category, as do the terms "Oriental" and "Asian." I retain the terms "West" and "Western," not only because there is no better term, but because the Japanese use the term *gaijin* (foreigners) to refer to all non-Japanese people, and *seiyōjin* (Westerners) to refer to all Western peoples, although both terms usually refer to Americans and West Europeans, including the French, the Germans, and the British.

2. This article draws from my book *Rice as Self: Japanese Identities through Time* (1993), although my argument here has been reformulated since then.

3. Braudel (1980:3) states that "a history of short, sharp, nervous vibrations" is "the most exciting and richest in human interest of histories," although "the most perilous" (see also Ricoeur 1980). Although I would not regard short-term oscillations dangerous unless they are prejudged as permanent changes, it is useful to note Ricoeur's distinction between long-term enduring changes and short-term oscillations whose impact on culture may be superficial and temporary. This approach of the *longue durée* is not a popular approach within the discipline of history, whose dominant approaches remain the exhaustive use of primary sources for a narrowly defined topic within a short period of time. Futhermore, in this approach to history, the roles and behaviors of historical actors are often subsumed in broad sweeps of historical flows. (For further discussion on the historical approaches in anthropology, see Ohnuki-Tierney 1990a, 1995.)

4. The concept of collective representation in anthropology has carried with it an unfortunate baggage, offering itself as a fair prey for criticism. Thus, it has reified several theses that have occupied a central place in anthropology but have come under question in the recent past. First, the Durkheimian collective representation falsely reified the notion of society as a universal social institution and assumed the universality of the abstract notion of society, with its concomitant assumption that individuals identify themselves as members of that abstract "society." Yet, in many "societies," it is concrete relationships that are "real" to people, who have no conceptualization of "society" as such. Second, the collective self and its representation have always been thought of as singular, when, depending upon the context, they should be thought of as mul-

tiple — multiple social groups constituting "a society" and individuals having multiple voices. Third, the notion of the collective self was often based on the Western notion of an autonomous individual, which may be an idealized model even in the West.

5. Orikuchi (1965a:78–82, 1965b:33–35, 1976:303–17) first called attention to this aspect of the *marebito* deities. For further discussions of the *marebito*, see Higo 1942:103–4; Matsudaira 1977; Ouwehand 1958–59; Suzuki 1974, 1979. For the continuation of the *marebito* concept into the present day, see the incisive analyses of folk festivals in contemporary Japan by Higo (1942) and Matsudaira (1977).

Some scholars link the *marebito* deities to the figure of the "stranger," who is simultaneously far and near, or belongs to and does not belong to the community in which he or she is in a position to exercise considerable power. The concept of the stranger, originally developed by Simmel (1950:402–8), is further developed by a number of scholars (see Ohnuki-Tierney 1987).

An intriguing question for both anthropologists and historians is whether the concept antedates in each of these societies the contact with the superior other, including the colonial power, or whether it was formulated in response to these historical forces.

6. The name of the grain soul is Masakatsu Akatsu Kachihaya Hiame no Oshihomimi no Mikoto (Kurano and Takeda 1958:111, 125). Another name for the grandson and first emperor is Amatsu Hiko Hiko Ho no Ninigi no Mikoto, which describes rice stalks with succulent grains (Kurano and Takeda 1958:125).

7. For a discussion of New Year's observances without rice cakes but with taro (*satoimo*), see Tsuboi 1984.

8. These are a series of woodblock prints executed by Katsushika Hokusai entitled *Hyakunin isshu uba ga etoki* (pictures of one hundred poems by one hundred poets, explained by the wet-nurse). They are illustrations of the well-known collection of one hundred poems (*Hyakunin isshu*; literally, one hundred poets, one poem each) selected and completed in 1235 by Fujiwara no Teika (1162–1241), as Hokusai interpreted them from the perspective of the mid–eighteenth century. Hokusai, who started to work on this series at age seventy-six, completed prints for only twenty-seven of the hundred poems but also left many line drawings. Eighty-nine of them are reproduced in the collection by Morse (1989).

9. They are numbers 1, 5, 8, 9, 12, 13, 14, 17, 19, 20, 22, 23, 30, 39, 44, 47, 65, 68, 70, 71, 77, 78, 79, 83, 84, and 90. For details of my interpretation, see Ohnuki-Tierney 1993b.

10. The prints in *Sixty-Nine Stations along the Kiso Road* (*Kiso Kaidō rokujū-kyū tsugi*) (Gotō 1976), which contains prints by both Hiroshige and Keisai Eisen (1790–?), contain similar motifs.

11. For details of the process of compilation of these myth-histories, see Sakamoto et al. 1967:6–12.

12. While the date when wet-rice agriculture was introduced is now set at around 400 B.C. (Pearson 1992), there is still some controversy as to its exact origin (Yoshida 1992). It was introduced to Japan in Kyūshū, the southernmost major island of the Japanese archipelago, via the Korean Peninsula. From there, it spread northeastward in three successive waves, reaching the northeastern region by the beginning of the Christian era (Kokuritsu Rekishi Minzoku Hakubutsukan 1987:14).

13. One of the ways in which nativist scholars of the late early modern period and Meiji scholars attempted to distinguish the Japanese from the Chinese was through the objectification of the Chinese through the label of *Shina*, a designation for China by other peoples. The term *Shina* first appeared in an Indian sutra and was adopted by the Japanese during the middle-early modern period and used until the end of

World War II. the Chinese designation for themselves is *Chūgoku* (the Middle Kingdom; literally, the country at the center), which expresses the centrality of China (*chū* = center) in their view (see Tanaka 1993). By adopting the label of *Shina,* the Japanese made a deliberate choice to ignore the significance that the Chinese expressed in their own representation to the world.

14. Some continued to eat meat, however, although they "converted" them into flowers; that is, names of flowers were given to animal meat, such as "cherry blossoms" for horse and "peony" for wild boar (see Harada 1993).

15. See also Okabe Saburō, director of the Science and Technology Division of the Liberal Democratic Party and a member of the House of Councilors, in the *Record of Sangiin Gaimu Iinkai Kaigiroku,* no. 5 (during the 118th session of the Diet), p. 7.

16. For a more nuanced interpretation of "structure" and its transformations, see Ohnuki-Tierney 1995.

17. See Ohnuki-Tierney (1993a) for the enormous importance of the equation of nature with plants but not animals and how it provides the symbolic basis for discrimination of special-status people (*burakumin*) and the Ainu, who are symbolically equated with the negative side of "beastly" nature, although each in a different sense.

18. Here I refer to the governmental policy to designate talented individuals, especially in the traditional arts, as human treasures (*ningen kokuhō*).

References

Amino Yoshihiko. 1984. "Chūsei no tabibitotachi" (Travelers during the medieval period). In *Hyōhaku to teijū* (Wandering and settling), edited by Y. Amino et al., pp. 153–266. Tokyo: Shōggakan.

Anderson, Benedict. 1991. *Imagined Communities.* London: Verso.

Augé, Marc. 1982 [1979]. *The Anthropological Circle: Symbol, Function, History.* Cambridge: Cambridge University Press.

Berger, Peter L., and Thomas Luckmann. 1967. *The Social Construction of Reality.* New York: Doubleday.

Berque, Augustin. 1990. *Nihon no fūkei, seiyō no keikan, soshite zōkei no jidai* (Comparative history of landscape in East Asia and Europe). Tokyo: Kōdansha.

Bolitho, Harold. 1977. *Meiji Japan.* Cambridge: Cambridge University Press.

Bourdieu, Pierre. 1984 [1979]. *Distinction: A Social Critique of the Judgement of Taste.* Cambridge, Mass.: Harvard University Press.

Braudel, Fernand. 1980 [1958]. *On History.* Chicago: University of Chicago Press.

Brettell, Richard R., and Caroline B. Brettell. 1983. *Painters and Peasants in the Nineteenth Century.* New York: Rizzoli International Publications.

Calder, Kent E. 1988. *Crisis and Compensation: Public Policy and Political Stability in Japan, 1949–1986.* Princeton, N.J.: Princeton University Press.

Chartier, Roger. 1982. "Intellectual History or Sociocultural History? The French Trajectories." In *Modern European Intellectual History: Reappraisals and New Perspectives,* edited by D. La Capra and S. Kaplan. Ithaca, N.Y.: Cornell University Press.

Cohn, Bernard S. 1980. "History and Anthropology: The State of Play." *Comparative Studies in Society and History* 12:198–221.

Dore, Ronald P. 1978. *Shinohata: A Portrait of a Japanese Village.* New York: Pantheon.

Dumont, Louis. 1970 [1966]. *Homo Hierarchicus.* Translated by M. Sainsbury. Chicago: University of Chicago Press.

———. 1977. *From Mandeville to Marx.* Chicago: University of Chicago Press.

———. 1986 [1983]. *Essays on Individualism: Modern Ideology in Anthropological Perspective.* Chicago: University of Chicago Press.

Gluck, Carol. 1985. *Japan's Modern Myth: Ideology in the Late Meiji Period.* Princeton, N.J.: Princeton University Press.

Gotō, Shigeki. 1975. *Tōkaidō gojū-san tsugi* (Fifty-three stations along the Tōkaidō). Tokyo: Shūeisha.

———. 1976. *Kiso Kaidō rokujū-kyū tsugi* (Sixty-nine stations along the Kiso Road). Tokyo: Shūeisha.

Handler, Richard. 1988. *Nationalism and the Politics of Culture in Quebec.* Madison: University of Wisconsin Press.

Harada Nobuo. 1993. *Rekishi no naka no kome to niku* (Rice and meat in history). Tokyo: Heibonsha.

Harootunian, Harry. 1988. *Things Seen and Unseen: Discourse and Ideology in Tokugawa Nativism.* Chicago: University of Chicago Press.

Herzfeld, Michael. 1987. *Anthropology through the Looking-Glass.* Cambridge: Cambridge University Press.

Higo Kazuo. 1942 [1938]. *Nihon shinwa kenkyū* (Research on Japanese myths). Tokyo: Kawade Shobō.

Hobsbawm, Eric J. 1992. "Ethnicity and Nationalism in Europe Today." *Anthropology Today* 8 (1):3–8.

Hunt, Lynn. 1986. "French History in the Last Twenty Years: The Rise and Fall of the *Annales* Paradigm." *Journal of Contemporary History* 21:209–24.

Inoue Hisashi. 1988. "Kome no hanashi (5)—Amerika no kome" (Discussion on rice (5)—American rice). *Days Japan* 1 (6):103.

Ishibashi Fushiha. 1914. "Minzokugaku no hōmen yori mitaru kagami" (Anthropological interpretations of mirrors). *Jinruigaku Zasshi* 29 (6):223–27.

Itoh Mikiharu. 1979. "Ta no kami" (Deity of the rice paddy). In *Kōsa Nihon no kodai shinkō* (Belief system in ancient Japan), edited by T. Matsumae, pp. 162–81. Tokyo: Gakuseisha.

———. 1988. "Inasaku girei ni mirareru kami kannen" (The concept of deity as expressed in rituals concerning rice production). *Nihon Bunka Kenkyū Hōkoku,* March, pp. 73–79.

Kawasoe Taketane. 1980 [1978]. *Kojiki no sekai* (The world of *Kojiki*). Tokyo: Kyōikusha.

Kokuritsu Rekishi Minzoku Hakubutsukan, ed. 1987 [1985]. *Nihon no rekishi to bunka* (Japanese history and culture). Tokyo: Daiichi Hōki Shuppan.

Kurano Kenji and Takeda Yūkichi, eds. 1958. *Kojiki Norito* (*Kojiki* and *Norito*). Tokyo: Iwanami Shoten.

Matsudaira Narimitsu. 1977. *Matsuri—honshitsu to shosō: Kodaijin no uchū* (Festivals—their essence and multiple dimensions: The universe of the ancient Japanese). Tokyo: Asahi Shimbusha.

Mauss, Marcel. 1985 [1938]. "A Category of the Human Mind: The Notion of Person, the Notion of Self." In *The Category of the Person,* edited by M. Carrithers, S. Collins, and S. Lukes, pp. 1–25. Cambridge: Cambridge University Press.

Morse, Peter. 1989. *Hokusai: One Hundred Poets.* New York: Braziller.

Murakami Shigeyoshi. 1977. *Tennō no saishi* (Imperial rituals). Tokyo: Iwanami Shoten.

Nakayama Tarō. 1976. "Mizukagami Tenjin" (Mizukagami Tenjin). *Nihon Minzokugaku* 1:181–88. Tokyo: Yamato Shobō.

Natsume Sōseki. 1984 [1965]. "Kōfu" (The miners). In *Sōseki zenshū* (The complete works of Sōseki), vol. 3. Tokyo: Iwanami Shoten. Originally published as a daily newspaper column beginning January 1, 1907.

Newby, Howard. 1979. *Green and Pleasant Land?* London: Hutchinson.

Nōda Tayoko. 1943. *Mura no josei* (Women of the village). Tokyo: Mikuni Shobō.

Ohnuki-Tierney, Emiko. 1987. *The Monkey as Mirror: Symbolic Transformations in Japanese History and Ritual.* Princeton, N.J.: Princeton University Press.

———. 1990a. "The Ambivalent Self of the Contemporary Japanese." *Cultural Anthropology* 5:196–215.

———. 1990b. *Monkey as Metaphor? Transformations of a Polytropic Symbol in Japanese Culture.* Man, n.s., 25 (1990):399–416.

———. 1991. "The Emperor of Japan as Deity (*Kami*): An Anthropology of the Imperial System in Historical Perspective." *Ethnology* 30 (3):199–215.

———. 1993a. "Nature, pureté et soi primordial: La nature japonaise dans une perspective comparative." *Géographie et Cultures,* no. 7 (1993):75–92.

———. 1993b. *Rice as Self: Japanese Identities through Time.* Princeton, N.J.: Princeton University Press.

———. 1994. "Brain Death and Organ Transplantation: Medical Technology as Cultural Construction." *Current Anthropology* 35 (2):233–54.

———. 1995. "Structure, Event, and Historical *Metaphor*: Rice and Identities in Japanese History." *Journal of the Royal Anthropological Institute* 30, no. 2 (June):1–27.

Orikuchi Shinobu. 1965a. "Marebito" (Marebito stranger). In *Orikuchi Shinobu zenshū* (The collected works of Orikuchi Shinobu), vol. 1, pp. 78–82. Tokyo: Chūōkōronsha.

———. 1965b. "*Marebito* [sic] no otozure" (Visits by Marebito). In *Orikuchi Shinobu zenshū* (The collected works of Orikuchi Shinobu), vol. 2, pp. 33–35. Tokyo: Chūōkōronsha.

———. 1976. "Ijin to Bungaku" (The stranger and literature). In *Orikuchi Shinobu zenshū* (The collected works of Orikuchi Shinobu), vol. 7, pp. 303–17. Tokyo: Chūōkōronsha.

Ōshima Kiyoshi. 1984. *Shokuryō to nōgyō o kangaeru* (Thoughts on food and agriculture). Tokyo: Iwanami Shoten.

Ouwehand, Cornelius. 1958–59. "Some Notes on the God Susano-o." *Monumenta Nipponica* 14 (3–4):138–61.

Pearson, Richard. 1992. *Ancient Japan.* New York: Braziller.

Pollack, David. 1986. *The Fracture of Meaning: Japan's Synthesis of China from the Eighth through the Eighteenth Centuries.* Princeton, N.J.: Princeton University Press.

Ricoeur, Paul. 1980. *The Contribution of French Historiography to the Theory of History.* Oxford: Clarendon Press.

Sahlins, Marshall. 1981. *Historical Metaphors and Mythical Realities: Structure in the Early History of the Sandwich Islands Kingdom.* Ann Arbor, Mich.: University of Michigan Press.

Saigō Nobutsuna. 1984 [1967]. *Kojiki no sekai* (The world of the *Kojiki*). Tokyo: Iwanami Shoten.

Sakamoto Tarō, Saburō Ienaga, Mitsusada Inoue, and Susumu Ōno, eds. 1965. "Nihonshoki (Ge)." In *Nihonshoki,* vol. 2. Tokyo: Iwanami Shoten.

———. 1967. "Nihonshoki (Jō)." *Nihonshoki,* vol. 1. Tokyo: Iwanami Shoten.

Sansom, George. 1961. *A History of Japan, 1334–1615.* Stanford, Calif.: Stanford University Press.

Shimogaito Hiroshi. 1986. *Okome to bunka* (Rice and culture). Osaka: Zen-Ōsaka Shōhisha Dantai Renrakuai.

———. 1988. *Zoku okome to bunka* (Rice and culture, continued). Osaka: Zen-Ōsaka Shōhisha Dantai Renrakuai.

Simmel, Georg. 1950. *The Sociology of Georg Simmel.* Glencoe, Ill.: Free Press.

Suzuki Mitsuo. 1974. *Marebito no kōzō* (The structure of *Marebito* [stranger]). Tokyo: Sanichi Shobō.

———. 1979. "Marebito" (Strangers). In *Kōza Nihon no minzoku* (Folk cultures of Japan), vol. 7, *Shinkō* (Belief systems), edited by T. Sakurai, pp. 211–39. Tokyo: Yūseidō Shuppan.

Tanaka, Stephan. 1993. *Japan's Orient: Rendering Pasts into History.* Berkeley: University of California Press.

Tsuboi Hirofumi. 1984 [1982]. *Ine o eranda Nihonjin* (The Japanese who chose the rice plant). Tokyo: Miraisha.

Tsukuba Tsuneharu. 1986 [1969]. *Beishoku, nikushoku no bunmei* (Civilizations of rice consumption and meat consumption). Tokyo: Nihon Hōsō Shuppankai.

Turner, Victor. 1975 [1974]. *Dramas, Fields, and Metaphors: Symbolic Action in Human Society.* Ithaca, N.Y.: Cornell University Press.

van Gennep, Arnold. 1961 [1909]. *The Rites of Passage.* Chicago: University of Chicago Press.

Vansina, Jan. 1985. *Oral Tradition as History.* Madison: University of Wisconsin Press.

———. 1990. *Paths in the Rainforests: Toward a History of Political Tradition in Equatorial Africa.* Madison: University of Wisconsin Press.

Williams, Brackette F. 1989. "A Class Act: Anthropology and the Race to Nation across Ethnic Terrain." *Annual Review of Anthropology* 18:401–44.

Williams, Raymond. 1973. *The Country and the City.* New York: Oxford University Press.

Yalman, Nur. 1992. "The Perfection of Man: The Question of Supra-Nationalism in Islam." Keynote address to the symposium on nationalism held at the Department of Anthropology, University of Osaka, March 1992; published in *Shisō* 823:34–49.

Yamaguchi Iwao. 1987. "Maintaining Japan's Self-Sufficiency in Rice." *Journal of Trade and Industry* 6 (2):40–42.

Yanagita Kunio. 1982a [1969]. "Kome no chikara" (Power of rice). In *Yanagita Kunioshū* (The collected works of Yanagita Kunio), vol. 14, pp. 240–58. Tokyo: Tsukuma Shobō.

———. 1982b [1970]. "Kura inadama kō" (Thoughts on the soul of rice). In *Yanagita Kunioshū* (The collected works of Yanagita Kunio), vol. 31, pp. 159–66. Tokyo: Tsukuma Shobō.

Yanagita Kunio, ed. 1951. *Minzokugaku jiten* (Ethnographic dictionary). Tokyo: Tōkyōdō.

Yoshida Shūji. 1992. "*Shimpojūmu idengaku ga shimeshita saibai ine no kigen*" (The origin of the rice plant as identified through genetic analysis). *Minpaku* 16 (6):18–19.

8 / Self, Agency, and Cultural Knowledge: Reflections on Three Japanese Films

Wimal Dissanayake

According to the conventional wisdom, the Japanese are so inextricably tied to the concept and practices of group loyalty and social obligations that the idea of human agency finds no place in Japanese culture. Groupism, according to this line of thinking, is the defining and foundational trait of Japanese social life. This idea finds repeated and emphatic articulation in most books on Japanese culture written for popular consumption. For example, the following observation from a popular book on Japanese culture is fairly representative of this mode of perception: "Modern Japan, as anyone who has ever watched a Japanese tourist group can tell, is still a group-oriented society. The desires of the individual are subordinated to the demands of his or her group. The concept of individual rights is not readily understood in Japan" (Buruma 1984:220).

What is interesting about passages such as this is that while there is some substance to these observations, there is a tendency to occlude the distinction between individuality and agency. Individuality is a distinctly Western concept that arose out of clearly discernible social and cultural formations and discursive practices, while the idea of human agency is prevalent in Japanese as well as all other cultures. How this agency finds articulation in culturally sanctioned behaviors and idioms of living is the more relevant and significant question that needs to be addressed.

The Japanese concept of self is usually delineated in relation to the socius; the social order in Japan and the Japanese self are perceived to be two sides of the same coin. The Japanese social order, most anthropologists who have specialized in Japanese culture argue, cannot be properly understood in isolation from the dynamics of the constitution of the self, just as much as the social order cannot be properly understood in isolation from the functioning of the social order.[1] Hence the examination of the nature, role, and significance of human agency, which is at the heart of theorizations of social scientists such as Anthony Giddens (1979) and Pierre Bourdieu (1977) and humanists such as Charles Taylor (1988), assumes a centrality of meaning and unignorable urgency.

Much of the most interesting contemporary writing on the concept of self in Japanese society, understandably enough, has been produced by cultural anthropologists, and to a lesser extent psychologically oriented social scientists. In this regard, three books that have profoundly influenced their own respective academic fields of origin as well as those outside are Ruth Benedict's *The Chrysanthemum and the Sword,* Chie Nakane's *Japanese Society,* and Takeo Doi's *The Anatomy of Dependence.* All three books, which in my judgment are conceptually flawed, have sought to theorize Japanese society in sociocentric terms. Clearly, Takeo Doi's book draws its inspiration from psychiatry, but ultimately it too lays emphasis on the sociocentric dimension.

Ruth Benedict's *The Chrysanthemum and the Sword* has been an immensely influential book and a continuing academic presence and reference point in the understanding of Japanese culture. Intrigued by the perceived contradictions of Japanese behavior she sought to inquire deeper into this and make greater sense of it. She observed, "The Japanese are, to the highest degree, both aggressive and unaggressive, both militaristic and aesthetic, both insolent and polite, rigid and adaptable, submissive and resentful of being pushed around, logical and brave and timid, conservative and hospitable to new ways" (1946:2). In seeking to resolve these paradoxical behaviors she made use of concepts such as "*on*" (social obligation) and "*giri*" (duty), which had very clear social resonances and content. The overpowering influence of social norms in the shaping of Japanese character emerges very strongly from her study.

Chie Nakane, in her book *Japanese Society* (1970) also contributes to the circulation of a sociocentric model of understanding Japanese self. She formulated a paradigm of a vertical society in which social hierarchies were central to the operation of society. She theorized the ways in which social groups are informed and activated by vertically structured interpersonal relationships, and how the Japanese society in general mirrors the ontology of these functional social groups. Kelly (1991) points out that Nakane put in place an analytic triad: "the social structure of subordination, the psychodynamics of dependence and the cultural obligations of debt and duty." And "vertical society," "socialization for achievement," and "ethics of indebtedness" all share an understanding of performance.

The Anatomy of Dependence by Takeo Doi (1973) thematizes the idea of *amae,* or dependence, and makes use of it as a heuristic device for understanding certain distinctive traits of Japanese selfhood. A trained medical doctor and a psychiatrist, Doi enunciates the idea that dependence is the guiding characteristic of Japanese culture. Grounding his analysis in linguistic investigations and clinical data, he argues that the desire of the infant to reintegrate with its mother and secure the comfort of the womb is a characteristic that is highly visible in Japan and that it could be profitably enlarged and expanded to reunderstand the dynamics of Japanese selfhood and social life. All three books, then, in their different ways and from their different viewpoints, foreground the idea of social obligation and social dependence as being pivotal to the construction and comprehension of the Japanese self.

Anthropologists and anthropologically minded scholars like Robert J. Smith (1983), Thomas Rohlen (1989), David Plath (1980), Takie Sugiyama Lebra (1976), Harumi Befu (1992), Emiko Ohnuki-Tierney (1984), Joseph J. Tobin (1991), Jane Bachnik (1992), and Nancy Rosenberger (1989) have refined these approaches to self and social order in Japan and have productively moved beyond the early conceptualizations. They in their different ways and from their distinct conceptual vantage points have sought to underline the importance of coming to grips with what Robert Smith has called the "interactional self" in Japan.

Despite the indubitable theoretical advances made by the aforementioned scholars in reunderstanding the Japanese self, there are two deficiencies in their conceptualization. First, there is still a residual tendency to perceive the self in unitary terms, and the fact that it is multiple, contradictory, riven by inner tension, and constantly reconstituting itself gets short shrift. Second, despite the declared and demonstrated emphasis on interaction and situationality, in the ultimate analysis the binarisms of subject/object, self/society, and inner/outer, which were the determining traits of earlier discourses, still retain their privileged status. As Dorrine Kondo observes, "Displacing the categories of 'personal' and 'political' through the introduction of myriad complicating multiplicities and ambiguities is a process that must occur on many different levels" (1990:44). What many of the even recent interrogations fail to take into consideration adequately is the fact that selfhoods are constituted contextually in specific historical and social situations and questions of power are inseparably linked to, and inscribed on, the formations of self. And it is important to remind ourselves, as Kondo points out, that "identity ... is not a unified essence, but a mobile site of contradictions and disunity, a node where various discourses temporarily interact in particular ways" (1990:47). In this essay, my terrain of exploration is Japanese cinema, and the specificities and particularities that characterize filmic discourse, I hope, will draw attention to this aspect of the construction of self. The philosopher Richard Rorty says, "The important thing about novelists as compared to theorists is that they are good at details" (1991: 817). This is even more true of cinema and the details that are vital to filmic diegesis, and representation should serve to foreground this aspect.

When discussing the question of self and its understanding in any culture, frames of intelligibility and interpretability associated with that culture assume a justifiably important position. Various indigenous concepts that have attained social articulation and legitimacy can be pressed into service with remarkable effect. In the case of Japan, in exploring the dynamics of the Japanese self, concepts such as *uchi* (inside), *soto* (outside), *omote* (in front), *ura* (in back), *giri* (social obligation), *ninjo* (personal emotion), *tatemae* (outer stance), *honne* (inner feelings), *amae* (dependence), *kokoro* (spiritual essence), *seishin* (spirituality), *kejime* (flexibility), *jinkaku* (personal character), *doo* (path), *on* (indebtedness), *wa* (harmony), and *ba* (frame) have been used. Clearly, the English translations do not capture the full plenitude of meaning and the nuanced understandings of the original terms. Many cultural analysts of Japanese society have used these and similar indigenous concepts in expanded senses to get at some of the deeper and more complicated aspects of Japanese self.

In this essay I wish to focus on the concept of *seishin* (spirituality) as a way of comprehending the discursive production of the Japanese self. Harumi Befu observes: "Among social values which make up the Japanese personhood, the Japanese terms 'jinkaku' (personal character) and 'seishin' (spirituality) come to mind immediately. A person with 'jinkaku' in Japan is respected for the virtues inherent in that person. It denotes moral and spiritual contents more than anything else. 'Seishin' (spirituality), therefore, is an integral component of 'jinkaku' in Japan. What is implied here is the inner strength, spirituality, and morality of a person" (1992:5). He then goes on to make the remark that, according to the Japanese way of thinking, one attains inner strength through the experiencing of hardships, and that hardship is indispensable for the acquisition of this strength. What is perhaps most noteworthy about this spiritual strength is that it seems to enlarge one's character, making one a wise, humane, understanding person and it generates a source of energy that could be productively channeled into constructive purposes. In examining the predicaments of the three protagonists in the three Japanese films that I have chosen to investigate in this essay, I wish to invoke this concept.

Culturally grounded concepts, such as the ones I have enumerated above, which are imbricated with cultural logics and cultural epistemologies, can be extremely helpful in analyzing the interplay between self and society. However, we can best make use of these concepts only if we refrain from totalizing them and absolutizing them, and if we recognize the complex ways in which they are inscribed by diverse forces of power. In other words, we need to historicize, politicize, and pluralize them. We need to attain a more complex understanding of these concepts, situating them in specific historical locations. This way, these culturally grounded concepts will enable us to reach a better grasp of the complexities, multiplicities, ambivalences, inner tensions, and fissures that characterize self in Japan, as indeed in any other country.

In this essay I wish to explore the question of human agency in Japanese culture in relation to three well-known Japanese films: Kon Ichikawa's *Harp of Burma,* Akira Kurosawa's *Ikiru,* and Hiroshi Teshigahara's *Woman in the Dunes.* All three films textualize this theme from their respective discursive spaces and suggest the validity of the concept of seishin as a way of probing more deeply into the meaning of the experiences of the three protagonists in the three films.[2]

The film *Harp of Burma* is based on a novel of the same name written by Takeyama Michio in 1946. It narrates the experiences of a company of Japanese soldiers who are compelled by force of circumstance to countenance the fury and brutality of war in Burma and who keep up their morale and sense of camaraderie by singing songs together. The real interest of the film resides in the character of Mizushima Yasuhiko, a well-liked member of the company, and his problems and privations. The complex way in which he acquires a sense of agency in the face of overwhelming odds, for me, constitutes the emotional and intellectual center of the film.

The vast majority of the Japanese who returned from the war presented a very sorry sight, looking exhausted, emaciated, and downcast. Many of them were sick and carried off on stretchers. However, the film portrays, among the returning soldiers, a company that was surprisingly cheerful and in good spirits. They were always singing and they sang exceptionally well. When they disembarked at Yokosuka, those who came to welcome them were surprised by their physical and mental strength. It so happened that the captain of the company was a young and talented musician just out of the school of music; he had made it a point to teach his fellow soldiers to sing. This enabled them to survive the hardships, overcome the inevitable boredom, and establish a sense of camaraderie. The man who was at the center of this interesting group was Mizushima, who grew up to be an accomplished harpist. Everyone in the company returned home except Mizushima, and the film recounts his life story.

Mizushima was a corporal. Although he had had no formal training as a musician prior to joining the company, very soon he became a highly accomplished musician; indeed, music was his passion. He made his own harp and played on it like a master. Although, through the instrumentality of communal singing, the company managed to keep its morale high, it was evident that the war was not going the way that the Japanese had expected, and the situation was becoming increasingly desperate. They were fleeing from mountain to mountain in the hope of eventually reaching Thailand. As they were moving from point to point, they encountered numerous dangerous experiences, and on those occasions it was Mizushima who could easily pass as a Burmese and who in addition played the Burmese harp with such professionalism that he saved them from certain destruction. As he could easily be mistaken for a Burmese, it was he who was sent out on perilous scouting missions.

One day the company came to learn that the war had ended three days earlier and that the Japanese had surrendered. They threw down their guns and became prisoners in the hands of the British. The captain of the company received intelligence reports to the effect that in a distant mountain range some Japanese soldiers were holed up and refusing to surrender. In his characteristic way, Mizushima volunteered to go and meet these erratic soldiers, explain the current situation, and persuade them to give up. In the meantime the company was taken to a P.O.W. camp in Mudon in Southern Burma. Weeks passed and there was no news about Mizushima. The company came to believe that he had died. One day, some members of the company chanced to see a Burmese monk who looked exactly like Mizushima and memories of him resurfaced. The captain who treated Mizushima as his own brother was overcome by guilt; he felt personally responsible for the latter's death. However, he did not totally give up hope of finding Mizushima. Meanwhile the company met that Burmese monk a number of times, and ultimately it was disclosed that he was none other than Mizushima himself. The members of the company invited him to rejoin them again, but their entreaties came to nothing.

In the meantime the company learned that it was to be repatriated. Just before they were to leave, the captain received a letter from Mizushima that is sent through an old Burmese woman who used to visit the camp to sell various things to the soldiers. The captain decided that he would read the letter later. The members of the company were clearly troubled by the thought that Mizushima, who served the company with such unwavering loyalty and deep dedication had ended up as a deserter. On the third day that they were on the ship on their way back to Japan, the captain called all the soldiers to read aloud Mizushima's letter. The contents of it came as a surprise, in many ways a relief, to those gathered there. Mizushima started out by conveying to his fellow soldiers how much he would like to return to his company and to work and sing with them as in former times. He said that he would never forget the moments of joy and agony that they shared together in Burma. He wanted very much to return to Japan and reunite with his family. However, his conscience would not permit such a course of action, as he felt deeply that he had a specific and important job to do in Burma.

The letter went on to narrate how he met the Japanese holed up in the mountain range. Despite his best efforts at persuasion they refused to surrender. He was himself injured in the crossfire between the Japanese and British soldiers. Mizushima realized that the corpses and skeletons of the Japanese soldiers who fell in battle were scattered in the woods, and came to the conclusion that it was his duty to give them a proper burial. He buried the bodies of the Japanese wherever he found them, and realized soon enough that it was no easy task. In the meantime he had learned to speak Burmese very fluently. He had also come to the realization that the world was full of misery and suffering and injustice and that it is our bound duty to alleviate them, in whatever way we can. It is our duty, he said, to work toward the creation of a more humane world that has less pain and suffering. Whatever the obstacles we might encounter in this effort, we need to carry out our duties undaunted and with mental tranquility. There are higher values than efficiency and empowerment, and we need to make a resolute attempt to reach them.

The life of Mizushima as textualized in *Harp of Burma* is most interesting, and we can usefully employ the concept of *seishin* to understand his metamorphosis. However, it is not a simple exercise of mechanically applying this concept to make sense of his behavior. There are a number of tensions within his self that foreground a clash between two sets of highly prized Japanese cultural values. For example, the whole concept of group loyalty, which is so positively valorized in Japanese culture and whose significance he knows only too well, has to be abandoned in his quest for the higher aims of life. Similarly, he has to forgo the opportunity to reunite with his family in order to fulfill his higher calling. To desert one's company is an act that is looked down upon with the utmost disfavor, yet Mizushima opts for this course of action. So what we see here is that Mizushima's attainment of a sense of agency through seishin is full of tensions, ambivalences, and fissures. This serves to convert the concept of seishin into a site of contestation of meaning. Did Mizushima, in countenancing the hardships and traumas that were placed in his path, take the right course of action? Would it have been better for him to reunite with his company and return to Japan? Such questions tend to underline the problematically multifaceted nature of the concept of seishin.

Ikiru, by Akira Kurosawa, is one of the greatest films of Japanese cinema and one that displays the depth of human understanding and the controlled artistry of the filmmaker. *Ikiru* is an intransitive verb meaning "to live," and the film explores the ramifications of this word in a complex and memorable way. The protagonist of the film is Watanabe Kenji, a minor official in the bureaucracy of the municipality. The film narrativizes his life and existential predicament. Watanabe learns, much to his consternation, that he has gastric cancer and has only six months to live. Naturally, his initial reaction is one of fear and trepidation. That night in bed he cries, bitterly overcome by a sense of indescribable helplessness. His next move is to involve himself in the family he has left, hoping for the solace of distraction. But this proves to be chimerical. His wife is dead and the only person close to him is his son. He is now married, and with the passage of time the son and his wife have become distanced and indifferent. In a curious sense, the encroaching death inculcates in him a sense of freedom—freedom and an opportunity to make the best use of the remainder of his life.

At first Watanabe's inclination is to immerse himself in pleasure and fulfill his physical desires. He withdraws his savings from the bank and goes into the city to have fun. He meets a writer of popular fiction who tells him:

> I see that adversity does have its virtues and that man finds truth in misfortune.... Having cancer has made you taste life. Man is such a fool. It is always when he is going to leave it that he finally discovers how beautiful life can be. And even then people who realize this are rare. Some die without even once knowing what life is. You're a fine man because you are fighting against death, and that is what impresses me. Up to now you've been life's slave, but now you are going to be its martyr. And it is man's duty to enjoy life. It is against nature not to. Man must have a greed for life. We are told that that is immoral, but it is not. The greed to live is a virtue.

The writer takes him to bars, strip shows, and *pachinko* (pinball machine) parlors. At one point, a rather abrasive prostitute takes his hat, and the writer admonishes him to buy a new one. He does—an anachronistically jaunty one.

One day, in the small hours of the morning, we see Watanabe singing a song that he has requested the pianist to play:

Life is too short
Fall in love, dear maiden
While your lips are still red
And before you are cold
For there will be no tomorrow
Life is so short
Fall in love, dear maiden
While your hair is still black
And before your heart withers
For today will not come again.

However, Watanabe realizes soon enough that pleasure does not bring him the anticipated happiness and contentment. He resolves that he should devote the rest of his life to the sustenance of a more meaningful relationship. Odagiri is one of the workers in his department. She comes to his house so that he can stamp her resignation. Watanabe and Odagiri start a relationship, and they are happy for a short period of time. They go to amusement parks, ice-skating rinks, and movies together. They enjoy themselves playing childish games. Watanabe finds her youthfulness and zest for life particularly appealing. One day, during dinner, he discloses to her the news about his impending death; he tells her that he has only a few months to live and that he finds himself increasingly drawn to her. He tells Toyo how as a boy he nearly drowned and that he has the same feeling of enveloping darkness and helplessness. She asks him about his son, and he responds by telling her not to mention his name.

Watanabe says that Toyo is so full of life and that he is envious of her. If only he could be like her for one day before his death. He says, "I won't be able to die unless I can be. Oh, I want something only you can show me. I don't know what to do. I don't know how to do it. Maybe you don't either, but please, if you can, show me how to be like you." She says that all she does is work and eat and make toys for children. She says that it is fun and that she feels as if she were friends with all the children in Japan. She says, "Mr. Watanabe, why don't you do something like that, too?" It is then that Watanabe makes up his mind to devote the remainder of his life for a worthy cause that would almost certainly invest his life with a greater measure of significance. He remembers a group of women dwelling in the slum had petitioned some time ago to have a fetid pool converted into a park for children. However, he recalls that they were given the usual bureaucratic runaround. Now Watanabe decides to expedite the plan and see it through to completion. He tells his colleagues that everyone in the bureaucracy should give their fullest cooperation to this worthwhile cause. Watanabe, despite his failing health, devotes all his time and energy to the construction of the children's park, and he succeeds in completing it before his death. There is a memorable scene in the film in which Watanabe rocks on the swing in the newly built children's park in the snow, as he sings an old song about living life to the fullest.

Once Watanabe decides to devote the remainder of his life to building the children's park and assumes agency, we see his conversion from a passive bureaucrat who led a routinized life in his office to a social activist and a humanitarian pursuing his chosen course with unwavering devotion. He fights the bureaucracy, galvanizes the workers, survives threats and intimidation, reenergizes himself, and achieves his ambition. After his death, ironically, various intepretations are put on his actions. His son, Mitsuo, is of the opinion that his father's strange behavior is due to his overhearing a conversation between him and his wife as to how they could obtain his retirement pay and use it for their own benefit. Watanabe's brother holds to the belief that his mistress should be held responsible for his recent eccentricities. Newspaper journalists have a theory of their own, namely, that his death was an act of suicide and that he was making a political statement about the corruption that was prevalent in the bureaucracy. The deputy mayor expresses the view that the park comes under the park section and that Watanabe was essentially promoting himself and seeking to get all the credit for the construction of the park for himself. What is interesting about these diverse interpretations is that they all miss the mark and make Watanabe's motives that much more noble.

Ikiru is a film that clearly deals with the acquisition of agency and its manifold implications. Watanabe's personal drama is played out against the social and moral degradation of postwar Japan, the one counterpointing the other. The indifference and coldheartedness of the bureaucracy, the selfishness of his son and daughter-in-law, the intimidations of the gangsters who are interested in building a red-light district instead of the park for children, the actions of the self-serving politicians all index this moral decline. Watanabe is an ordinary man leading an ordinary life until he learns of his terminal disease. Confronted with the dark threat of his impending death, he seeks to capture a sense of agency and impart a depth of meaning and significance to his life. In doing so he elevates himself to a higher plane. Although I have summarized Watanabe's life in a linear sequence, the film itself adopts a much more complex narrative strategy, with flashbacks, multiple viewpoints, and an interplay between the information given by the narrator and the actions of Watanabe in order to promote reflection and ratiocination on the part of the spectator rather than mere empathy.

Once again we can invoke the concept of seishin to understand the character of Watanabe. Watanabe is a very different man from Mizushima in *Harp of Burma*. Mizushima is young, an endearing character from the beginning. He assumes a sense of agency through grappling with a moral dilemma. Watanabe, on the other hand, is an older man who led a routine and uneventful life until told of his impending death. It is then that he seeks to assume a sense of agency. Initially he takes a number of false steps until he settles on the project of constructing the children's park. Here we see, then, that although the broad concept of seishin can be used to plumb the behavior of the two characters, the way in which they relate to this concept are very different and demand different hermeneutic strategies.

Let us consider the third film, *The Woman in the Dunes* (*Suna no onna*) by Teshigahara. This film is based on the celebrated novel by Abe Kobo (1972). Abe is one of the most distinguished novelists and playwrights in contemporary Japan and is the author of such well-known works as *The Face of Another, The Ruined Map, The Box Man,* and *The Woman in the Dunes,* Abe's most successful novel, which was awarded the Yomiuri Prize for literature in 1960. The highly gifted Japanese filmmaker Teshigahara made a film out of this novel that became a remarkable critical success, winning the Jury Prize at the prestigious Cannes film festival in 1963.

One of Abe's abiding themes has been the alienation of human beings in modern society and their ceaseless quest for identity and agency. This certainly is the case with *The Woman in the Dunes*. It narrates the predicament of a man held captive with a young woman at the bottom of a perilous sand pit in a remote seaside village, and his desperate attempts to make sense of the bizarre world into which he has been inserted, much against his will, and to acquire a sense of agency in order to take control of the situation. The protagonist of the narrative is Niki Jumpei, a schoolteacher and a dedicated insect collector.

He disappears, quite mysteriously, one August afternoon. Investigations by the police and inquiries by the media draw a blank. While passionately searching for insects, Niki Jumpei unknowingly arrives at a desolate seaside village near the sand dunes. Absorbed with the insects, he is hardly aware of the grim and forbidding terrain into which he has accidentally wandered. When he eventually surveys the surroundings, he is struck by its strangeness and dullness.

As fate would have it, he misses the last bus, and now he cannot go home; he is stranded in an incomprehensibly bizarre world. The villagers, sensing his plight, invite him to spend the night in the village, and he readily accepts. He is asked to spend the night in a shack at the bottom of the sand pit, and this, for Niki Jumpei, is the beginning of a chain of bizarre incidents. He comes to be held captive in this nightmarish world, along with a young woman. The only reality is the ever-present sand. In this almost unlivable shack at the bottom of the sand pit he could not sleep or keep his eyes open; sand was everywhere and menacing in its presence. It so happens that the young woman, whose husband and daughter had died the previous year when their shack caved in, is now destined to live with him. He is in effect a prisoner in the hands of the villagers. His feelings toward this woman range from anger and irritation to erotic love and compassion. Niki Jumpei finds himself in a hopeless and baffling situation. He attempts to flee from this nightmarish world five times, but never succeeds in his aim. His efforts to outwit his captors fail repeatedly.

Niki begins to come to terms with the unexpected and unpalatable reality that has been foisted on him. One day he comes to the realization that he is able to obtain water through the capillary action of sand, a discovery that serves to bring about a fundamental change in his attitude and outlook. He now has acquired a new agency, and with the acquisition of this agency, he feels that he has opened a new chapter in his life. Niki Jumpei is no longer interested in escaping the sand pits and returning home; he is now far more interested in talking about his discovery with others.

The Woman in the Dunes thematizes the issue of human agency in a vividly fabulist mode of imagining. Sand is the regnant trope of the film, as indeed it is of the novel. It is everywhere—pervading the body, the thoughts, the imagination, the ruminations, and the actions of the protagonist. As Currie (1976) has rightly observed, sand is the novel's central metaphor, standing for the shifting reality in which the protagonist needs to sink roots to anchor his existence. This is equally discernible in the film. Many critics have sought to interpret the symbolism of the sand in diverse ways. It is my conviction that despite Abe's Catholic background, the symbolism has certain Buddhist connotations. According to Buddhism, sand signifies *samsara,* or worldly existence that is full of suffering, and water signifies wisdom and insight.

The message that emerges from the film is clearly the message that is inscribed in the novel as well. It is evident that director Teshigahara has aimed to stick as close as possible to the novel; even the dialogue, by and large, is taken directly from the novel. He has added a few episodes like the rape scene and the scene dealing with Niki's old girlfriend that occurs at the beginning of the film, and he has truncated the escape scenes, which are much longer in the novel. But apart from these few changes, the filmic text adheres with great fidelity to the original work. A memorable feature of *The Woman in the Dunes,* in both the novel and the film, is the imbrication of self and place. The discursive productions of self and place are vitally linked and inform the meaning of the film. Niki Jumpei is actualized, defined, and assessed in relation to place. First, we are privy to his attempt to escape from the city environment that he inhabits; next we see him against the background of the desolate and remote seaside village; the third stage, which constitutes the bulk of the film, enacts the encounter with the omnipresent sand in the shack at the bottom of the sand pit; finally his struggle with the environment and his triumph over it, with the discovery of water, results in the emergence of a newer self. At one point in the novel it is stated that "the change in the sand corresponded to a change in himself. Perhaps along with the water in the sand, he had found a new self." This point is enforced very powerfully in the film. This interplay between self and place is vital to understanding the way in which Niki acquired a newer sense of agency.

The Woman in the Dunes textualizes powerfully how the protagonist comes to acquire a new sense of agency as a consequence of struggling with the inhospitable environment in which he was compelled to live. Naturally, this is accompanied by a significant shift in the cognitive style. We are shown how human beings are prone to adhere to specific cognitive styles and to structure and reify reality in accordance with that preferred style. What the novel and the film point to is the importance of liberating oneself from rigidly constricting cognitive styles as a means of realizing one's potentialities to the full. This ties in with the concept of seishin, which presupposes such a shift in cognitive apprehensions as a consequence of facing up to hardships and seeking to understand their meaning. Needless to say, these cognitive styles are products of, and embedded in, specific discourses, and hence a change in cognitive style implies a discursive change.

Niki Jumpei is a product of the modern urban environment and the attendant discursivities that go along with it. He may not be totally happy with its discursive imperatives, but he certainly operated within its parameters. He strives to structure his reality in relation to the signification systems that he has inherited from his environment. In addition he is a resolute insect collector; the entomological and scientific modes of apprehension and analysis have deeply penetrated his being. He possesses a rational and analytic frame of mind; he has a penchant for reducing things to their basic constituent elements; he privileges reductionism over holism. Early on in the novel we are given the following description of Niki Jumpei: "His head bent down, he began to walk following the crescent-shaped line of dunes that surround the village like a rampart and towered above it. He paid almost no attention to the distant landscapes. An entomologist must concentrate his whole attention within a radius of about three yards around his feet" (15).

He was in the habit of employing classification and atomization as a way of understanding rather than seeing things holistically. As a consequence of his experiences in the shack with the woman, and as he became more and more acquainted with her ways of thinking and feeling and modes of perception, his cognitive style began to change. As the author says toward the end of the novel, "He was still in the hole, but it seemed as if he were already outside. Turning around, he could see the whole scene. You can't really judge a mosaic if you don't look at it from a distance. If you really get close to it you get lost in detail. You get away from one detail only to get caught in another. Perhaps what he had been seeing up until now was not the sand but a grain of sand" (235). As a result of Niki Jumpei's experiences in the shack — the interaction between self and place — he acquires a new cognitive style that is more holistic, as well as a newer image of his self. Once again, as with the life stories of Mizushima in *Harp of Burma* and Watanabe in *Ikiru,* we can make use of the concept of seishin to make better sense of Niki Jumpei's predicament and his eventual overcoming of it. However, there are distinct features in Niki's biography that distinguish him from the other two characters. He is a man with a scientific cast of mind, unlike the other two, and is a victim of the geography of power. Although he discovers water, it is more through an accident than through a conscious effort on his part. Moreover, there is a greater emphasis on seishin and the locatedness of experience in Niki Jumpei's transformation than in the case of the other two.

The protagonists of the three films share many features in common that are of relevance to the thematics of this essay. They are not larger-than-life figures but ordinary citizens preoccupied with the day-to-day issues of living that any average citizen has to contend with. The three characters are complex and display multiplicities, contradictions, and ambivalences that we normally ignore in our desire to come up with concepts of cohesive selves. They are compelled by force of circumstances to confront a predicament that underlines their helplessness. They are the victims of different forms of power and have to face numerous and demanding tribulations. As a consequence of facing up to their respective hardships and seeking to overcome them, they each acquire a sense of human agency. The concept of seishin, as we saw, could be invoked usefully to understand the plight of the protagonists in the three films. During the course of their privations, in seeking to confront the hardships that have befallen them and to overcome them, all three acquire a deeper sense of self-knowledge, which they clearly lacked at the beginning of their trying journeys. However, as we alluded to earlier, there are also significant differences among them. The process of self-formation in each of them bears the distinct imprint of his background, in relation to questions of power, insideness and outsideness, and displacements and relocations. It is because of this that the concept of seishin has to be applied in a way that does justice to the distinctiveness and the unique biographical trajectories of each of them.

In *Harp of Burma* we find a man torn between his desire to rejoin his fellow soldiers and return to Japan and his wish to fulfill what he perceives as his moral obligation and to achieve a sense of inner peace. Many observations of Japanese society are accepted as accurate; it is widely believed, for example, that a central characteristic of the Japanese is their strong group identity. It is thought to be present at every level of the society. Group ties are so developed that members take a collective sense of responsibility for other members' actions. Hence, betraying group loyalty is an action that is deeply negatively valorized. What is interesting about Mizushima's behavior is that he has been fiercely loyal to his company and has been an exemplar, and he suddenly decides to abandon his loyalty in pursuit of an alternate vision. He comes to the realization that the world is brutal and cruel and that suffering is everywhere. Japan had lost the war; he resists his temptation to rejoin the company. These are hard and painful choices, and Mizushima rises to the occasion with the strength of his inner convictions. As Befu remarks, "Mizushima, the main character of 'Harp of Burma,' is a man of 'jinkaku,' for his moral fiber is so strong that he is willing to sacrifice rejoining his platoon and returning to Japan" (1992:5). His moral fiber acquires the requisite strength as a consequence of honestly facing up to his predicament and reflecting on its deeper nuances.

In *Ikiru*, the protagonist Watanabe suddenly learns, much to his horror, that he has gastric cancer and that his death is imminent. In sheer desperation, he tries to live as fully as he can the remainder of his life. He takes many wrong steps that lead not to fulfillment but to greater despair and discontent until he hits upon the idea of building a park for children. He devotes all his time in the pursuit of this goal and succeeds. Watanabe faces up to his misery, takes control of the situation, and achieves his goal. Once again we see the manifestation of seishin in a distinctively different form. Michel Foucault once remarked, "It is in death that the individual becomes at one with himself, escaping from monotonous lives and their levelling effect; in the slow, half-subterranean, but already visible approach to death, the dull, common life at last becomes an individuality." In the life and death of Watanabe, the sense of seishin is inseparably linked with death.

In *The Woman in the Dunes*, the protagonist is thrust into the center of a bewilderingly miserable situation that he could have hardly anticipated. With each step the misery deepens, and he becomes helpless and powerless; he is at the mercy of the villagers who have imprisoned him. It is only as a result of facing up to his hardships and seeking to come to terms with his newer reality that he begins to acquire a sense of agency and master the situation. Here again we see the concept of seishin at play in a highly particularized situation.

The predicaments encountered by all three protagonists could be usefully reunderstood in terms of the concept of seishin. However, it is important to bear in mind that the biographies and emotional trajectories of the three are very different from each other; each has inscribed his very distinctive vector of progress on the concept of seishin, thereby extending its discursive horizons. Hence the concept of seishin and the individual life stories of each of them should be allowed to interrogate each other, thereby promoting a more nuanced understanding of seishin and a more finely grained comprehension of the ways in which the protagonists of the three films achieved their sense of agency.

Another significant advantage in using the concept of seishin to explore the privations faced by Mizushima, Watanabe, and Niki Jumpei is that it underscores the fact that the self is neither an autonomous, self-present, self-identical, sovereign subject who is the originator of meaning and action, nor a totally passive entity that is shaped and molded by exogenous forces. The three characters are products of various social and cultural discourses, but at the same time are capable of assuming a sense of agency in response to the challenges confronting them. The concept of seishin allows us to understand the limited but important discursive space opened up by that notion.

The danger with using concepts such as *amae, ura, uchi, soto, giri, ninjo, tatemae,* and *honne,* which I mentioned earlier, is that it is all too often easy to convert them into totalizing master concepts. Such a move would be counterproductive, because it would serve to put in place more reified and essentialized polarities. What we need to do, therefore, is to use these concepts not as master concepts, but rather as strategies of reading social and cultural situations imbricated with self.[3] The concept of seishin, too, should be pressed into service in such a way as to achieve this objective.

Brian Moeran (1984) has described how ambivalences characterize the concept of seishin and says that it is not easy to delineate precisely what constitutes seishin. Hence it is important to examine the ways in which it is variously and discursively produced in specific social and historical situations. Frager and Rohlen (1976:270) remark, "The 'seishin' outlook does not see the world as inherently divided into class or other interest groups; it chooses to view individuals less in terms of age, wealth, and the like, and more in terms of 'spiritual strength or weakness.'" However, the interesting point about seishin as a discourse is precisely the complex ways in which it is inscribed by age, wealth, class, and other interests. It is a terrain in which these intersect, giving rise to polysemic signifiers.

The danger with this kind of approach is that it tends to essentialize the concept and remove it from historical specificities and social particularities. In our examination of this concept in relation to the three Japanese films, the importance of locating it in specific situationalities became clear.

The ambivalences associated with the concept of seishin are demonstrated by Moeran when he points out how seishin and *kokoro* (spiritual essence) are at times in alliance and at other times in opposition. Useful as these concepts are, then, in reunderstanding Japanese self, we need to deconstruct them and display the inner tensions and aporias contained in them. They can best be understood not as manifestations of theory but as framers of diverse practices.

The concept of seishin, as it manifests itself in the three films we have discussed, has a vital bearing on the human body. It points to the fact that human selves are not disembodied selves and that somaticity forms a crucial and defining element of selfhood. In *Harp of Burma*, Mizushima sees death and destruction and seeks to rise above the bodily efficaciousness he has been trained to valorize. In *Ikiru*, we see how Watanabe fights bodily decline by turning his gaze toward a higher calling. In *The Woman in the Dunes*, Niki Jumpei turns his bodily entrapment into a mode of human achievement. In all three cases, then, the idea of seishin is deeply embedded in somaticity and in point of fact emerges from it. Seishin has a marked Buddhist connotation to it, and in Buddhism the idea of wrestling with one's body in order to gain spiritual strength is common. Here again the interplay between body and spiritual strength is differently defined depending on the specificities of the situation. Postmodernist thinkers have placed great emphasis on the human body and elevated it to a privileged hermeneutic position in social inquiry and cultural description. Michel Foucault is a case in point. He in his studies of what he calls "disciplinary society" has demonstrated interesting and fruitful ways of reconceptualizing the human body in relation to society. However, there is one principal deficiency in his writing—he leaves little room for the play of agency. In his works the body becomes an effect of the mechanisms of knowledge and power. The body emerges as a product of modern rationalism and the various institutions associated with the modern disciplinary society. This has the effect of making the human body into a passive entity and robbing it of its active and initiatory capacities. What the concept of seishin, on the other hand, clearly does is to focalize on the ways in which the body and the idea of human agency are mutually constitutive.

The concept of seishin, as we saw in the three films, has a close relationship with the idea of authenticity. Here I use the term "authenticity" in the same way that the philosopher Jean-Paul Sartre has employed it in his philosophical writings to reference the possession of a true and lucid consciousness of a situation and assumption of the responsibility and risks that it entails. All three protagonists of the films display this consciousness as a mark of their emotional and intellectual growth. However, what their experiences also point to is that the concept of authenticity can be most profitably understood not in the totalizing manner proposed by Sartre, but as one embedded in specific situations and differently produced by discourse.

The characters of Mizushima, Watanabe, and Jumpei are textually produced, and we need to factor this into our explorations. They are representations and hence are refashioned, refabricated, and recoded in terms of cinematic rhetoric. Edward Said (1993) has pointed out that the construction of a narrative subject is a social act par excellence, and hence contains behind or inside it the authority of society and history. He sees the authority as being formed by the convergence of three subauthorities: the authority of the author, the authority of the narrator whose discourse grounds the narrative in recognizable circumstances, and the authority of the community whose representatives most often are the family but also the nation. If we apply this formulation to the three films we have been discussing in this essay, we see that Ichikawa, Kurosawa, and Teshigahara, the authors of the three films, are historical people who have enriched Japanese cinema by interrogating various aspects of Japanese culture. The narrators in all three films adopt an omniscient viewpoint, and we observe a stimulating interplay between the vision of the omniscient narrator and the individual sensibility and perceptions of the protagonists. Finally, there is the authority of the community, without which the filmic experience means nothing. The frames of intelligibility offered, directly or obliquely, by the filmic discourse, which constitute a part of the cultural knowledge and cultural logic of the Japanese, serve to procure this authority. In this case it is the idea of seishin that serves to bring into play this authority of community. Hence it is important to recognize that the problems, predicaments, hardships, and eventual mastery of them by Mizushima, Watanabe, and Jumpei are textually produced and are imbricated with forms of cultural knowledge.[4]

Agency and structure are usually compartmentalized and presented as reified polarities. Instead we need to recognize them as mutually reinforcing entities that are interconnected with overlapping conceptual cartographies. What the concept of seishin and its applicability in the understanding of the experiences textualized in the three films tell us is that agency and structure are inscribed at a number of different levels and that each is embedded in the other's field of operation. The concept of seishin calls attention to the complex ways in which individuals acquire spiritual strength and a sense of agency by facing up to diverse forms of hardships. But at the same time the concept of seishin is very much a part of the Japanese cultural discourse and representative of the axiomatics of cultural understanding and valuation.

This essay began by pointing out the need to adopt a more complex and nuanced approach to the study of self and collectivism in Japanese culture and the importance of recognizing the discursive space that it provides for the emergence of agency. I sought to demonstrate this by examining three well-known and critically acclaimed Japanese films. In examining these films we saw the heuristic value of the concept of seishin as a way of framing the predicaments and dilemmas of the protagonists and their eventual acquisition of spiritual strength. While this concept is important and useful in our reunderstanding of Japanese selfhood, the concept can be most productively employed only if we refrain from totalizing it and using it as a reading strategy to get at the complexities and ambivalences of specific social and historical situations. This should be regarded as a site in which, directly or obliquely, an incessant contestation of meaning takes place. Selves are embedded in specific situations and discursively produced. Selfhood is a construct inseparable from rhetoricity and performativity and is imbricated with questions of power and cultural axiomatics. Hence the importance of these dimensions in the constitution of the self.

Notes

1. Discussions of the Japanese concept of self in relation to the self-society binarism are in large part inspired by Western scholarly discourses on this theme. This can, at one level, be regarded as a classic example of a privileged and imported idea that people feel must have a Japanese referent. As Pollack (1992:39) has pointed out, it was during the Meiji period (1868–1916) that the Japanese initially countenanced the notion of an autonomous individual self along with the other newer concepts, ideas, and accoutrements of modernity. At the same time, the concept of self as opposed to the group plays a vital role in the thought worlds of the Japanese. As Fujii observes (1993:1), in Japan, a nation constantly mischaracterized by foreigners and Japanese alike as a society in which the group displaces the self, Western-type romantic notions of the individual continue to be embraced with much enthusiasm. As for the question of agency, scholars like Sakai (1992), Field (1987), and Okada (1991) have demonstrated how even premodern Japanese literature contains clear articulations of subjective agency.

2. In all three films, it is interesting to observe, there are two phases in the protagonists' similar trajectories, and a dialectic leading from one to the other. The first half is rather ordinary and mundane, and contains nothing spectacular. It is in the latter half that we observe the manifestation of seishin; something extraordinary occurs in the lives of the protagonists to marshal forth the strength of seishin—facing death and seeing multitudes of corpses, being informed of terminal cancer, being trapped and held prisoner in a sand dune.

3. In order to comprehend the full heuristic value of concepts such as *uchi, soto, giri, ninjo, amae,* and so forth, we need to examine their historical evolution. These concepts emerged during certain historical conjunctures and evolved over time, being inflected by the circumambient social and cultural discourses at specific times. Without such a historically informed perspective, we are likely to turn these concepts into essentialized and transhistorical concepts.

4. An interesting question is whether these three films could have been made in, say, India or Mexico or France and succeeded in carrying the same freight of meaning. Clearly, the story line would translate across cultures, but the frames of intelligibility would not. What is the etiology and ontology of the self, society, and agency discourse textualized in the films that make it especially meaningful in the Japanese context? How are the goals, behaviors, and life changes cognitively processed and legitimated in Japan, and what epistemological conditions promote particular proceedings and justifications? In this regard, one can usefully invoke Charles Taylor's (1985:39) distinction between shared meanings and common meanings. As he says, "It is part of the meaning of a common aspiration, belief, celebration, etc. that it be not just shared but part of the common reference world. Or to put it another way, its being shared is a collective act. Common meanings are the basis of community. Intersubjective meanings give a people a common language to talk about social reality and a common understanding of certain norms, but only with common meaning does this common reference world contain significant common actions, celebrations, and feelings. These are objects in the world that everybody shares. This is what makes a community."

References

Abe Kobo. 1972. *The Woman in the Dunes*. Translated by E. Dale Saunders. New York: Vintage Books.

Bachnik, Jane M. 1992. "The Two 'Faces' of Self and Society in Japan." *Ethos* 20 (1).

Befu, Harumi. 1992. "Self and Society in Contemporary Japan." Typescript.

Benedict, Ruth. 1946. *The Chrysanthemum and the Sword: Patterns of Japanese Culture*. Boston: Houghton, Mifflin.

Bourdieu, Pierre. 1977. *Outline of a Theory of Practice*. Cambridge: Cambridge University Press.

Buruma, Ian. 1984. *Behind the Mask: On Sexual Demons, Sacred Mothers, Transvestites and Other Japanese Cultural Heroes*. New York: Pantheon.

Currie, William. 1976. *"The Woman in the Dunes,"* in K. Tsuruta and T. E. Swan, *Approaches to the Modern Japanese Novel*. Tokyo: Sophia University.

Deleuze, Gilles. 1989. *Cinema 2: The Time-Image*. Translated by Hugh Tomlinson and Robert Galeta. Minneapolis: University of Minnesota Press.

Doi, Takeo. 1973. *The Anatomy of Dependence*. Tokyo: Kodasha International.

Field, Norma F. 1987. *The Splendor of Language in* The Tale of Genji. Princeton, N.J.: Princeton University Press.

Frager, Robert, and Thomas P. Rohlen. 1976. "The Future of Tradition: Japanese Spirit in the 1980s," in *Japan — The Paradox of Progress*, edited by Lewis Austin. New Haven, Conn.: Yale University Press.

Fujii, James A. 1993. *Complicit Fictions*. Berkeley: University of California Press.

Giddens, Anthony. 1979. *Central Problems in Social Theory*. Berkeley: University of California Press.

———. 1984. *The Constitution of Society*. Berkeley: University of California Press.

Kelly, William. 1991. Paper presented at the Conference on Self and Social Order in China, India, and Japan, Honolulu, Hawaii.

Kondo, Dorinne. 1990. *Crafting Selves: Work, Identity, and the Politics in a Japanese Factory*. Chicago: University of Chicago Press.

Lebra, Takie Sugiyama. 1976. *Japanese Patterns of Behavior*. Honolulu: University of Hawaii Press.

Moeran, Brian. 1984. "Individual, Group, and Seishin: Japan's Internal Cultural Debate." *Man* 19:252–66.

Nakane, Chie. 1970. *Japanese Society*. Berkeley: University of California Press.

Ohnuki-Tierney, Emiko. 1984. *Illness and Culture in Contemporary Japan*. New York: Cambridge University Press.

———. 1990. "The Ambivalent Self of the Contemporary Japanese." *Cultural Anthropology* 5:197–216.

Okada, Richard. 1991. *Figures of Resistance: Poetry Narrating and the Politics of Fiction in* The Tale of Genji *and Other Mid-Heian Texts*. Durham, N.C.: Duke University Press.

Plath, David. 1980. *Long Engagements: Maturity in Modern Japan*. Stanford, Calif.: Stanford University Press.

Pollack, David. 1992. *Reading against Culture: Ideology and Narrative in the Japanese Novel*. Ithaca, N.Y.: Cornell University Press.

Rohlen, Thomas P. 1989. "Order in Japanese Society: Attachment, Authority, and Routine." *Journal of Japanese Studies* 15 (1):5–40.

Rorty, Richard. 1989. *Contingency, Irony, and Solidarity*. Cambridge: Cambridge University Press.

———. 1991. *Essays on Heidegger and Others*. New York: Cambridge University Press.

Rosenberger, Nancy R. 1989. "Dialectic Balance in the Polar Model of Self: The Japanese Case." *Ethos* 17:88–113.

Said, Edward. 1993. *Culture and Imperialism.* New York: Knopf.

Sakai, Naoki. 1992. *Voices of the Part: The Status of Language in Eighteenth Century Japanese Discourse.* Ithaca, N.Y.: Cornell University Press.

Smith, Robert J. 1983. *Japanese Society: Tradition, Self, and the Social Order.* Cambridge: Cambridge University Press.

Taylor, Charles. 1985. *Philosophy and the Human Sciences.* Cambridge: Cambridge University Press.

———. 1989. *Sources of the Self: The Making of the Modern Identity.* Cambridge, Mass.: Harvard University Press.

Tobin, Joseph J. 1992. "Japanese Preschools and the Pedagogy of Selfhood," in *Japanese Sense of Self,* edited by Nancy R. Rosenberger. New York: Cambridge University Press.

9 / The Nail That Came Out All the Way: Hayashi Takeshi's Case against the Regulation of the Japanese Student Body

Marie Thorsten Morimoto

The nail that protrudes gets hammered down.
TRADITIONAL JAPANESE SAYING

The nail that comes out all the way never gets hammered down.
CONTEMPORARY JAPANESE SAYING

In May 1985, a young high school student was on a school trip to the Tsukuba Expo, a world science exhibition. In violation of school regulations, he borrowed his friend's hair dryer to style his hair. When his teacher caught him in the act, the boy apologized and began crying, but his remorse was in vain. The teacher forced him to kneel down while he beat and kicked the young student to his death.

At that time, another student, Hayashi Takeshi, was beginning his third year of high school in Chiba prefecture. Impressed by the incident at Tsukuba as an indication of the severity of Japanese student regulations, Hayashi led a group of fifteen students in protesting the regulations of their own prefectural high school. Their movement successfully resulted in a relaxation of many of the more rigid stipulations.

Less than a year after graduating from high school, Hayashi published his first book protesting Japan's *kōsoku*, the codes of school regulations and sanctions. The response to *Down with School Regulations!* was overwhelming; a second volume quickly followed, compiling excerpts from more than three thousand letters from students informing Hayashi of their personal situations with the kōsoku. Now, over a decade later, Hayashi's career has been completely shaped by his movement against school regulations. He writes an advice column on school regulations for a young women's magazine, for which he receives about one hundred letters per month. He works with an attorney's group to help solve problems of children's educational rights, and he has been interviewed by several foreign media sources, including *Newsweek* and the *New York Times*. He has planned a fourth volume of *Down with School Regulations!*

I became interested in the young education critic not only for the substance of his argument against kōsoku, but for the author's own style as a remarkable exception to everything the kōsoku seemed aimed to produce—in Hayashi's own frequently used epithet, robots. *Down with School Regulations!* is an adolescent catharsis, no doubt, but it is anything but robotic. It is a highly creative work of investigative journalism interspersed with self-penned poetry, personal anecdotes, inevitable teeny-bop illustrations, and last but not least, a manifesto for teenagers to hone up on constitutional law and stand up for their rights.

Interviewing Hayashi, I asked him at the outset why he was an exception to the oft-heard dictum "The nail that protrudes gets hammered down," which defines a social structure believed to inhibit the development of the self. While there is little doubt that group adherence is more important in Japan and elsewhere in Asia than it is in the West, it must also be true that if no nail ever protruded, Japan would still be a land of sword-wielding samurai and airy aristocrats ruling over the masses of farmers and merchants. Hayashi explained that he and other student activists have taken as their motto a more contemporary saying, "The nail that comes out all the way never gets hammered down." They believe their self-identities are masked and manipulated, but not muted. They aim to instill confidence in their role as active human agents assailing a solid but not invincible structure: the Japanese school regulations.

Hayashi's extracted nail may protrude from our usual impression of "things Japanese," impressions of conformity, discipline, and obedience to authority. Yet Hayashi's case represents not only the interstices of the "typically Japanese," but perhaps more pertinently, the interstices of "East" and "West." The geopolitical "orders" of nation and civilization are becoming increasingly fluid in today's world, just as new, belated definitions of identity defying traditional borders are on the rise. Perhaps the most conspicuous of new identities is that of the "East," the general region of "Asia" or the "Pacific Rim." Several questions thus converge around the extracted nail: Does Hayashi's work mean young Japanese are defying the "Asian"? Does his project exemplify the plurality of identities of "Asia"? Will Westerners soon find Japanese-style corporal discipline more attractive?

Even keeping these panoramic questions in mind, however, I am not sure that it is fair to hammer down Hayashi's case in the flurry of identity reconstruction going on in the "global" picture, especially without first focusing on the "local" nature of his work. Most of our understanding of new identities taking shape on the global front is that of elites, yet it is readily apparent from Hayashi's case that he is not "elite": his work of answering letters and commenting on specific cases of corporal abuse is personal, particular, and pragmatic. Therefore, the purpose of this chapter will be to look more deeply at Hayashi's resistance itself, to understand that whatever the broader, ambivalent issues of national or civilizational identity that may be refracted in the topic of student regulations, the work of young educational assailants such as Hayashi remains more concisely local, concerned with the basic freedom of the human body.

The first goal of this chapter will be to outline Hayashi's basic position that the student regulations are unconstitutional, illegitimate, and inhumane. Second, I will explain how his definition of "rights" is not universally but relatively defined, in a way that pragmatically fits his needs as a protestor of violations against the most basic, bodily freedom of students. Third, I will outline some reasons why the scenario of East and West, which might easily place Hayashi's case into an outmoded role of "modernization," would not be appropriate. Finally, I will suggest some recent circumstances that may affect the kōsoku and the silencing of educational criticism.

Certainly Hayashi's gumption to write and get published on this otherwise silenced subject is remarkable; before meeting him, I had pictured him as a lone nail protruding. But my conversation with him, and my continued reading of his books, suggested to me that the message in his well-articulated frustration may be neither unusual nor un-Japanese. I was impressed much less by the legal code he defends than by the simple issue of seeking freedom of the body. I decided thus to explore whether it is the kōsoku—the system of regulations governing the minutiae of student "bodies"—that may be less traditionally "Japanese" than Hayashi himself.

Foucault distinguishes between "power" as the system of rights and duties governed through officials and institutions and "power" that works subtly, often anonymously, through the technique of disciplining human bodies. The latter form of control, "biopower," concentrates on the management of entire populations as well as the discipline of the individual body. If formal laws have been less significant in Japan than informal sanctions—as is the case with the kōsoku issue—then Foucault's notion of biopower is all the more fitting. Biopower has not replaced traditional power in the modern era; rather, it has "infiltrated" and co-opted the more recognizable forms of power, making possible "an infinitesimal distribution of the power relations." In this chapter, Hayashi's work is presented to convey the significance of power acting directly upon the individual body. The continuous surveillance of clothing, behavior, and movement has made the student body into an object of knowledge, a "docile body" to be improved at each academic or vocational transition. Hayashi's project is to defy this socially constructed docile body.

Introduction to Student Regulations and Hayashi's Case against Them

Nearly all Japanese junior high and high schools have some form of student regulations. The majority of schools regulate such things as hairstyle, clothing, school cleaning, and behavior while commuting to and from school. Some schools also regulate personal possessions, manners and greetings, and behavior and appearance off-campus and even in the home.[1] Many students are not allowed to hold part-time jobs or to fraternize with students from other schools. They often cannot enter public places such as game centers, bowling alleys, restaurants, parks, and even supermarkets. Following the publicity surrounding Hayashi's first book, several foreign media services began interviewing students about the severity of their student regulations. Even this may have broken the rules: it is not unusual for students to be forbidden to write letters to the opinion sections of newspapers or to speak to reporters.

Regulations vary from school to school according to the elaboration of the details and the disciplinary enforcement. The punishment for violations is so often physical that the two issues—the control of the body through detailed regulations and the punishment of the body for failure to keep the rules—are usually merged whenever the subject of kōsoku is addressed as a social problem, especially in Hayashi's work. Another, broader, term to define this phenomenon is *kanri kyōiku*—or "overregulated education."

A general example of the regulated student bodies can be found in the accompanying diagram. Part of the task of *Down with School Regulations!* is to collect samples of the myriad forms of such regulations and their enforcement, rules that often are as elaborate as they

Winter Dress Code of "K" Junior High School in Fukui Prefecture

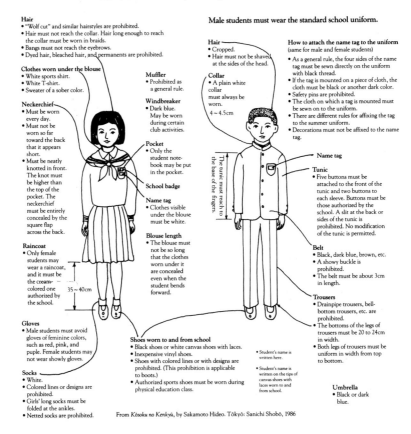

Male students must wear the standard school uniform.

Hair
• "Wolf cut" and similar hairstyles are prohibited.
• Hair must not reach the collar. Hair long enough to reach the collar must be worn in braids.
• Bangs must not reach the eyebrows.
• Dyed hair, bleached hair, and permanents are prohibited.

Clothes worn under the blouse
• White sports shirt.
• White T-shirt.
• Sweater of a sober color.

Neckerchief
• Must be worn every day.
• Must not be worn so far toward the back that it appears short.
• Must be neatly knotted in front. The knot must be higher than the top of the pocket. The neckerchief must be entirely concealed by the square flap across the back.

Raincoat
• Only female students may wear a raincoat, and it must be the cream-colored one authorized by the school. 35 – 40cm

Gloves
• Male students must avoid gloves of feminine colors, such as red, pink, and puple. Female students may not wear showly gloves.

Socks
• White.
• Colored lines or designs are prohibited.
• Girls' long socks must be folded at the ankles.
• Netted socks are prohibited.

Muffler
• Prohibited as a general rule.

Windbreaker
• Dark blue. May be worn during certain club activities.

Pocket
• Only the student notebook may be put in the pocket.

School badge

Name tag
• Clothes visible under the blouse must be white.

Blouse length
• The blouse must not be so long that the clothes worn under it are concealed even when the student bends forward.

Hair
• Cropped.
• Hair must not be shaved at the sides of the head.

Collar
• A plain white collar must always be worn.
4 – 4.5cm

The tunic must reach to the base of the fingers.

Shoes worn to and from school
• Black shoes or white canvas shoes with laces.
• Inexpensive vinyl shoes.
• Shoes with colored lines or with designs are prohibited. (This prohibition is applicable to boots.)
• Authorized sports shoes must be worn during physical education class.

• Student's name is written here.

• Student's name is written on the tips of canvas shoes with laces worn to and from school.

How to attach the name tag to the uniform
(same for male and female students)
• As a general rule, the four sides of the name tag must be sewn directly on the uniform with black thread.
• If the tag is mounted on a piece of cloth, the cloth must be black or another dark color.
• Safety pins are prohibited.
• The cloth on which a tag is mounted must be sewn on to the uniform.
• There are different rules for affixing the tag to the summer uniform.
• Decorations must not be affixed to the name tag.

Name tag

Tunic
• Five buttons must be attached to the front of the tunic and two buttons to each sleeve. Buttons must be those authorized by the school. A slit at the back or sides of the tunic is prohibited. No modification of the tunic is permitted.

Belt
• Black, dark blue, brown, etc.
• A showy buckle is prohibited.
• The belt must be about 3cm in length.

Trousers
• Drainpipe trousers, bell-bottom trousers, etc. are prohibited.
• The bottoms of the trousers must be 20 to 24cm in width.
• Both legs of trousers must be uniform in width from top to bottom.

Umbrella
• Black or dark blue.

From *Kōsoku no Kenkyū*, by Sakamoto Hideo. Tōkyō: Sanichi Shobō, 1986 are esoteric. Below is an excerpt from a public junior high school in Kobe—a section of the code that also demonstrates the gender discrimination sometimes found in the rules:[2]

On campus:

• Boys and girls may be friends but may not enter into relationships. Exchange of gifts, borrowing and lending, or any other reciprocal relationship is absolutely forbidden.

• Boys and girls who are friends must act according to appropriate junior high school behavior whenever they are seen by anyone. Whenever criticism is received, irrespective of the reason, guidance must be enforced by parents.

• When boys and girls talk to one another, there should be at least three students together whenever possible, and there should be more than two meters between the students.

• Conversation between the sexes for more than three consecutive minutes, or walking together for more than three meters, is forbidden. Naturally, an exception will be made for assemblies.

Punishment for scandalous occurrences between boys and girls will be as follows:

• Third-year boys: Write a self-reflection essay of no less than two thousand characters and do *seiza* sitting for three hours.[3]

• Third-year girls: Write a self-reflection essay of no less than two thousand characters and do *seiza* sitting for six hours.

• Second-year boys: Write a self-reflection essay of no less than two thousand characters and do *seiza* sitting for one and a half hours.

• Second-year girls: Write a self-reflection essay of no less than two thousand characters and do *seiza* sitting for three hours.

• First-year boys: Exempt.

• First-year girls: Do *seiza* sitting for one and a half hours.

Not all school regulations may be this severe, yet a few may be worse (Hayashi cites one school requiring seven hours of seiza). There is considerable variation among all types of schools. Some students do not mind the regulations; they may find it easier to put on a uniform every day than join up in a fashion competition—one of the reasons often given for the persistence of the rules. For some students, school regulations are so important that they set their aspirations on entering a school where the regulations are more relaxed. This variation indicates how elusive the locus of power is—or appears to be—in the school system. Japan's Ministry of Education does control the school curriculum and university entrance exam from its centralized location. However, the ministry does not control the student regulations directly; these are set to some extent by local governments but mostly by individual schools.

The case can be made, however, that kōsoku are indirectly governed by the uniform entrance exam system. As long as parents believe that education is directly linked to employment and that this linkage must be established in the early stages of childhood through the irreversible outcome of exams, they will do whatever they can to ensure their children's success in education.

Obeying the rules is a large part of ensuring that success. One of the main requirements for passing from junior high to high school, and again from high school to university, is (along with the exam itself) the *naishinshō,* or secret report card. The naishinshō is the annual report of a student's progress in his or her grade. It includes quantitative criteria (scaled from one to five on a bell-shaped curve) to measure students' performance in basic subjects, as well as qualitative criteria to explain students' special characteristics or special concerns and problems. The naishinshō is usually of secondary importance to the entrance exam, and in most cases where students have been "average" the teacher will write perfunctory responses (such as "nothing special") in the spaces reserved for qualitative judgments.

Teachers will not skimp on words to describe delinquent behavior on the part of the student, however, and such words could irreversibly hinder the student's progress. The most common form of delinquent behavior is violation of the school regulations; thus the code of regulations becomes the teacher's empowerment, often described as a "weapon" or "invisible whip." The teacher can always threaten a student by admonishing, "If you disobey the rules, it will permanently tarnish your naishinshō!" Because the naishinshō is always kept private from students and parents, the power disadvantage of the student is considerable. It is like a one-way glass: students know they are being watched, they just don't know how they are *seen.*[4] (An analogy can be found in Japanese medical practices, in which doctors are legally permitted to withold information from patients.)

The naishinshō represented, as Foucault would put it, an "apparatus of writing" that enabled the functioning of disciplinary power. It made possible the objectification of the individual "under the gaze of a permanent corpus of knowledge," and it (along with other methods of evaluation, namely official exams and commercial mock exams) made possible a comparative system to analyze collective character-istics of students.[5] Perhaps most important, reinforcement of student regulations through the secret naishinshō made the student's experi-ence something like one continuous classroom from junior high school to university entrance. Students and parents, whether in Japan or Amer-ica, often fail to speak out on issues that concern them if they have reason to believe the teacher can retaliate by issuing poor grades or references. Because the naishinshō is passed from grade to grade without a chance for the student to ever start afresh, silence is also maintained from grade to grade.

During the 1970s and 1980s the code of kōsoku became increas-ingly severe, as did violent acts committed against students by teach-ers, against teachers by students, and between students. The latter form of violence, *ijime,* or bullying, has been especially disconcerting to the Japanese. The bullies sometimes act out the role of teachers and authority figures; they act as young vigilantes who take the rules and regulations into their own hands by harming those who violate the mandated codes of conduct.

It is helpful to review what else was going on at this time to see how the escalation of severity of the regulations figures in with the rest of the terrain of Japanese education. It was also at this time, during the seventies and eighties, or the immediate aftermath of the postwar high-growth boom period, that the "entrance examination war" became increasingly competitive, with the swelling in population of school-age children wanting to enter the "good schools" leading to "good jobs." This atmosphere became an ideal business market for the now ubiquitous cram schools (*juku*), which tended to specialize either in preparing children for the entrance exam or in "remedial" learning, which gave students the opportunity not to be left out by attending a juku that was remedial at best or a babysitting service at worst.

The cram schools had the edge in doing exactly what the formal schools were supposed to be doing—training students to pass ex-ams—but they offered more time, freedom, money, and, perhaps most important, computerization to continuously calculate test scores. Con-sequently, as cram schools proliferated, teachers in regular schools came to feel that their own importance was diminished: why have a regular school system when students get their best training from the cram schools? Their response was sometimes to use the naishinshō for securing their own foothold. The naishinshō represented "the only weapon" teachers had to justify the broader spectrum of curriculum not covered by the entrance exam, including school activities, sports, and arts. Thus it could legitimate their own role as teachers in the formal school system.[6] Many public and private schools that wanted to present an image of effectiveness, reflected in well-rounded, ambitious college-bound youngsters, turned up the heat on the enforcement of regulations.

The ideological underpinnings of the two systems of measurement thus pulled students in two different directions. Continual mock exams, calculated as often as once a month at the junior high level, admonish students to rise above the statistical mean in order to gain a sense of accomplishment, that is, to become eligible to enter a "good" high school. Thus they encourage and demand fierce *competition.*

Educators justify the student regulations, on the other hand, by the doctrine of *equality.* The rules admonish students *not* to be competitive, to be just like any other typical junior high or high school student: *gakuseirashii,* or "studentlike," embodying the model of an ordinary student. Thus the numbers that define a student's appearance, as the length of the hair, contents of the bag, folds in the anklets, and so on are held in check. Students are not allowed to individuate themselves by clothing or personal possessions; even things as small as mechanical pencils are often prohibited in order to prevent competition. Meanwhile, one's individual ability to perform in exams is supposedly unleashed, for in this category students are compelled to compete and rise above one another. Each evaluation method is intended as a counterbalance to mitigate the deleterious effects of the other.

Yet either method of precise and quantitative control, whether aimed toward competitive liberalism or egalitarianism, suffocates the nourishment of the student's qualitative individuality — the kind Hayashi and other young students yearn for. Thus Hayashi's purpose (along with other student and lawyers associations who have taken up the mission of battling the kōsoku) is to protest against this loss, the "robbing" of identity. Hayashi's own signature on this theme, if you will pardon the pun, is the writing of his pen name in the phonetic, generic hiragana script, as would a kindergartner, rather than in personalized, individualized Chinese characters (*kanji*) — the usual way of writing adult names. The metaphors of his books, moreover, are those that portray the restriction of the body, depicting the school as a prison, as a military unit, or as an animal cage, and the student as a subject bound by head and by foot (*ganjigarame*).

While at times his creative vignettes and illustrations seem to disburden more than discuss, Hayashi never fails to drive home his unwavering position that the kōsoku are unconstitutional, illegitimate, and inhumane. At the close of his first book, he cites from tracts published by legal organizations that answer basic questions concerning the legality of the student regulations. This chapter, along with commentary in *Part 2* and *Part 3*, address three of the most important legal documents in Japan—the Constitution of Japan, the Fundamental Law of Education, and the School Education Law (1947), all of which were enacted during the early years of the Allied Occupation of Japan. The following excerpts summarize what are considered by Hayashi and other educational rights activists as the most relevant articles demonstrating the illegality of kōsoku.

Unconstitutionality of Kōsoku

Most important is the law expressly forbidding corporal punishment:[7] "Principals and teachers of schools may punish their students, pupils, and children, when they recognize it [to be] necessary in the light of education, in compliance with the regulations issued by the competent authorities. They shall not, however, inflict corporal punishment" (Article 11 in the School Education Law).

To protect against the violation of children's rights and to defend respect for individuality,[8] "All of the people shall be respected as individuals. Their right to life, liberty, and the pursuit of happiness shall, to the extent that it does not interfere with the public welfare, be the supreme consideration in legislation and in other governmental affairs" (Article 13 in the Constitution of Japan).

To protect against the searching of private bags and belongings,[9] "The right of all persons to be secure in their homes, papers and effects against entries, searches and seizures shall not be impaired except upon warrant issued for adequate cause and particularly describing the place to be searched and things to be seized. . . .

. . . Each search or seizure shall be made upon separate warrant issued by a competent judicial officer" (Article 35 in the Constitution of Japan).

Hayashi closes the first volume with the entire copies of the constitution and the Fundamental Law of Education, and an enthusiastic recommendation for students to study up on them.

Illegitimacy of Kōsoku

While the extent to which the constitutional provisions are applicable to children's rights may be debatable, the prohibition against corporal punishment in schools is succinctly stipulated. Yet, as with other legal codes, informal sanctions bear more weight than formal laws. The definition of corporal punishment as cited in Hayashi's work includes any type of physical hitting such as kicking or inflicting other sorts of injury, as well as signs of physical distress such as that incurred from long hours of maintaining the seiza posture alluded to above. If seiza is legitimately mentioned in some schools' official regulations, it is perhaps because people still sit seiza-style in many normal situations and it is not a recognizable form of punishment unless one does too many minutes of it.

Another form of cultural legitimation must exist, therefore, to account for why the kōsoku have persisted and even worsened in some cases. Hayashi names this process in his third volume, labeling it as a disease: that of "homogenitis" (*minna onaji byō*, literally, the "every-one-the-same disease"):[10]

Exam-centered education, the attention given to names of schools, the prevention of school violence—these are the usual reasons offered [to account for the severity of Japan's school regulations]. Yet the deeper and more fundamental reason is that the Japanese people, especially teachers, have poisoned junior high and high schools with the disease of "homogenitis" (group conformism). This is a very dreadful disease in which blending oneself with the prevailing surroundings is considered better than stating one's own opinion or way of thinking in terms of, "I am such and such," or "I believe in such and such." ... The unfortunate thing is, the majority of students contract "homogenitis" from the teachers who are inflicted with the disease. Because of the strange regulations that govern them from the tops of their heads to the tips of their toes, they follow along without making judgment and without nourishing any suspicion or dissatisfaction, becoming like elephants or tigers in the zoo, who can't do anything without orders. Thus they turn into "wait-for-the-order humans" [*shiji-machiningen*] who can't do anything without their homogenitis-inflicted teachers telling them, "Do this! Do that!"

Hayashi thus implies that conformity is structure and not culture, nurture and not nature. The school regulations have "robbed" children of what is originally and rightfully theirs: their individuality. Conformity, therefore, is the illness and individuality is the norm. Likewise, his handwritten decree at the opening of *Part 1*:

Somewhere today there is a student getting beaten up.
We must not give in!
To all the schools that rob students of their individuality:
"Down with school regulations!" ... Hang in there, all junior high and high school students of Japan!

Inhumanity of Kōsoku

Three junior high boys explained their plight to Hayashi: "If we go to Harajuku with haircuts like these, people will think we're on a school trip from out in the sticks somewhere." The kids were concerned with more than their reputations at Tokyo's famous juvenile hangout, however. According to Hayashi, when young boys have to shave their heads or young girls are forbidden from letting their hair touch the shoulders, they feel they are denied freedom of the body, freedom of speech, freedom of self-determination, and freedom to have their belongings kept private unless approached with a search warrant.[11]

More fundamentally, when students are made to look like monks, prisoners, or soldiers, when they have teachers hover over them ready to shave or cut their hair, their *human rights* are violated, stresses Hayashi. Since 1988, it has become increasingly common to hear of kōsoku problems discussed as human rights issues. In April of that year, a lawyers' association called the Defense Counsel for Children's Human Rights formed to deal with complaints, "Declarations of Human Rights Violations," from students about serious abuses of teachers' authority. Such organizations have become extremely helpful in helping students and their parents receive apologies and compensations, both in and out of court, for their problems with school authorities.

The following imaginary dialogue, from Hayashi's first book, depicts the way in which students would like to argue with and subvert educational authorities, if their voices could be heard, and summarizes Hayashi's position that the kōsoku are unconstitutional, illegitimate, and inhumane:[12]

> TEACHER: Hey, you! No perms allowed!
>
> STUDENT: Yes, sir. I have a perm. Is there something wrong with that?
>
> TEACHER: Don't smart aleck me! It's written in the regulations! Check your student handbook!
>
> STUDENT: But why can't we have perms?
>
> TEACHER: Because it says so in the rules, that's why you can't have a perm!
>
> STUDENT: But those regulations ignore human rights. Please have them reformed. So why can't we have perms?
>
> TEACHER: Because people will think you're delinquent if you have a perm.
>
> STUDENT: But there are so many people on the street who have perms. Are you telling me they are all delinquent? I'm sure even people you know have perms.
>
> TEACHER: For adults it's OK.
>
> STUDENT: Why is it wrong only for students?
>
> TEACHER: Because perms cost a lot of money. It's a burden on your parents.
>
> STUDENT: I got a perm with my own pocket money that I saved up. My parents said it was OK. That's why I don't want you telling me perms are forbidden. And I still don't get why perms are forbidden, anyway.
>
> TEACHER: OK! When you get a perm you pay so much attention to your hair that could otherwise be spent on your studies.
>
> STUDENT: Oh? There is no connection between perming your hair and studying! Give me proof if there is. Show me some statistics from the Ministry of Education!
>
> TEACHER: You cheeky little brat! I'm going to write this down on your naishinshō! A rule's a rule, so you just have to follow it, that's all!
>
> STUDENT: There now, please don't threaten me. Wearing one's own hair according to one's own taste should be the freedom of each individual. The School Education Law emphasizes the individual freedom and independence of students, as in, "Education shall aim for the actualization of human character ... the value of the individual shall be honored ... fulfillment of the independent spirit ..."

TEACHER: I get it, I get it. That's fine with me but I don't know what the other teachers will do when they catch you.
STUDENT: At that time, I'll count on you as my ally.

Human Rights and the Student Body

It would be fairly easy for some to dismiss Hayashi's work as a typical product of the rebellion of youth. In some ways it is, but it is not similar to the way that young people of the previous generation rebelled. In the sixties and seventies, the dictum that "if you are not a Marxist at twenty, you have no heart, but if you are still a Marxist at age thirty, you have no brain" was popular in Japan, as many of Japan's young radicals were quick to join the workaholic, conservative white-collar labor force and leave their peace signs behind them. For young people of Hayashi's generation, however, the story is different. The entire system of kōsoku and academic credentialism militates against forgiveness for the ephemeral turbulence of youth. A violation reported on the naishinshō may damage a student's academic goals for life, and unlike the situation for their parents, most of these violations are not in the same category as holding sit-ins, protesting war, or advocating a political ideology. They are in the category of letting the hair grow a centimeter too long, forgetting to fold the anklets in the proper trifold, wearing colored underwear, taking a part-time job at McDonald's, driving a motorcycle, or using a hair dryer.

Even the time spent to organize a protest movement, as Hayashi and other students have done, can impede the pace of scholastic progress necessary to enter university. Hayashi himself spent two years at a *yobiko* (a full-time cram school to prepare students for university) before entering the Nihon University Faculty of Law. Disillusioned, he dropped out and returned to his writing—a move that is indeed unusual, since university education in Japan is not considered difficult, once all of the hurdles to gain admission are met. The other fourteen boys who joined his signature drive have all taken regular "salaryman" jobs, Hayashi says, but as for their movement in high school to challenge school regulations, "They have not forgotten."

Dropping out of university, establishing himself as a writer at a young age, successfully rebelling against entrenched structures of authoritarianism with little support from his elders, not even his parents—these are not typical life experiences for Japanese young people. Yet what makes this young rebel more typical of his generation is the ahistorical nature of his argument. This is true for many of his older educational rights mentors as well: they draw from the well of democratic language as though constitutional protection, human rights, and individual liberty were indigenous to Japan.

But it is important to remember that while the democratic lexicon was largely imported from the West in the late nineteenth century and popularized at the start of the Occupation period, the system of emperor worship imposed on the Japanese people in the nineteenth century also seemed alien; yet it was such an ideology that degenerated into the ultranationalism exploited by the Japanese military. As a result of Japan's defeat in World War II, young people of Hayashi's generation were brought up in an educational system that disdained the prewar educational system, with its mythmaking aspects of Japanese history. But the postwar educational system has thrown the baby out with the bathwater in avoiding Japan's recent past rather than seeking to understand and interpret it. At the time Hayashi was in high school (he graduated in 1986), it was the social norm to shun conversation about the emperor, the national flag, and other reminders of nationalism. It was the norm to be seen as neither for nor against nor even neutral about love and pride for one's country, but more preferably, avoidant.

Critical of American education, I often got cornered, in my conversation with Hayashi, into denying a self-congratulatory posture every time he insisted that American schools, even with their gun-toters and drug dealers, were better than those of Japan. Yet I began to see that when he made his comparative remarks, he drove home a simple point: the Japanese do not defend their rights; Americans do. In the following conversation, on the matter of "underwear inspection," he convinced me. In the more "innocuous" instances of this rare but infamous practice, teachers will inspect girls' suitcases before embarking on a school excursion. In the more egregious cases, students are strip-searched and told they are as worthless as prostitutes or bar hostesses if their underwear is anything but unfrilled regulation white:[13]

> H. T.: Do American schools have anything such as the underwear inspection?
>
> M. T. M.: I've heard about that in the news. No, America has nothing like it. It's unbelievable.
>
> H. T. (strongly): Yes, that's what I'm saying, you may hear about it in the news but that's all. As for students who go to

such schools, no matter how disgusting they think it is, they just reluctantly go along with it. And their parents are stupid. Everyone just keeps silent. But if this were an American school, what would happen? It would be a huge problem.

M. T. M.: You're right.

H. T.: The students would flatly refuse to allow such a thing and their parents would naturally complain on their behalf. But there's no such thing in Japan. That's why I'm saying America is wonderful. I think it's a good place. It's because their consciousness of rights is very high.

In Hayashi's work the issue is not just conformity versus individuality, where his argument is well pronounced but sociologically thin; nor is the topic America versus Japan, where his comments in the interview were employed liberally but with functional pragmatism. Hayashi speaks no English and has never been to the United States or any other foreign country. His first two volumes address virtually no international comparisons. Exceptions include the cover of his first book, which features a delinquent-looking character extending his middle finger, a better approximation, perhaps, of the sentiments behind the expression, "Down with …!" *Part 2* features a small illustration of two faces, a Japanese labeled "gloomy" and a foreigner labeled "bright." The caption states: "How enjoyable it would be to live in a foreign country where everyone is free! Japanese schools are terrible in comparison." It is not until the end of his more mature and somber third volume that he discusses his topic of "homogenitis" as the way he would have to explain Japan's educational system if he were in a conversation with foreigners. (At this point, he says he has been collecting a great deal of material concerning education in Europe and America; we can perhaps expect more comparative notations from his upcoming fourth volume.)

Set in this ahistorical context, therefore, his more provocative, more exclamatory message surrounds the issue of constraint of the body versus freedom of the body. He is no doubt naively influenced by the West, as Japanese educators have long been. Yet as the words "democracy," "freedom," and "rights" are trumpeted throughout the opus, the weighty concepts are streamlined to serve a utilitarian purpose, disengaged from their historical or cultural contexts. Hayashi merely points out the regulations that the schools invent and the principles that they violate.

There are no "grand themes" in Hayashi's book. And why should there be? It would be unfair to compare Hayashi with other protestors of other generations, whose mantras were "the war to end all wars," "peace and love," and so on. Hayashi's theme is neither global nor national but as local as one's own body, one's own self. The weight of the argument is concisely, consistently corporeal: it seeks the freedom to dress as one pleases, to wear one's individual hairstyle, to walk home from school with friends of one's choice and in the direction one pleases, to have the privacy of one's belongings protected. It has nothing to do with curriculum, ideology, education in the United States versus education in Japan, the past, or the future.

"Rights," as Hayashi uses the term, means simply that either you have freedom of the body or you don't. In his view, America does and Japan doesn't. He doesn't open a space for discussing the universality or relativity of his position, but neither does he close it.

Yet his unaffected approach of attacking all of Japanese education in terms of the way students feel the constraint of bodily freedom and movement is not the weakness of this work; it is its strength and its poignancy. Perhaps the imported words of "freedom," "individuality," and "rights" have structured the verbalization of pain and the way that distress is mediated to the individual. Yet to focus on the basic emotions of that distress rather than the origins of the language used to express it, we can sense that the young student body that expresses the pain of educational experiences, whether psychological or physical, has become the target space onto which the assaults of more complex problems in education and the larger political economy have been directed.

Beyond "East" and "West"

While studying Hayashi's case against student regulations, a formal incident of corporal punishment occurred in Singapore and developed into an international commotion. In May 1994, a nineteen-year-old American, Michael Fay, was sentenced to six lashes of a cane by the Singapore government for the charge of vandalism. The highly publicized incident created the impression on the part of many Americans that "controlled"—that is, politically sanctioned—violence such as corporal punishment, as well as the benefits of social order created by fear of punishment, is a distinctively "Asian" norm. In contrast, lack of discipline and uncontrolled violence, such as rioting, were seen as the more characteristically "Western" way to violate the rights of children. The Singapore incident also coincided with a political climate in the People's Republic of China that rejected the Western definition of human rights, especially the definition in the United States, which failed to acknowledge its own hypocritical treatment of its citizens. Such a context opened the possibility that the "national" images of America and Japan would become highlighted in their "civilizational" forms, as in "Western," or "Euro-American," and "Eastern," or "Asian."

I started to imagine apprehensively that if Hayashi's case were to be heard now in America of 1994, in the wake of the Michael Fay incident and in the climate beckoning the dawn of a Pacific age, the narrative of *Down with School Regulations!* would follow a plotline similar to the Michael Fay story. The kōsoku might be seen as the "Asian" way of discipline. Hayashi might be cast as the lone dissenter applying universal human rights in a way that mimics Americanization. The application of human rights to specific situations in the context of Japanese education, as depicted in the foregoing section, would be surrounded either by smugly imagined connotations of the righteousness of the democratic way, or, conversely, by a view of the failure of Western democracy to realize anything like the stabilized social order characteristic of Asia. What I am concerned with in this writing, however, are the interests of the "non-elite," the children and adults who support critiques of corporal discipline such as that of Hayashi. Voices of such individuals would be lost in any reifying "civilizational" framework that only interprets national identities as culturally unchallenged and fails likewise to steer a course between absolutism and relativism.

Again and again in *Down with School Regulations!* the reasons provided for students and parents failing to speak out against regulations have to do with the naishinshō and its volatility as an impediment that can permanently thwart a child's path to success. Likewise, the reasons children often do not inform their parents of egregious violations is for fear the parents will not believe them or take them seriously—all in the name of keeping the path clear for entrance exam drills. The kōsoku and the political economy that values such conformity and discipline of future workers thus inhibit the expression of the students' legitimate frustrations and pain.

It is this aspect of the kōsoku as a strategy of silencing that facile national stereotypes bulldoze over. Images of national identity privilege their own standards and ignore the myriad "local" voices; in the case of the kōsoku problem, the accepted cultural standard is the nail that dares not protrude. That standard ignores the political conditions that inhibit other nails from letting the constructions they support reveal their worm-eaten holes. National or "civilizational" identities also ignore global issues that transcend borders, factors such as technological linkages, macroeconomic strategies, and knowledge convergence. Finally, national identities have been subject to a grammar that until recently posited West or North as "subject," acting upon East or South as "object," rather than looking at the vulnerablity of borders, the exchange between and among nations, and the continuous state of cultural realignment.

For these reasons I would like to invite another possiblity of understanding: the consideration that Hayashi, as a human agent arguing against severe regulation of the human body, is not alone in his protest, nor is such a role as his historically unprecedented. In the following sections, I have outlined six other possibilities for problematizing our knowledge of kōsoku so as to question the self-limiting categories of "Japan" and "America," or "East" and "West." The possiblities cited thus help to situate the significance of *Down with School Regulations!* as more consistent with changing Japanese cultural patterns than it might seem at first blush.

The Kōsoku as a Reminder of Militarism

To begin with, the precisionism dictated by the kōsoku—socializing children to obey the microscopic school regulations verbatim or to risk potentially irreversible punishment—seems inconsistent with other commonly recognized characteristics of Japanese culture, such as relativity, flexibility, or tolerance of ambiguity. True, Japan is also known for delicate rules of conduct and speech, but these are generally subject to informal social sanctions rather than the formal disciplinary mechanisms of schools. It is also true that many of the indigenous Japanese arts, as well as traditional and modern sports, demand rigorous self-discipline, characterized by such concepts as *seishin* (spirit), *shitsuke* (discipline), and *gaman* (endurance). But as anthropologist Robert J. Smith reveals, the relationship between instructor and pupil in such an instance must be built on trust and mutual acknowledgment of the benefits of the training, for "what makes such treatment tolerable is one thing alone; the pupil must remain firmly convinced of the absolute justice and impartiality of the teacher's assessment of his or her progress."[14] Clearly, the contribution of *Down with School Regulations!* is to reveal that it is not only the opinion of one young rebel but of the thousands of young people and their parents who have written to him that today's students are not at all convinced of the "absolute justice and impartiality of the teacher's assessment." The perception instead is that teachers are out of touch with basic humanitarian needs of students.

Japan's kōsoku, after all, signify a strict model of logocentrism, the supremacy of written law or words usually associated with Western civilization. Some schools even consider that the regulation codes are an analogous extension of the constitution, as in one rule stating, "Just as the nation has the constitution, the schools have the kōsoku. Just as we obey the constitution, we must obey the kōsoku." According to education critic Sakamoto Hideo, such a stipulation is not uncommon.[15] It is a sadly ironic analogy, however, considering the unconstitutionality of the corporal punishment used to enforce the regulations.

The rules may also be less redolent of the particularist features of Japanese culture than of the features of militarism or a police state—features that are both universal, in the sense that all cultures have had some sort of militarism, and particular, in that Japan's educational system was heavily yoked to militarism prior to World War II.

If we examine the historical precedent, the roots of the Japanese connection between militarism and education date from the Tokugawa era (1600–1868) when the civil and military arts, *bun* and *bu* respectively, were joined in the formal education of the samurai class. But we find less evidence here for unbroken cultural continuity of the strict discipline characteristic of today's kōsoku. The grounds for military training were often located on or very near school premises, and a typical regimen was to study book learning in the morning and military training in the afternoon. In such schools, etiquette was strictly observed, but formal school rules were apparently limited to school-related concerns. R. P. Dore, the leading scholar on Tokugawa education, lists the most common of them as "quarrelling, talking during classes, running in corridors, banging doors and partitions, scrambling for clogs when leaving, talking or laughing in a loud voice, leaving one's seat without permission, illegally delaying one's return from the lavatory, abusive speech, late arrival, illegal absence, the offering of false excuses, and in one case, lewd talk of women." The most common forms of punishment were expulsion and cleaning chores, and corporal punishment was rare. Dore cites two schools that used caning and one that used moxa cautery, burning powder on the skin.[16] Moxa cautery is a disciplinary technique still used in some Japanese households today, but it is supposed to have a medicinal quality traditionally believed to exorcise evil spirits. (The method causes some Westerners to cringe but it is perhaps no less unpleasant than cod liver oil.) While Dore does not compare military regulations with the academic regulations, he does imply that the academic portion of a samurai boy's education was probably more rigorous and challenging in general than the military portion of his schooling.[17]

The population of samurai in this era, however, was less than 10 percent of the population. If their educational methods utilized but a few forms of corporal discipline, the education of commoners provided even fewer, Dore implies. One of the prominent and coveted features of Japanese history was the country's widespread education of commoners; it is believed (based on Dore's research) that about 40 percent of boys and 10 percent of girls received basic education outside the home during the Tokugawa period. The commoners' schools were considerably less strict than those of the military class and, as Dore depicts them, were quite relaxed: "It seems to have been a genial kind of education, predicated on the assumption that children were basically well-disposed creatures who could be easily persuaded to co-operate, whose delinquencies were mostly harmless and who had a right to their occasional fun. They did not necessarily have to be beaten for every sneeze in order to tame the devil in them." Forms of punishment were rarely corporal and, at worst, usually aimed to produce noise rather than pain.[18] One might have a weak case, therefore, in justifying the kōsoku as traditionally Japanese.

In letter less than spirit, today's elaborate codes of kōsoku recall the nationalistic education instituted in the late nineteenth century, which, along with military conscription, consolidated the nation of Japan. At first, in preparation for the establishment of universal education, Japan was mostly impressed by the pedagogical ideas of the Swiss and the Americans and by the highly centralized administrative structure of the French. With the defeat of France in the Franco-Prussian war, Prussian models of discipline and militarism became favored at the same time that American-style individual-centered learning was brought into serious question. In 1880, under the guidance of Motoda Eifu, an adviser who favored a return to Confucian principles, an ordinance was passed introducing military drills for educational discipline. Mori Arinori, Japan's first minister of education, who had studied American and European models of education and social organization extensively, had also decided to favor the more collective ideas of the Germans when, in 1885, he issued a series of ordinances establishing the organization of Japan's modern educational system into elementary, middle, and normal schools and universities. The goals for the new system, according to Ronald Anderson, stressed "(1) loyalty to the Emperor-state, (2) productive ability, and (3) military training."[19] At the start of Japan's entry into war in 1937, schools were again reorganized as Prussian-style "people's schools" (*kokumin gakko*), and both the pedagogy and physical training were geared more directly to filling the needs of the military until the defeat of Japan in 1945.

The schools that use kōsoku thus resemble prewar schools in their linkage of education with military discipline, but such a linkage does not represent the entire picture of today's educational system. The schools Hayashi decries for the severity of their kōsoku are largely junior and senior high schools. Joseph Tobin's work on preschools in Japan demonstrates that children begin their foothold on the education ladder with a pedagogy often quite tolerant of variations in children's development and, in some cases, perhaps too undisciplined for Americans.[20] Few elementary schools have rigid school regulations; Hayashi opens his first book reminiscing about his pleasant days in elementary school, when teachers played dodgeball with children who did not even know how to read the characters spelling "corporal punishment." And on the final rung of the education ladder, with the exception of a handful of traditional women's colleges, the colleges and universities have not only abandoned most forms of kōsoku, they have become notorious "leisurelands" where formalized compliance often seems the exception rather than the rule.

In the broader cultural and historical context, therefore, there may not be enough consistency to label kōsoku as the unchallenged "Japanese way." But what can be said about the period of intensive regulating in today's education is that it clearly overlaps with the period of intense competitiveness in entrance examinations. Although one evaluation method pulls the student toward a value system of equality (kōsoku) and the other toward a value system of competitiveness (exams), both are largely products of the postwar frenzy to achieve economic stability—for individual families as well as the nation—in a short period of time, and to do it through education.

Furthermore, while critics suggest a continuity between the prewar character of the Japanese police state and the present condition of overregulating in Japanese education, there is, of course, a fundamental difference: the present educational system does not buttress the foundations of the militarist nation by inculcating the ideology of emperor worship in the schools. The point has often been made, however, that the present system now serves the nation by supplying a compliant, well-organized workforce to the labor pools, with the aim of economic rather than military nationalism. In addition, some changes that are said to glorify militarism have been introduced in the curriculum, but amid widespread publicity and controversy. The possibility that the schools could return to the cozy relationship with militarism as it existed in the past still remains remote, however. Instead, other signifiers, such as militaristic school uniforms and regulations, along with frequently used sayings referring to exam pressure as the "entrance exam war," students as "soldiers," and major exams as "critical battles," function as subtle, metaphoric reminders of the strategic importance of educational competitiveness on the national scale.

The salient point here is that the implied connection today between education and militarism, even if atavistic and symbolic, pinpoints why Hayashi's emphasis on bodily freedom is poignantly on target. Both militaristic discipline and the kōsoku have been perceived as practices that violate the human body. Japan, after all, has not always been a rationally unified state as it is today, nor has it been a heavily militarized state as it was during World War II. At the start of the Meiji period (1868), which ushered in Japan's modernization, the newly formed nation was highly decentralized, divided into 240 *han* (prefectures). Thus, when the new army began to conscript young soldiers from the provinces, as historian Takashi Fujitani notes, the standardized stipulations, governing not only military technique but control of the body over such things as sleep patterns and bowel movements, created a tremendous psychological impact on the young men and on all villagers in general. This control of the body through militarization perhaps became "normalized"—made into the standard of "normal" by authoritarian governance—but it was never something that became naturalized among individual men. To this day, soldiers and their loved ones, asked to recall some aspect of their miliary experiences, are likely to express some way that the military affected their *bodies* above all else.[21]

In a similar way, Hayashi remembers how dismayed he was when he first entered junior high school and had his own body regulated by the kōsoku. He had to wear the regulation black uniform, cap, and white socks and to cut his hair in the "nerdy" nearly shaven crew cut. In the beginning, he had every intention of obeying the rules compliantly, for not to do so would be to accept the label of "juvenile delinquent." After several months, however, he started looking on the teachers as his enemies. In contrast to his halcyon days in elementary school, he remembers little else about his three years of junior high school except for the practice of corporal punishment—that inflicted by one teacher in particular. The teacher straddled young boys like a pro wrestler to beat them and delivered rounds of face-slapping to students who skimped on their cleaning chores. In a manner Hayashi says was more like that of a gorilla than an educator, he caused severe injuries while beating up a boy who was watching television past the curfew hour on a school trip.[22]

For Hayashi to remember first and foremost this pain of injury to the student body was not without precedent in Japanese history. Soldiers of the military superpower and students of the economic superpower both wore the blueprint of authoritarianism on their bodies, bodies that in turn became building blocks for the continuous reproduction of that authoritarianism. During Japan's transition to modernity, as Fujitani's study illustrates, this "standardizing" of bodies was the mission rationalizing the nation: it was necessary for the central government to "homogenize" its populace as a way to achieve greater social control.[23]

In the contemporary situation, however, the control is more elusively directed, in the sense, as I have already mentioned, that it is not the central government that *directly* dictates the standard uniforms, behavior, and discipline of students. The central government governs the standardization of the curriculum and university entrance exam; most other standards are established by the direct actions of local governments, school boards (nonelected), individual schools, and, in the case of testing methods and procedures, commercialized cram schools.

Hayashi as a Mediator

Another point of comparison between the early phase of military discipline and the contemporary state of educational discipline has to
do with the role of mediating structures. Because premodern Japan
was greatly decentralized, early authorities of the central government
who entered villages to recruit soldiers and reconstruct their standards
of behavior were not synchronized with the attitudes of local officials. The latter often gave more allegiance to the needs of the draftees
rather than to the purposes of the state, and were known to offer assistance to those who wished to evade their conscription.[24]

In the contemporary situation, it is true that local boards of education and other local government officials have some degree of administrative autonomy from the Ministry of Education, more than is
often realized. Nevertheless, the policies and procedures, the general
intentions, and certainly the language used are highly synchronized
and uniform in comparison with early modern Japan. It would be a
rare situation for any official to play the role of advocate on behalf
of students against educational authorities, whether local, prefectural,
or national, whether public or private. Instead, the role of advocacy
is now being belatedly undertaken by various lawyers' associations,
under the theme of children's rights or human rights in general.

Hayashi's role is not only to support frustrated students through
his empathic power of the pen, which allows students to vent their
frustrations through his books and advice column. He also offers tips
on legal courses of action to take, and he has also taken up the direct
role of mediator himself. In 1988 he received a telephone call from
the mother of a girl in a large municipal junior high school located in
Hayashi's home prefecture. Hayashi agreed to meet the mother, her
daughter, and her daughter's friend to discuss the severity of student
beatings at their school. The mother's daughter had been labeled an
"insubordinate" for taking a stand asking teachers to be "a little more
considerate of the feelings of students." The teachers obviously did not
appreciate these words of constructive criticism, and they responded
with humiliation and corporal punishment against her and her friend.
Other girls at the school had their hair pulled and their perms dunked
into water. One group of girls was severely beaten for possession of
Valentine's Day chocolates. Another group of students was beaten un-

til bloody for walking away from their desks during study hour. Some students were beaten for going to noodle shops, talking while cleaning, or wearing ribbons in their hair. Most ominously, students believed that at least one student per day was brought to a secluded meeting room on the second floor for a "lynching" (severe bullying).

Hayashi acted on behalf of concerned students and parents by filing a "Declaration of Human Rights" to an attorneys' association, calling attention to the inhumanity of four named teachers and seeking an end to student regulations. In so doing, he took the heat of inevitable negative reaction away from the students and parents. As an established writer, he was also able to get the incident well publicized. The principal and the teachers of the school staunchly denied any wrongdoing, but finally it was agreed that three of the four teachers would be transferred to other schools.[25]

Westernized Language, Japanized Syntax

As revealed in the foregoing example, the constitutional and legal language sounds Americanized (as it in fact often is), while the non-litigious method of dealing with problems as they occur is more characteristically Japanese. Citing from the counsel of attorneys, *Down with School Regulations, Part 1* advises students who have been beaten by teachers to see a physician, get a certified assessment of their injuries, and tape record statements from any witnesses. Then they should consider the following steps. First, they should obtain an apology from the perpetrating teacher and principal and obtain consolation money as a settlement. If this does not work, they should contact the mass media and cause embarrassment to the school. The third course of action, if the media fail to intimidate the school, is for the student to seek the help of an attorney. The final course of action, if an out-of-court settlement cannot be reached by any other means, is to file a lawsuit and contact the police.[26]

Xenophilia as "Ordinarily Japanese"

Some might regard Hayashi as infatuated with American legalese, yet even this is historically precedented in other instances of xenophilia. China was Japan's cultural mentor for several centuries, and Japanese education borrowed abundantly from Chinese knowledge. It is not surprising, then, that the Confucianist scholars of the feudal era were known (according to the rival "National Learning" scholars) to "adulate the traditions of China and scorn those of their own country." The same criticism resounded against the important "Dutch scholars" of the nineteenth century, who introduced Western learning to Japan. In Dore's paraphrasing, critics claimed the Dutch scholars would "allow themselves to be fascinated with useless toy devices and theories of no practical value; they have a taste for foreign luxuries and they would even flirt with Christianity."[27] Yet both the Confucian and the Dutch scholars were, of course, important catalysts of change in Japanese education, history, and culture.

All the while, of course, Japan never became another China or another Holland. The exchange of information across borders is important, but it should not be forgotten that cultures adapt and realign themselves in continuous adjustment to new phenomena. There may be evidence to support the notion that Hayashi's outcry against "homogenitis" and the regulation of the student body are indeed influenced by American ideas of educational freedom, but this is not new, and in the history of Japanese education it might make him more usual than otherwise. Since the founding of the Japanese nation in 1868, the country has made the institution of education its priority, and as part of that process, ideas were generously imported from the West—from France, Prussia, and the United States—all of them structurally amalgamated with the more traditional Chinese and indigenous Japanese features.

Mutability of Boundaries East and West

On the Japanese side, Hayashi's work and movement might be taken less seriously, not so much because of "Americanization" per se as because of his youthfulness and failure to complete his education. Seniority and pedigree are still the leading indicators for respect among the posse of Japanese social critics. The danger of trivializing Hayashi's work as "Americanization" may be more likely to occur from the ranks of Western scholars and journalists themselves. On the one hand, critics emphasize that the Western imagination greatly exaggerated the potential and probability that Japan would eventually become Americanized. Journalist James Fallows (catching up to what academic scholars have been saying all along), for example, recalls a *Life Magazine* special edition from 1964 in which various portents on the

Japanese social landscape, such as the tendency of Japanese young people to decry their workaholic fathers (a lament also voiced by Hayashi), were marshaled to usher in the coming Westernization of Japan. Of course, it never happened.[28]

On the other hand, thirty years later, an increasingly popular position is to suggest the need for increased Asianization of the West. Kishore Mahbubani, permanent secretary of the Ministry of Foreign Affairs in Singapore, for example, hopes that more Americans will visit Asia and thus "come to realize that their society has swung too much in one direction: liberating the individual while imprisoning society." The experience Americans would have in feeling safety on the streets in Asia would help them "begin to understand that freedom can also result from greater social order and discipline."[29]

Thus the boundary guarding the exclusiveness of East and West, or Japan and the United States, has exposed its vulnerability. There is no longer the expectation that the East will become like the West, or that the twain shall never meet. Many in America would not disagree with Mahbubani. Some critics even sided with Singapore's caning method, believing it to be preferable or superior to America's own disciplinary negligence. Surely many agree with the point made by Asian leaders that the United States should also recognize its own forms of abuse as another form of human rights violations. At the same time, many people both inside and outside of Asia feared that the new assertiveness of Asian leaders, such as Singapore's former president Lee Kuan Yew, who deny the universality of "human rights" while campaigning to restore traditional values such as those of Confucianism, might become a mandate for the legitimization of despotism.

What is less well known, moreover, is that legally sanctioned corporal punishment still does exist in some American schools. The unexpected cheerleading around the Michael Fay incident prompted two education specialists who are also attorneys, Charles H. Rathbone and Ronald T. Hyman, to draw attention to the overlooked fact that many American schools do practice legally mandated corporal punishment. In the United States, there is no federal statute prohibiting corporal punishment, and only one-half of the states expressly forbid it. Some local districts that permit corporal punishment "merely specify the length, width, and thickness of the paddle to be used." Other districts allow carefully supervised corporal punishment only when proven that all other disciplinary methods have failed. Both attorneys believe, however, that the tendency for states to enact legislation justifying physical force may be on the rise.[30]

The Myriad "Americanizations"

In such a scenario that undoes or counterbalances the long legacy of "modernization theory," which falsely imagined the perfectly linear Westernization of the East, the voice of a Japanese youth beaming with some naive Americanisms would be out of synch. It can no longer be assumed, however, that the "Westernized" veneer of youth has anything to do with Westernization, Americanization, or modernization. For instance, Hayashi implied that xenophilia for Western countries can be a regretful condition of national self-abnegation and distrust of elites, as is his own. Critics such as Hayashi hope to insulate themselves from a possible new "Asianism" that might amount to a fast-forwarding of wartime pan-Japanism, a re-creation of the prewar "great East Asia Co-Prosperity Sphere." Many foreigners in Japan have also had the experience of believing a Japanese friend to be Westernized or cosmopolitan only to find out how much that person is unaware of his or her own feelings of national exclusion. This was the theme of *Tokyo Pop*, a film from the mid-1980s, in which a young American woman breaks up with her Japanese boyfriend when he is unable to let go of his prejudice that she will never understand him as a Japanese.

Perhaps the more likely significance of the Japanese touting of Western images is that often there is little significance at all. I have met some Japanese young people who do not know that Coke, Big Macs, or Mickey Mouse are American in origin, just as some American youngsters don't know their Panasonic stereos or Sony TVs are Japanese in origin. American males are now wearing the shaved hairdo that Hayashi's retinue are railing against, while their adventurous Japanese counterparts get perms to sport the Elvis or Jimmy Dean look.

If there is no single theme connecting the kaleidoscope of Westernized pop culture signs, or the language of human rights and individual rights, other than the fact of their popularity among Japanese young people, then Hayashi's embrace of these signs should identify him as nothing more than an ordinary Japanese young adult. To read "Americanization" into his work, the possibility that I feared, would be not only to recognize the ordinariness of the language he latches onto, it would also be to attach labels of national identity that are no longer as restrictive as they once were and to therefore misread the thrust of his argument as an aberration rather than a natural consequence of overly regulated education.

Thus, the space for understanding Hayashi's case against the homogenitis of the Japanese student body would not seem to neatly locate itself in the language of modernization, which implies a typology of convergence, the loosening of national identities, of pointing out that the Japanese are becoming more like Americans, or vice versa. Hayashi's Americanization is naive at worst—since he does not seem to recognize America's own educational "human rights" record—or pragmatic at best—since he borrows legal codes that originated in America to counter the violence inherent in the codes of school regulations. And surely there is even less reason to believe that *Down with School Regulations!* is intended to consolidate any sort of meaning of "being Japanese." Instead, it is important to recognize that both of the categories of understanding, whether pointing to the loosening or the tightening of national identity, presuppose an immutably unitarian model of "being Japanese." This essay questions that model of unity. It proposes instead that arguments springing forth from young "rebels" such as Hayashi Takeshi be seen not as un-Japanese but as suppressed or subdued voices of the *ordinarily* Japanese—of the "other nails" that dare to protrude "all the way" and never get hammered down.

Some changes on the contemporary Japanese landscape may also heighten the audibility of such underheard voices. In 1988, the ministry advised local boards of education to do away with the more detailed and severe regulations in their schools. Yet, in Hayashi's words, this amounted to "sprinkling some water on hot lava."[31] According to a survey of seventy-seven junior and senior high schools conducted by the National Education Institute, some senior high schools eased their regulations, while many junior high schools made some regulations even stricter, especially on dress codes (31 percent, stricter; 25 percent, more relaxed) and hairstyles (25 percent, stricter; 15 percent, more relaxed).[32]

If public consciousness on the severity of kōsoku began to increase since then, it probably had less to do with the ministry's guidance, or efforts such as Hayashi's, than with broadly changing socioeconomic and political conditions. Labor economists of advanced nations increasingly warn that militaristic, mass-production methods of schooling and labor are no longer conducive to the changing technological environment that values creativity and individualized consumerism. Japan has had to adjust to this change during its longest postwar recession, in an international atmosphere compelling the country to soften its image and improve the welfare of its citizens. The declaration of a "lifestyle superpower" in 1992 resulted in educational changes such as reduced dependence on commercial mock exams, a shortened (five-day) school week, and a renaissance of admonitions to respect and elevate the importance of the individual in education.

Meanwhile, a few particular incidents gained international notoriety—another reason why the case against kōsoku may become more audible. Perhaps the most widely publicized incident occurred on July 6, 1990, when fifteen-year-old Ishida Ryōko was rushing to her morning class. She had never been late to school before. Her school, Takatsuka High School in Kobe, maintained a strict policy of shutting their 1.5-meter-high sliding metal gate at precisely 8:30 A.M. to discourage students from tardiness. "Tardiness and absence lead to delinquency," according to the principal, Nomura Atsuo. The teacher in charge of operating the gate that morning, Hosoi Toshikiko, was disappointed with his record of letting five or six tardy boys slip by the gate. "Since then, I made up my mind to close the gate in an abrupt manner," he later told police. That morning, Ryōko barely made it to the gate by the 8:30 deadline. But she failed to pass through before Hosoi abruptly and punctually lowered the gate, crushing the young girl's head against the entrance post. Ryōko was rushed to a hospital where she later died of a fractured skull.[33]

Afterward, Nomura explained the "accident" to students by telling them it could have been avoided if students were tardy less often. The public, however, was greatly moved, and various symposia were held throughout Japan to discuss excessive kōsoku. The parents' and students' most vocalized concern, however, remained the risk of speaking out against the kōsoku, considering the power teachers have to prevent students from entering high school or university if they have violated the regulations.[34]

A significant challenge is thus posed by changing socioeconomic conditions to the traditional, but often criticized, dominance of bureaucrats over the people (kansonminpi), a system that legitimates the practice of kōsoku and the persistence of rigidly enforced group conformism. This challenge coincides with other phenomenal changes in Japan in the mid-1990s, such as the end of thirty-eight years of single-party dominance by the Liberal Democratic Party (LDP); the subsequent formation of a coalition between the LDP and the Social Democratic Party of Japan and election of the latter's party leader, Murayama Tomiichi, to the office of prime minister; the recovery of the nation from the massive 1995 Hanshin earthquake; the split among financial elites over the high yen; the confrontation with history in the fiftieth anniversary of World War II's end; and the rise of an apocalyptic religious cult that killed several people in a Tokyo subway with nerve gas. The cloudy conditions could also open up a silver lining, however, if the atmosphere becomes more conducive to discussion and debate of critical social and political issues. Perhaps then, dissenting ideas such as those of Hayashi Takeshi might generate some more productive results.

In August 1993, for example, a junior high school group formed in Japan's Kansai area to protest student regulations. Like Hayashi, they also took as their motto "The nail that protrudes all the way never gets hammered down." The youngsters sent a letter calling for an immediate end to the kōsoku to Akamatsu Ryōko, recently named education minister by then prime minister Hosokawa. While conceding that an end to all regulations was out of the question, Akamatsu, considered somewhat of a maverick, did have some acerbic words for the dreaded *marugari,* the close-cropped haircuts that are the easily recognized insignia of many Japanese junior high school boys. One-third of all public junior high schools require marugari, and teachers will sometimes stand by with shears or have students abide by a written contract to keep their hair cut short. Answering the students' letter publicly, the minister candidly stated, "As an individual, whenever I see the marugari, I am dismayed, because it reminds me of the soldiers who wore their hair that way during the war." She urged junior high schools and local authorities to follow the trend of the times and reconsider the necessity of the militaristic haircuts. In so doing, however, she stopped short—as the ministry did in 1988—of assuming authority to end needless or outmoded regulations.[35]

Nevertheless, the Osaka Municipal Board of Education took the unexpected step of abolishing the marugari after hearing her remarks. An adult group also formed in the Kansai area to give direct support to the junior high school students. The group has since then asked another thirteen schools to abolish the marugari, and it remains active in attempts to abolish the kōsoku.[36]

Such developments still do not seem promising to an activist such as Hayashi Takeshi, for whom work is never finished. As stated at the outset, Hayashi is skeptical about the way the Japanese government and businesses are now touting the importance of the individual. The rhetoric does not mesh with the present reality of what you see from day to day in urban Tokyo: husbands and wives who rarely see one another because of the expectations of company life on working men.

But Hayashi himself will not break away from his own workaholic schedule of reading hundreds of letters per month, writing his books and columns, helping troubled students seek legal advice, and collecting his own library of books on educational problems. Hayashi believes there are few Japanese young people like himself. He prefers to compare his spunk to that of popular entertainers than to that of the other "new species" (*shinjinrui*, like America's "generation X").

While it is true that few Japanese young people have his willpower, my impression of him as more "ordinary" than I first suspected was directed at the basic substance and style of his argument. He effectively demonstrates that thousands of young people have tremendous conflicts with school regulations, and he relays their frustrations in the common language of young people, with defiance, directness, and desire to subvert the existing structures of authority.

Learning about Hayashi was for me also a process of self-learning. As conditioned as I am to be wary of *nihonjinron* (the theory of Japanese uniqueness and superiority), I felt sorrow when Hayashi outwardly expressed hatred of Japan. There must be another way to open the history books for young people without the prejudice of inducing debilitating nationalism. Having no educational mentors in history, Hayashi's most frequently mentioned educational heroes are a television creation of the 1980s, "Mr. Kimpatsu" (Kimpatsu Sensei), a long-haired, empathic teacher who took time to understand his students and their problems on an individual basis, and real-life teachers who resemble Mr. Kimpatsu.

At the same time, *Down with School Regulations!* represents an alternative and overdue cultural artifact that recognizes and takes seriously the presence of dissenting voices in Japan. When we think merely in terms of the unitary images of national or civilizational identity, we often react only to the dominant images of the mass media, the sanctioned stereotypes and worn-out dictums of collective identity. This is especially true of the popular image of Japan and of Asia as highly conformist societies where nails that stick out do get hammered down. Often, however, as I have tried to demonstrate, the many nails that have suppressed their nonconformist urges also deserve to be included in the cultural landscape. Lately, young people such as Hayashi Takeshi have ventured to portray a new impression of the subjective human agency in Japan: that by persisting "all the way" with one's ideals, or by becoming nails that resist getting hammered down, the obsolescent constructions of human enterprise can be affected.

Notes

1. According to a public survey of 2,900 schools cited by education critic Hideo Sakamoto, 88.9 percent of junior high schools and 94.9 percent of senior high schools regulate clothing. Other regulations are as follows: hairstyle (81.7 percent junior high, 89 percent senior high); cleaning (83.4 percent junior high, 79.8 percent senior high); commuting behavior (85.4 percent junior high, 75.3 percent senior high); personal possessions (63.6 percent junior high, 42 percent senior high); off-campus and home behavior (58.1 percent junior high, 41.8 percent senior high); and manners and greetings (47.7 percent junior high, 33 percent senior high). Sakamoto Hideo, *Kōsoku no hanashi: Seito no tame no kenri tokuhon* (Tokyo: San-ichi Shinsho, 1992).

2. Hayashi Takeshi, *Fuzakeruna! Kōsoku: Part 3* (Down with School Regulations!) (Tokyo: Kuso, 1990), p. 151. Henceforth *DWSR!*

3. *Seiza* is the traditional, rigid seating position in which the legs are folded straight under the body. It is comfortably tolerable for no more than twenty minutes by today's long-legged youth. Afterward the legs become tremendously painful and numb.

4. For a discussion on the relationship between the naishinshō and the general issue of academic freedom in Japan in the legal context, see Horio Teruhisa, *Educational Thought and Ideology in Modern Japan: State Authority and Intellectual Freedom*, ed. and trans. Steven Platzer (Tokyo: University of Tokyo Press, 1988), pp. 279–94. Horio also reveals that the one exception to finding out the contents of the naishinshō may come when parents hire a private detective to conduct research on a prospective marriage partner for their child.

5. Michel Foucault, *Discipline and Punish* (New York: Pantheon, 1977), p. 190.

6. Sakamoto, *Kōsoku no hanashi*, p. 190.

7. Cited in *EHS Law Bulletin Series: Japan*, vol. 3 (Tokyo: Eibun-Horei-Sha, 1977), p. BA3.

8. Cited in *The Constitution of Japan and Criminal Statutes* (Tokyo: Ministry of Justice, 1958), p. 6.

9. Ibid., p. 9.

10. Hayashi, *DWSR! Part 3*, p. 170.

11. Hayashi, *DWSR! Part 1* (Tokyo: Kuso, 1987), pp. 48–49, 65.

12. Ibid., pp. 62–64.

13. Interview with Hayashi Takeshi, October 1, 1993.

14. Robert J. Smith, *Japanese Society: Tradition, Self and the Social Order* (Cambridge: Cambridge University Press, 1983; reprint, 1987), p. 100.

15. Sakamoto, *Kōsoku no hanashi,* p. 22.

16. R. P. Dore, *Education in Tokugawa Japan* (Berkeley: University of California Press, 1965), pp. 95, 102.

17. Ibid., p. 313.

18. Ibid., pp. 254, 273.

19. Ronald S. Anderson, *Education in Japan: A Century of Modern Development* (Washington, D.C.: U.S. Department of Health, Education and Welfare, 1975), p. 27.

20. Joseph J. Tobin, David Y. H. Wu, and Dana H. Davidson, *Preschool in Three Cultures: Japan, China and the United States* (New Haven, Conn.: Yale University Press, 1988), pp. 12–71.

21. Takashi Fujitani, "Local Cultures/Military Cultures: Discipline and Nationalism in Modern Japan," presentation at East-West Center, Honolulu, Hawaii, April 12, 1994.

22. Hayashi, *DWSR! Part 1,* pp. 12–13.

23. Fujitani, "Local Cultures/Military Cultures."

24. Ibid.

25. Hayashi, *DWSR, Part 3,* pp. 79–128.

26. Hayashi, *DWSR! Part 1,* pp. 170–71.

27. Dore, *Education in Tokugawa Japan,* pp. 30, 168.

28. James Fallows, *Looking at the Sun* (New York: Pantheon, 1994).

29. Kishore Mahbubani, "Go East, Young Man," *Far Eastern Economic Review* 157, no. 20 (1994):32.

30. Charles H. Rathbone and Ronald T. Hyman, "Singapore-Style Discipline: Corporal Punishment Is Educationally Unsound and Fundamentally Wrong," Commentary in *Education Week,* June 1, 1994, p. 36.

31. Hayashi, *DWSR! Part 3,* p. 49.

32. *Japan Times,* May 12, 1990, p. 2. The survey followed up a 1984 study that looked at the regulations of 257 schools. The National Education Institute is affiliated with the Japan Teachers' Union, usually considered a rival of the Ministry of Education, although conflict between them has dwindled over the past decade. The Ministry of Education also conducted its own survey of regulations at that time, but the results were not revealed to the press.

33. Ibid., July 17, 1990, p. 4.

34. Ibid., August 23, 1990, p. 2.

35. *Asahi Shimbun,* September 4, 1993, p. 3.

36. *Mainichi Daily News,* September 13, 1993, p. 12.

Contributors

Wimal Dissanayake is a senior fellow at the East-West Center, Honolulu, Hawaii, and a member of the graduate faculty of the Department of Communication at the University of Hawaii. He is the author of several books on literature, cinema, and the concept of self in Asian theory and practice. Among his other books are *Melodrama and Asian Cinema* (1993), *Colonialism and Nationalism in Asian Cinema* (1994), and the *Penguin Book of Modern Indian Short Stories* (1989). He is the editor of the *East-West Film Journal*.

Richard G. Fox is professor of anthropology at Washington University in Saint Louis and the editor of *Current Anthropology*. Other recent works on India include *Lions of the Punjab: Culture in the Making* (1985) and *Gandhian Utopia: Experiments with Culture* (1989).

Lydia H. Liu teaches Chinese and comparative literature at the University of California, Berkeley. Her forthcoming book, *Translingual Practice: Literature, National Culture, and Translated Modernity* will be published by Stanford University Press.

Owen M. Lynch is Charles F. Noyes Professor of urban anthropology at New York University. He has done research in India on scheduled castes, urban squatters, pilgrimage, and the Chaubes of Mathura.

He is the author of *The Politics of Untouchability: Social Mobility and Social Change in a City of India* (1969), and editor of *Divine Passions: The Social Construction of Emotion in India* (1990) and *Culture and Community in Europe: Essays in Honor of Conrad M. Arensberg* (1984). He has published numerous articles on India, urban anthropology, pilgrimage, identity, and the social construction of emotion.

Vijay Mishra is an associate professor of English and Comparative Literature at Murdoch University in Perth, Western Australia. His most recent publications include *Dark Side of the Dream: Australian Literature and the Postcolonial Mind* (1990) (with Bob Hodge) and *The Gothic Sublime* (1994). He is currently revising two further books, *Devotional Poetics: Toward a Theory of the Indian Sublime* and *Bombay Cinema: Defining a Genre*, for publication.

Marie Thorsten Morimoto received her Ph.D. from the University of Hawaii. She wrote her dissertation on Japanese education and the question of economic nationalism.

Emiko Ohnuki-Tierney, a native of Japan, is Vilas Research Professor at the University of Wisconsin, Madison. She began her work with the Sakhalin Ainu; that work resulted in *Illness and Healing among the Sakhalin Ainu* (1981), *The Ainu of the Northwest Coast of Southern Sakhalin* (1974), and *Sakhalin Ainu Folklore* (1969). She has since then turned her attention to Japanese culture. She is the author of *Illness and Culture in Contemporary Japan* (1984), *The Monkey as Mirror: Symbolic Transformations in Japanese History and Ritual* (1987), and *Rice as Self: Japanese Identities through Time* (1993). Her visiting appointments include Harvard University (1993–94); Ecole des Hautes Etudes en Sciences Sociales (1992); University of Manchester (1990); Center for Advanced Study in the Behavioral Sciences, Stanford (1988–89); Institute for Advanced Study, Princeton (1986–87); and Oxford University (1986).

Eugene Yuejin Wang is assistant professor in the Department of Art at the University of Chicago. He has published articles in *Framework, Public Culture, Wide Angle, East-West Film Journal,* the *Art Bulletin,* and elsewhere. He has also translated Roland Barthes's *Fragments d'un discours amoureux* into Chinese.

Ming-Bao Yue is an assistant professor of Modern Chinese literature who teaches in the Department of East Asian Languages and Literatures at the University of Hawaii at Manoa. She received her Ph.D. degree from Stanford University and has published on modern Chinese literature and contemporary Chinese film and culture. She is also the author of a forthcoming book on feminist readings of modern Chinese fiction.

Index